THE CAMBRIDGE
ANCIENT HISTORY

PLATES TO VOLUMES V AND VI

THE CAMBRIDGE
ANCIENT HISTORY

PLATES TO VOLUMES V AND VI

The Fifth and Fourth Centuries B.C.

NEW EDITION

Edited by

JOHN BOARDMAN F.B.A.

*Lincoln Professor of Classical Archaeology and Art
in the University of Oxford*

CAMBRIDGE
UNIVERSITY PRESS

Published by the Press Syndicate of the University of Cambridge
The Pitt Building, Trumpington Street, Cambridge CB2 1RP
40 West 20th Street, New York, NY 10011–4211, USA
10 Stamford Road, Oakleigh, Melbourne 3166, Australia

© Cambridge University Press 1994

First published 1994

Printed in Great Britain at the University Press, Cambridge

A catalogue record for this book is available from the British Library

Library of Congress Cataloging-in-Publication Data applied for

ISBN 0 521 23349 6 hardback

CONTENTS

ACKNOWLEDGEMENTS

The following are thanked for supplying photographs or drawings and granting permission for reproduction. The sources for illustrations derived from publications are indicated in the notes to each item.

Amsterdam, Allard Pierson Museum: 201d; Andreiomenou, A.: 187; Andronikos, M.: 49; Athens, American School of Classical Studies: 53, 64a, 82c, 106, 112, 116–25, 130a, 132, 138, 155; Athens, Ecole Française: 52, 137; Athens, German Archaeological Institute: 3c, 34, 38–9, 44, 78, 105, 208, 210; Athens, National Museum: 131a, 152, 158, 185, 200, 206–7, 214, 216; Athens, Swiss Archaeological School: 128a; Baatz, D.: 209; Basel, Antikenmuseum: 48, 162; Berlin, Staatliche Museen, Antikensammlung: 14, 107, 154, 161, 183, 193, 203; Bern, Historisches Museum: 113; Boardman, J.: 24, 30, 61a, 67; Boston Museum of Fine Arts: 110, 141, 165, 168; Brauron Museum: 18, 151; Brussels, Mus.du Cinquantenaire: 133b; Cahn, H.A.: 191b; Capellani, G.: 80; Catling, H.W.: 213a; Cefalù, Museo Mandralisca: 114; Chicago, Loyola University (photo R. Schoder): 111; Cleveland Museum of Art: 177; Copenhagen, Ny Carlsberg Glyptothek: 167; Coulton, J.J.: 61b, 62, 68; Ferrara, Mus. Naz. Arch.: 149, 170; Florence, Soprintendenza: 22a–b; Frankfurt, Mus. für Vor- und Früh-Geschichte: 142; Frantz, Alison: 1c, 3a, 7; Editions Gallimard: 1a, 1d, 1e, 2, 6, 10a, 11b, 12, 13, 20, 27, 31; Hamburg, Mus. für Kunst und Gewerbe: 90; Hartford (Conn.), Wadsworth Athenaeum: 179; Hirmer Verlag: 3d, 8, 17, 43, 47, 69, 156, 217; Istanbul, German Archaeological Institute: 218; Jackson, Peter: 11a; Jones, J.E.: 93a, 97; Karlsruhe, Badisches Landesmuseum: 150; Kassel, Staatlichen Kunstsamm- lungen: 28; Kienast, H.: 102, 103b; Köln, Forschungsarchiv für röm. Plastik: 176; Lohmann, Hans: 87; London, British Museum: 9, 26b, 36–7, 108, 140, 171, 196, 202, 221–78; London, Courtauld Inst., Conway Library (Photo A.W. Lawrence): 213b; London, Ministry of Defence: 89; Los Angeles, University of California Institute of Archaeology: 92, 100; Maier, F.-G.: 181; Malibu, J. Paul Getty Mus.: 32, 45, 172; Motya, Whitaker Mus.: 21; Munich, Antikensammlungen: 33, 182; Naples, Mus. Naz. Arch.: 29; Newcastle, Shefton Museum: 220; New York, Metropolitan Museum of Art: 41, 127, 135a, 144, 175; Oliver, Graham: 98–9; Osborne, R.G.: 88, 93b, 101, 103a, 104; Oxford, Ashmolean Museum: 198, 201c; Paris, Louvre Museum: 55, 135b, 204, 211, 215; Parker, R.: 136; Providence (Rhode Island), School of Design: 190; Reggio, Mus. Arch.: 25; Rome, Conservatori Mus.: 5; Rome, German Archaeological Institute: 26a, 69; Rome, Vatican Museums: 164; Simon, Erika: 139; Smith, Candace: 1b, 71; Sparkes, B.A.: 94; St Petersburg, Hermitage Museum: 46; Sydney, University Museum: 178; Taranto, Mus. Arch. Naz.: 157; Toledo, Museum of Art: 115; Toronto, Royal Ontario Museum: 4; Vienna, Kunsthistorischesmuseum: 188; Wellesley College Museum: 194; Wilkie, N.C.: 109; Wilkins, R.L.: 57; Worcester (Mass.) Art Museum: 192; Würzburg, Martin von Wagner Museum: 160, 166, 174; Yalouris, N.: 10b; Young, G.M.: 23.

PREFACE

The fifth and fourth centuries B.C., the Classical period *par excellence*, are the first in which a modern scholar can turn readily to a great range of written sources to record the history, life and religion of the Greek world. In earlier periods the material evidence played a major role, but it can be of no less value in the Classical period. The fifth-century 'Classical revolution' in the arts represents Greece's first major contribution to world art, with an influence that stretches through Rome and the Renaissance to the present day, at least in the western world. But even for conventional historical studies, in the broadest sense, the material world provides more than simple illustration. Excavations in Athens have revealed the workings of civic life, while the character of Athenian art, especially its vase-painting, allows a view of contemporary life and behaviour which is fuller than anything available for almost any other period of antiquity. It lacks only a Pompeii. Recent exploration and study of the Greek countryside has illuminated subjects which are out of the mainstream of conventional history but which were crucial to Greek society, while even the mechanics of the Greek theatre, which we seem to know well from texts, can be studied through architecture and representational art, and this may even improve our understanding of how Greek poets used and manipulated their stock of myth.

The new edition of *CAH* Volume VI has lengthy chapters of regional studies devoted to places and peoples on the periphery of the Greek world. These have been illustrated in the text volume, leaving the Plates Volume to concentrate on the Classical Greek homeland. Readers are also referred to *Plates to Volume IV* (1988) where areas of the Persian Empire in the fifth and fourth centuries are considered.

The editor and authors are grateful to the many scholars and institutions who have provided photographs for this volume. Several of the line drawings have been specially prepared by Marion Cox, and in chapter 2 by Alison Wilkins.

Oxford, June 1993   J.B.

ABBREVIATIONS

AA	*Archäologischer Anzeiger*
ABV	J.D. Beazley, *Attic Black-Figure Vase-Painters* (Oxford, 1956)
Add²	T.H. Carpenter, *Beazley Addenda* (2nd edn; Oxford, 1989)
AJA	*American Journal of Archaeology*
AK	*Antike Kunst*
APl	*Antike Plastik*
Arch.Eph.	*Archaiologike Ephemeris*
ARV	J.D. Beazley, *Attic Red-Figure Vase-Painters* (2nd edn; Oxford, 1963)
Ashmole, *ASCG*	B. Ashmole, *Architect and Sculptor in Classical Greece* (London, 1972)
Ath.Mitt.	*Athenische Mitteilungen*
BCH	*Bulletin de Correspondance Hellénique*
Berve–Gruben–Hirmer	H. Berve, G. Gruben and M. Hirmer, *Temples, Theatres and Shrines* (London, 1963)
BICS	*Bulletin of the Institute of Classical Studies, London*
BMC	*British Museum Catalogue of Coins*
Boardman, *ARFV* I	J. Boardman, *Athenian Red Figure Vases: Archaic Period* (London, 1975)
Boardman, *ARFV* II	J. Boardman, *Athenian Red Figure Vases: Classical Period* (London, 1989)
Boardman, *GSCP*	J. Boardman, *Greek Sculpture: Classical Period* (London, 1985)
BSA	*Annual of the British School at Athens*
CVA	*Corpus Vasorum Antiquorum*
GRBS	*Greek, Roman and Byzantine Studies*
GVGetty	*Greek Vases in the J. Paul Getty Museum*
Haus und Stadt	W. Hoepfner and E.-L. Schwandner, *Haus und Stadt im klassischen Griechenland* (Munich, 1986)
IG	*Inscriptiones Graecae*
IGCH	*Index of Greek Coin Hoards*
IGD	A.D. Trendall and T.B.L. Webster, *Illustrations of Greek Drama* (London, 1971)
Ist.Mitt.	*Istanbuler Mitteilungen*
JDAI	*Jahrbuch des Deutschen Archäologischen Instituts*
JHS	*Journal of Hellenic Studies*
Kraay, *ACGC*	C.M. Kraay, *Archaic and Classical Greek Coins* (London, 1976)
Kraay–Hirmer	C.M. Kraay and M. Hirmer, *Greek Coins* (London, 1966)
Kyrieleis, *AKGP*	H. Kyrieleis (ed.), *Archaische und Klassische Griechische Plastik* I, II (Berlin, 1986)

LIMC	*Lexicon Iconographicum Mythologiae Classicae* I- (Zurich/ Munich, 1981–)
Mattusch, *GBS*	C. Mattusch, *Greek Bronze Sculpture* (Cornell, 1988)
M–L	R. Meiggs and D.M. Lewis, *Greek Historical Inscriptions* (Oxford, 1969)
*MMC*³	T.B.L. Webster, *Monuments Illustrating Old and Middle Comedy* (3rd edn; London, 1978)
*MTS*²	T.B.L. Webster, *Monuments Illustrating Tragedy and Satyr Play* (London, 1967)
NC	*Numismatic Chronicle*
Olynthus	D.M. Robinson *et al.*, *Excavations at Olynthus* I–XIV (1929–52)
Para	J.D. Beazley, *Paralipomena to ABV, ARV* (Oxford, 1971)
PCG	*A Guide to the Principal Coins of the Greeks, British Museum* (1959)
Pickard-Cambridge, *Festivals*	*The Dramatic Festivals of Athens* (2nd edn; rev. J. Gould and D.M. Lewis, Oxford, 1968)
RA	*Revue Archéologique*
Richter, *Portraits*	G.M.A. Richter, *Portraits of the Greeks* (revised by R.R.R. Smith; Oxford, 1984)
Ridgway, *FC*	B.S. Ridgway, *Fifth-century Styles in Greek Sculpture* (Princeton, 1981)
Ridgway, *SS*	B.S. Ridgway, *The Severe Style in Greek Sculpture* (Princeton, 1970)
Robertson, *HGA*	M. Robertson, *A History of Greek Art* (Cambridge, 1975)
RVAp	A.D. Trendall and A. Cambitoglou, *The Red-Figured Vases of Apulia* (Oxford 1978, 1982)
Simon, *Theatre*	E. Simon, *The Ancient Theatre* (London, 1982)
Simon–Hirmer	E. Simon and M. and A. Hirmer, *Die griechischen Vasen* (Munich, 1976)
SNG	*Sylloge Nummorum Graecorum*
Stewart, *GS*	A. Stewart, *Greek Sculpture: An Exploration* (New Haven, 1990)
Travlos, *Athens*	J. Travlos, *Pictorial Dictionary of Ancient Athens* (London, 1971)
Travlos, *Attika*	J. Travlos, *Bildlexikon zur Topographie der antiken Attika* (Tübingen, 1988)

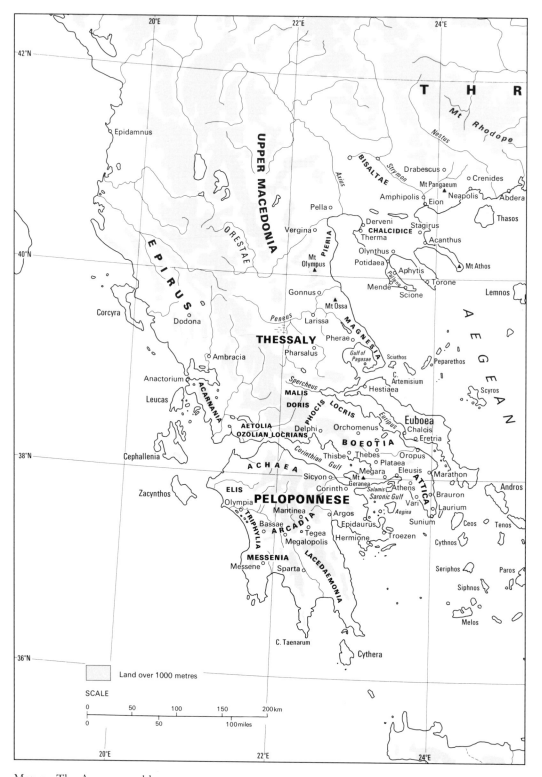

Map 1. The Aegean world

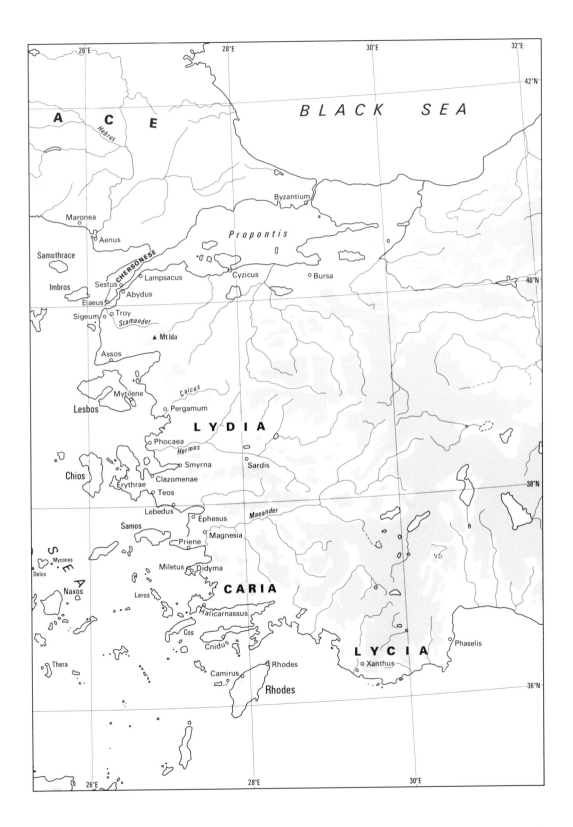

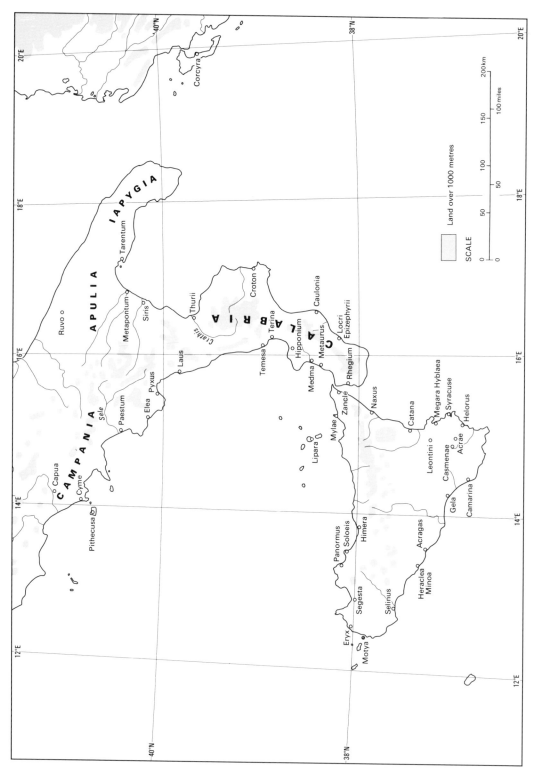

Map 2. South Italy and Sicily

xii

1. CLASSICAL ART

B. A. SPARKES

The Persian invasion of Greece in 480 B.C. was successfully repulsed. Whether impelled by that success or not, Greek artists and craftsmen rapidly developed those formal advances that had been initiated in the late sixth and early fifth centuries. For the most part the social functions of their work remained the same: architectural decoration often with political meaning; free-standing dedications in sanctuaries and public places; and products for private purposes, whether funerary, domestic or personal. In free-standing sculpture concern with the mechanism of the human body gives way to a deepened expression of the inner life that activates physical movement. Formal order begins to take a less prominent position, the emphasis on pattern lessens, and the single figure, realized in more complex movements in space, becomes dominant. In architectural sculpture and in vase-painting the compositions become bolder and more complicated and once again states of consciousness are emphasized. Myths remain the powerhouse for subject-matter, though alongside the old myths there are new stories and episodes and novel ways of treating those Archaic images that endured. In the more private sphere the life of the everyday world has an important role to play, and even in myth and worship artists reduce the gap between gods and men by humanizing the loftiness of the Olympians. By the end of the hundred and fifty years that mark the life of 'Classical art' in the Greek world, the figures have become more natural and more individualized, whilst still retaining a basic adherence to the unspecific.

Our understanding of the Early Classical period (c. 480–450 B.C.) is dominated by the sculptures of the Zeus temple at Olympia (1) and by the life-size bronze statues (20, 22–23, 25) that are a derisory percentage of the original number shaped. There is simplicity, not to say austerity of form, and a seriousness of look that contrasts with the smiling figures of the Archaic period.

Pose and gesture project the will, and the expressive faces begin to mirror the feelings and thoughts of the participants. In this context the figures from the Zeus temple have rightly been compared with the contemporary tragedies of Aeschylus. States of rest before and after movement give some idea of the meaning of *rhythmos* which is mentioned in art-historical literature; this is exemplified in such bronzes as the Zeus of Artemisium (23) and the marble copy of Myron's bronze discus-thrower (27). The Early Classical period also sees a move in the direction of the representation of historical figures (e.g. Themistocles 26a) and of historical events (such as Marathon in the Painted Stoa at Athens). It is at this time too that we seem to see the emergence of the individual as artist in such personalities as the sculptor Myron and the wall-painter Polygnotus.

In the Early Classical period the balance between underlying formality and surface fluctuation had tipped in favour of the transient; in the following generation (450–420 B.C.), with Athens at her zenith, individuality is rejected, and the emphasis swings back to the harmonious perfection of unspecific form. None the less, the timeless and cosmic quality of the Parthenon sculptures (3–4) is rooted in the political realities of the Periclean age. The influence of the Phidian style is to be seen in allied crafts in Athens and in work produced in other parts of the Greek world and beyond, e.g. Lycia, Caria and Phoenicia.

By the close of the fifth century (420–400 B.C.), a flamboyant, not to say mannered elegance is in place, and richness of effect is achieved through a better understanding of perspective (by the Samian Agatharchus) and of shading (by the Athenian Apollodorus). The choice and treatment of the subject-matter, with figures of lovelorn women and scenes of romance in myth and ordinary life (e.g. 44), would seem to suggest that the products of the time were a reaction to the turmoil of the protracted civil war.

The display of emotions found in the late fifth century is extended in the fourth century (400–330 B.C.) to a stress on individualism, now more emphatic in portraits of orators, poets, philosophers (**26c**) and such which are realistic in intent, if not in truthfulness; in private worship, especially that devoted to Asclepius at Epidaurus (**10**); in heightened states of feeling and sentiment such as pain, anger, yearning, exemplified in the series of funerary stelae (**15–17**); and in an emphasis on the erotic, now carried to an extreme in the public field of sculpture with Praxiteles' Cnidian Aphrodite (**35**). Personifications are also characteristic of the time (e.g. **33**). Themes in art that reflect the ethos and patronage of the polis are less frequent; private commissions become more important (e.g. **11**).

Classical art, which barely extends over five generations, moved from the decorative formality that had been the hallmark of the Archaic period, to the naturalism that was to inform ways of seeing for centuries in the future. In all this, the appearance of man was the measure; his deeds, whether divine, heroic or human, were the active ingredients.

GENERAL BIBLIOGRAPHY

B. Ashmole, *Architect and Sculptor in Classical Greece* (London, 1972); J.J. Pollitt, *Art and Experience in Classical Greece* (Cambridge, 1972); J. Charbonneaux, R. Martin and F. Villard, *Classical Greek Art* (London, 1973); M. Robertson, *A History of Greek Art* (Cambridge, 1975); P. Kidson, 'The Figural Arts' in M.I. Finley (ed.), *The Legacy of Greece, a New Appraisal*, (Oxford, 1981) ch. 14.

Architectural Sculpture

1. The temple of Zeus at Olympia, *c.* 470–457 B.C. In the Archaic period there had been no temple of Zeus in the sanctuary at Olympia; the temple constructed in the Early Classical period was built from the spoils of the war that Elis won over Pisa. The architect is said to have been Libon, a local man (Paus. v.10.3). The architectural sculpture of metopes and pediments was made of marble (most likely Parian) and contrasted with the plaster-covered shelly limestone of the building itself. The metopes, set above the entrances at front and back, showed the twelve labours of Heracles, son of Zeus and founder of the Olympic games, as a progression from inexperienced youth to triumphantly successful hero (a has Atlas delivering the Apples of the Hesperides to Heracles who is holding up the heavens with the help of Athena). The pediments (b) are contrasted in subject and composition: on the east the still, inner tension of the moment of sacrifice to Zeus before the decisive chariot-race between Oinomaus and Pelops, and on the west the physical turmoil of Lapiths against centaurs

3

(**c**) aided by Apollo (**d**). The subject on the east is local to Olympia, that on the west has Athenian connexions and has been seen in detail (cf. **41**) and composition to lend itself to political interpretations. The style of the figures is heavy and sober, with an interest in youth and age (**e** is an old seer foreseeing the outcome of the race). Pausanias (v.10.8) informs us that Paionius (see **31**) was the sculptor of the east pediment and Alcamenes of the west, but these attributions have generally been discounted.

(Olympia, Museum. **a** Metope 10. Height 1.6 m; **b** Drawing of pediments © Candace H. Smith 1990. Height of pediments 3.3 m, length 26.4 m; **c** West pediment figures RST. Height *c.* 1.65 m; **d** West pediment figure L. Height of Apollo 3.1 m; **e** East pediment figure N. Height 1.38 m)

B. Ashmole, N. Yalouris and A. Frantz, *Olympia, the Sculptures of the Temple of Zeus* (London, 1967); Ridgway, *SS* 17–23; Ashmole, *ASCG* chs. 1–3; Robertson, *HGA* 271–91; Boardman, *GSCP* ch. 4; Stewart, *GS* chs. 12.2 and 21.1, T 39.

2. Limestone and marble metope from temple E (Hera) at Selinus, *c.* 470–450 B.C. Zeus reclines on Ida and imperiously grasps the arm of an upright Hera to draw her towards him, the *hieros gamos*. The figures are in high relief, and Hera's head, feet and arms are in marble, contrasting with the local limestone of the rest of the figures. All the extant metopes of temple E show confrontations between male and female (Zeus v Hera; Athena v. Giant; Heracles v. Amazon; Artemis v. Actaeon; Apollo v. Daphne), and it is suggested that this theme may derive from the local philosophies of e.g. Pythagoras and Empedocles. For an earlier metope at Selinus, see *Pls. to Vol. IV*, pl. 245.

(Palermo, Museo Nazionale Archeologico 3921 B. Height 1.62 m)
    E. Langlotz and M. Hirmer, *The Art of Magna Graecia* (London, 1965) pls. 105–8; Ridgway, *SS* 23–4; V. Tusa, *La scultura in pietra di Selinunte* (Palermo, 1983) 119–23 and pls. 11–21.

3. The temple of Athena Parthenos, the Acropolis, Athens, *c.* 447–432 B.C. The sculptural programme of the Parthenon (**a**) has been shown to have as much of a political message as a religious meaning: Athena as patroness of the Athenians, Athens and her importance in the Greek world, the glorious military triumph over the Persians, and success in peacetime. The very elaboration of the decoration, all in Pentelic marble, declares the prime position that Athens held amongst the Greeks of the day. The sculptor Phidias was Pericles' choice of overseer of the building programme and was doubtless responsible for the design of the architectural sculpture as well as

being personally concerned with the making of the cult statue (see **4**). Ictinus and Callicrates are named as architects.

The metopes (92 in all) encircled the outer colonnade and divide into four sets of which many are missing. The north presents the Sack of Troy, the east the Gigantomachy, the west the Amazonomachy, whilst the south has a central section (now missing, but known from drawings) that is as yet not satisfactorily explained, framed by centaur battles (**b**). The style and quality of the work varies, as the metopes were the earliest blocks carved. The frieze, which encircled the whole of the cella, has the Panathenaic procession for its basic theme, but with the emphasis on the cavalry and with omissions that have suggested a non-contemporary procession, may be linked to the Panathenaea held before Marathon. The movement is from west to east and culminates in two groups of Olympian deities observing the parade (**c**, Poseidon, Apollo, Artemis, Aphrodite and Eros); between

the two groups the ritual of the robe woven every four years for Athena, an important element in the festival, is centred over the main east doorway. The relief is low, and there is much overlap between blocks. The pediments concern

Athena: at the west end she is shown in her struggle with Poseidon for the land of Attica, framed by chariots and local ancient kings, whilst at the east end she stands newly born from her father's head in the presence of other deities (d, Hestia (?), Dione (?) and Aphrodite) and framed by the sun and moon with their horses. The massive figures of the pediments were the latest carved and are the culmination of the style which presents unspecific types in human form with the contrast between bodily surface and the texture of clothing that lies above it.

(**a** Athens, Parthenon; **b** metope S1, Acropolis Museum. Height 1.36 m; **c** frieze East VI 38–42, London, British Museum 324. Height 1.06 m, length of frieze 160 m; **d** East pediment figures KLM, London, British Museum 303. Height of K 1.30 m, height of pediments *c.* 3.50 m)

General: Ashmole, *ASCG* chs. 4–5; Robertson, *HGA* 292–311; F. Brommer, *The Sculptures of the Parthenon* (London, 1979); Ridgway, *FC* chs. 2–4; *Parthenon-Kongress Basel* (Mainz, 1984) Section IV; J. Boardman and D. Finn, *The Parthenon and its Sculptures* (London, 1985); Boardman, *GSCP* chs. 9–12; Stewart, *GS* ch. 13.2. Metopes: F. Brommer, *Die Metopen des Parthenon* (Mainz, 1967); E. Berger, *Der Parthenon in Basel, Dokumentation zu den Metopen* (Mainz, 1986). Frieze: M. Robertson and A. Frantz, *The Parthenon Frieze* (London, 1975); F. Brommer, *Der Parthenonfries* (Mainz, 1977); J. Boardman, 'The Parthenon Frieze: another view', in *Festschrift für Frank Brommer* (Mainz, 1977) 39–49. Pediments: F. Brommer, *Die Skulpturen der Parthenon-Giebel* (Mainz, 1963); O. Palagia, *The Pediments of the Parthenon* (Leiden, 1993). For the building accounts, see *IG* I³ nos. 436–51, and M–L, no. 59.

4

4. Model of the cult statue of Athena Parthenos for the Parthenon, the Acropolis, Athens, *c.* 447–438 B.C. Nothing remains of the original gold and ivory statue of Athena Parthenos, and we are dependent on literary descriptions, later copies (large and small, whole and part) and contemporary allusions in vase-painting. Athena was fully armed with triple-crested helmet, aegis, spear and shield (with a snake beside it), and held a winged Victory on her right hand (the column may not have been an original feature). The statue was made of detachable gold plates for the dress and accoutrements, and ivory for the exposed parts of the skin of both the figures and for the Medusa head on Athena's aegis. As with the architectural decoration (see **3**), there were mythological narratives to emphasize her power and the success that she shared with the Athenians: on the outside of the shield an Amazonomachy (often copied), on the inside a Gigantomachy; on her sandals a Centauromachy, and on the base on which the statue stood, the birth of Pandora.

(Model in the Royal Ontario Museum, Toronto. Original height of statue *c.* 11.5 m, height of model one tenth of original)

N. Leipen, *The Athena Parthenos, a reconstruction* (Toronto, 1971); A. Schiff, *AK* 16 (1973) 4–44; *Parthenon-Kongress Basel* (Mainz, 1984) Section III; *LIMC* Athena nos. 219–33; Boardman, *GSCP* 110–12; K.W. Arafat, *BSA* 81 (1986) 1–6 (on the shield); Stewart, *GS* ch. 21.2. On chryselephantine statues, see Mattusch, *GBS* 176–81. For the accounts, see IG I³ nos. 453–60 and M–L, no. 54.

5

5. Marble pedimental figure from the Apollo Sosianus temple, Rome, *c.* 430 B.C. Fragments that make up into a pedimental composition have been found in the area of the Apollo Sosianus temple in the Campus Martius, Rome, in an area noted for its display of plundered works of art. The figures, which include Theseus (**5**), Heracles and Amazons, indicate that the subject was an Amazon battle. The marble may be Parian and the workmanship also suggests an island origin for the sculptors. The pediment (with its matching pair) was originally erected in Greece and at some time transferred to Rome where it was eventually set up on or in the Apollo Sosianus temple which was built in the 20s B.C. The original location for the temple is not known;

that of Apollo Daphnephoros at Eretria has been suggested.

(Rome, Conservatori inv. 2768. Height 1.52 m)

E. Langlotz and M. Hirmer, *The Art of Magna Graecia* (London, 1965) pls. 115–17; E. La Rocca, *Amazzonomachia, le sculture frontonali del tempio di Apollo Sosiano* (Rome, 1985); E. La Rocca, 'Le sculture frontonali del tempio di Apollo Sosiano a Roma', in Kyrieleis *AKGP* II 51–8; R.M. Cook, *AA* 1989, 525–8.

6. Marble acroterium from the east pediment of the temple of Apollo on Delos, *c.* 425–417 B.C. A Doric temple was built for Apollo by the Athenians after the purification of the island of Delos in 426 B.C. when a new festival was instituted. The metopes and pediments were left unfilled, but the roof was decorated with apex and angle figures. The angle figures were girls fleeing from the rapes of the central groups. On the west Eos was carrying off Cephalus and on the east Boreas

6

was flying away with the Attic princess Oreithyia (**6**). The figures are badly eroded, but the strong pyramidal composition is still clear, with a mature and bearded Boreas hoisting the slighter figure of the girl with fluttering and clinging draperies. Acroteria were either floral or figured, and the subjects chosen for the latter were usually suited to the position (winged victories, breezes, winds, etc.).

(Delos Museum inv. A 4287. Height 1.70 m)

U. Wester, *Die Akroterfiguren des Tempels der Athener auf Delos* (diss., Heidelberg, 1969) 25–31; A. Delivorrias, *Attische Giebelskulpturen und Akrotere des fünften Jahrhunderts* (Tübingen, 1974) 187–8; Ridgway, *FC* 59–64; *Exploration Archéologique de Délos* 34 (1984) 'La sculpture archaïque et classique', 23–42, pls. 11–21; no. 15, pls. 14–16; *LIMC* Boreas no. 67.

7. Marble Caryatids from the south porch of the Erechtheum, the Acropolis, Athens, *c.* 420–415 B.C. The false southern porch which faced towards the Parthenon was furnished with six *korai* ('maidens') in place of columns to hold up the flat roof. This was rare substitution, found already in Archaic, see *Pls. to Vol. IV*, pls. 117a and 124. The maidens, whom later copies show to have held phialae in their right hands, wear heavy garments that fall in rich folds to their feet. The frieze figures of the Erechtheum were attached separately on a background of dark Eleusinian stone and concerned cult subjects. The name 'Caryatid', which has been adopted from Vitruvius, is first found in extant inscriptions of the fourth century B.C.

(Athens, Acropolis Museum. Height 2.31 m)

E.M. Schmidt, *APl* 13 (1973); H. Lauter, *APl* 16 (1976); Ridgway, *FC* 105–8. For an attempt to make sense of the name 'Caryatid', see M. Vickers, *RA* 1985, 3–28. For the frieze figures, see P.N. Boulter, *APl* 10 (1970) 7–28; M. Brouskari, 'ΖΩΙΔΙΑ ΛΑΙΝΕΑ: nouvelles figures de la frise de l'Erechtheion', in *Kanon, Festschrift Ernst Berger* (*AK* Beiheft 15, 1988) 60–8. For the building accounts, see *IG* I³ nos. 474–9 (nos. 475–6 the frieze figures).

Robertson, *HGA* 349–50; Ridgway, *FC* 97–8; E. Simon, 'Zur Sandalenlöserin der Nikebalustrade', in *Kanon, Festschrift Ernst Berger* (*AK* Beiheft 15, 1988) 69–73.

8. Marble block from the balustrade of the Athena Nike bastion, the Acropolis, Athens, *c.* 410–400 B.C. The small Ionic temple of Athena Nike erected *c.* 420 B.C. on the south-west bastion of the Acropolis was surrounded about a decade later by a life-saving balustrade. The slabs show winged victories at various tasks: bringing a bull to sacrifice, dressing a trophy with Persian spoils, etc. The draperies are full and flowing, taking further the stage of development seen on **3d**, best shown by the Nike unfastening her sandal where the catenary folds are most marked.

(Athens, Acropolis Museum 973. Height 1.06 m)
  R. Carpenter and B. Ashmole, *The Sculpture of the Athena Nike Parapet* (Cambridge, Mass., 1929);

9. Marble slab of the frieze from the temple of Apollo Epicurius at Bassae (Phigaleia), Arcadia, *c.* 400 B.C. Pausanias (VIII.41. 7–9), who set the Bassae temple second only to the temple at Tegea (see **12**), linked it with the name of the designer Ictinus (also responsible for the Parthenon) and with the assistance that Apollo Epicurius ('the Helper') gave to the local people in delivering them from the plague that struck Athens in 430–429 B.C. Both connexions have been contested. Stylistically, the frieze belongs to the end of the century. A few fragments of the metopes have survived; they were set at either end of the temple, i.e. north and south because of the unusual orientation of the temple. The continuous frieze was set internally and framed the main room of the cella. It was divided unevenly between an Amazonomachy and a Centauro-

machy, the latter the version in the open air, with women grasping an Archaic-style statue. The two battles are marked by brutal scenes of carnage, with clinging and flying draperies, diagonal lines, and staccato compositions which the confinement to single blocks underlines.

(London, British Museum 524. Height 64 cm)

C. Hofkes-Brukker and A. Mallwitz, *Der Bassai-Fries* (Munich, 1975); N. Yalouris, 'Problems relating to the temple of Apollo Epikourios at Bassai', in *Acta of the XI ICCA: Greece and Italy in the Classical World* (London, 1979) 89–104; Ridgway, *FC* 94–6; Stewart, *GS* ch. 14.2; B.C. Madigan, *The Temple of Apollo Bassitas* II (The Sculptures. Ed., F.A. Cooper. Princeton, 1992).

10. Marble acroterium and figures from the east pediment of the temple of Asclepius at Epidaurus, *c.* 380–370 B.C. Asclepius was a major deity in the fourth century B.C., and his sanctuary at Epidaurus was furnished with a temple that was small but elaborately decorated with architectural sculpture and a chryselephantine statue (Paus. II.27.2). The acroteria survive in fragments; on the East Apollo was shown carrying off Coronis flanked by winged figures (Nike and Eros?), on the West a central Nike was flanked by horse-borne Breezes (**a**). Asclepius had little mythology with which to fill out the narratives; his sons fought at Troy, so the pediments showed the Amazons before Troy on the West (**b**) and the sack of Troy on the East. The figures are in violent poses with three-quarter turns and double twists, underlining the three-dimensional turmoil. Inscriptions name Timotheus, Thrasy-

medes, Hectoridas and Theo[; Pausanias (II.27.2) read an inscription naming Thrasymedes as the maker of the cult statue.

(**a**: Athens, National Museum 157. Height 78 cm; **b**: Athens, National Museum 4752. Height 55 cm)

B.R. Brown, *Anticlassicism in Greek Sculpture of the fourth century* (New York, 1973) figs. 8, 10–17, 19–21, 26, 29–35; Robertson, *HGA* 399–402; N. Yalouris, 'Die Skulpturen des Asklepiostempels von Epidauros', in Kyrieleis, *AKGP* II 175–86 and *APl* 21 (1992); Stewart, *GS* chs. 14.2 and 22.2, T 88 and T 89.

10a

11. Section of a frieze and free-standing figure from the Mausoleum, Halicarnassus, *c.* 360–345 B.C. Accounted one of the seven wonders of the ancient world, the Mausoleum, through recent excavation and more detailed study of its remaining sculpture, is beginning to resemble its original shape more closely (see **74**) and to have its sculptures placed in their correct positions. The tomb was most likely begun before Mausolus' death (*pace* Pliny, *NH* XXXVI.30) and was continued after it by his sister-wife Artemisia (Pliny, *NH* XXXVI.31). The designer was Pytheus of Priene, along with Satyrus (of Paros?). Four sculptors were also named in the sources, each in charge of one side: Scopas (east), Bryaxis (north), Timotheus (south) and Leochares (west); Praxiteles was substituted for Timotheus by Vitruvius (VII. Praef.13). It is now suggested that the named sculptors were in charge of the free-standing sculptures, not the friezes. Some relief sculpture is well preserved: the Amazonomachy (**a**) ran along the top of the stepped podium, the Centauromachy below the pedestal of the chariot group on top of the pyramid; the frieze of racing chariots may have been set up inside. The sub-

jects are traditional Greek themes; the compositions are repeated, with a stress on diagonal lines and widely spaced figures.

Some fragments of free-standing sculpture at different sizes survive. The best known and preserved is that usually called 'Mausolus' (**b**) but now thought likely to be an ancestor. It is over lifesize and was most likely one of the many statues that were set between the columns of the colonnades. The features are made to suggest a non-Greek figure: thickened lips, moustache, long shaggy hair swept back. Such 'individual' traits are often found on statues at the edges of the Greek world and may have been one of the elements that went towards the development of portraiture.

The temple-tomb and its sculptures emphasize the growing importance of the individual and of spectacular display in non-religious contexts.

a London, British Museum 1015 (with new fragment in Bodrum). Height 90 cm; **b** London, British Museum 1001. Height 3.00 m)

General: Ashmole, *ASCG* ch. 6; Robertson, *HGA* 447–63; K. Jeppesen, F. Hojlund and K. Aaris-Sorensen, *The Maussoleion at Halikarnassos I. The Sacrificial Deposit* (Jutland, 1981); S. Hornblower, *Mausolus* (Oxford, 1982) ch. 9; K. Jeppesen and A. Luttrell, *The Maussoleion at Halikarnassos II. The Written Sources* (Jutland, 1986). Friezes: D. Strong and K. Jeppesen, *Acta Archaeologica* 35 (1964) 195-203; B.F. Cook, 'The Sculptors of the Mausoleum Friezes', in T. Linders and P. Hellström (eds.), *Architecture and Society in Hecatomnid Caria* (Uppsala, 1989) 31–42. Free-standing sculptures: G.B. Waywell, *The Free-Standing Sculptures of the Mausoleum at Halikarnassus in the British Museum: A Catalogue* (London, 1978). For Pytheus, see J.C. Carter, 'Pytheos', in *Akten des XIII Internationalen Kongresses für klassische Archäologie Berlin 1988* (Mainz, 1990) 129-36.

11b

12. Marble head from the west pediment of the temple of Athena Alea at Tegea, *c.* 345–335 B.C. Pausanias (VIII.45.5) considered the Athena Alea temple to be far superior to all other temples in the Peloponnese and also said that Scopas was responsible for its design and for the statues of Asclepius and Hygieia (VIII.47.1), now thought not to have been originally installed in the temple. The pedimental sculptures have also been ascribed to him in modern times. The east pediment showed the hunt for the Calydonian Boar and the west the battle between Telephus and Achilles on the Caicus plain in Mysia. It has been difficult to reassemble the design of the pediments from the fragmentary remains, and no reconstruction has yet been convincing. The head of Telephus (**12**) has been considered to resemble the style of Scopas, with the turn of the head, the uplifted face, the piercing, deep-sunk eyes and the open mouth. The choice of subjects has been seen to reflect anti-Spartan feeling.

(Tegea Museum 60. Height 31.4 cm)
Robertson, *HGA* 452–5; A.F. Stewart, *Skopas of Paros* (Park Ridge, 1977) 5–84; N.J. Norman, *AJA* 88 (1984) 169–94 and *AJA* 90 (1986) 425–30; Stewart, *GS* 182–5 and 284–6. On Scopas, see now B.S. Ridgway, *Hellenistic Sculpture I The Styles of c. 323–200 B.C.* (Madison, 1990) 82–90.

Relief Sculpture

13. Marble votive relief from the Acropolis, Athens, *c.* 470 B.C. This small relief shows Athena in heavy peplos typical of the period (cf. **1a**), right hand on hip, leaning slightly forward against the spear that she holds in her left hand; her Corinthian helmet is pushed back from her face. She is gazing down at a squared pillar which has been variously interpreted as a *terma* (finishing post), a *horos* (boundary stone) or a stele (funerary monument) listing the names of Athenian dead. It is uncertain whether she is lost in contemplation or is sorrowing for the fallen.

(Athens, Acropolis Museum 695. Height 54 cm)
Ridgway, *SS* 48–9; F. Chamoux, *RA* 1972, 263–6; F. Magi, *Parola del Passato* 31 (1976) 324–35; G. Neumann, *Probleme des griechischen Weihreliefs* (Tübingen, 1979) pl. 20a; *LIMC* Athena no. 625.

14. Marble funerary relief (the 'Giustiniani Stele'), perhaps from Paros, c. 460–450 B.C. There is a gap in Athenian funerary reliefs between late Archaic (cf. *Pls. to Vol. III*, pl. 332) and the latter part of the fifth century. Early Classical funerary reliefs were however still being made in the rest of Greece (the islands, central Greece, Thessaly and Western Greece); some are furnished above with a floral finial. Paros has yielded well-executed studies of young

girls as **14**. The thin peplos is ungirt, the hair bound up, and the girl lifts a piece of jewellery (rendered originally in paint) from a box. The personal funerary subjects are conveyed with understated emotion (cf. **15**).

(Berlin, Staatliche Museen inv. 1482 (K19). Height 1.43 m)

Ridgway, *SS* 47–8; H. Hiller, *Ist. Mitt.* Beiheft 12 (1975) 175–6, pls. 17, 2 and 30, 3, K8; A. Kostoglou-Despoine, *Problemata tes Parianes Plastikes tou 5ou Aiona p. Ch.* (Thessaloniki, 1979). For the Classical period, see Ridgway, *FC* 144–9 and B. Schmaltz, *Griechische Grabreliefs* (Darmstadt, 1983) 189–222.

15. Marble funerary relief from the Ceramicus cemetery, Athens, c. 400 B.C. After a gap of more than two generations, Attic sculptors again produced figured funerary reliefs; it is possible that the craftsmen were those who until 430 B.C. had been employed on the Periclean building programme. The new shape is wider than the archaic version (see *Pls. to Vol. III*, pl. 332), allowing room for two or three figures. Pediment and antae frame the scene with an overlap allowed by the figures who are set in the foreground. A seated woman, named Hegeso, daughter of Pro-

14

15

xenos, takes a (painted) piece of jewellery from a lidded box held by the slave girl (cf. **14**); the background was blue. A melancholic abstraction pervades the composition.

(Athens, National Museum 3624. Height 1.49 m)

J. Frel, *Les sculpteurs attiques anonymes* (Prague, 1969) pl. 1, no. 17; D.C. Kurtz and J. Boardman, *Greek Burial Customs* (London, 1971) 130–2; Travlos, *Athens* fig. 410; B. Schmaltz, *Griechische Grabreliefs* (Darmstadt, 1983) 1–18.

16. Marble funerary relief from the Ceramicus cemetery, Athens, *c.* 394 B.C. This funerary relief is more precisely dated than others, as the inscription below names the war in which Dexileos was killed: the 'Corinthian War' of 394/393 B.C. The stele was set up by the family above a cenotaph; Dexileos' body was buried with the other war-dead in the state cemetery. The work itself is a rather frigid exercise with borrowings from the Parthenon (the rider's and horse's heads) and from the Nike balustrade (swirling draperies), and with hard crosslines of the fallen opponent's right side and Dexileos' (missing) spear.

16

(Athens, Kerameikos Museum P 1130. Height 1.40 m (with base, 1.75 m))

K.F. Johansen, *The Attic Grave Reliefs of the Classical Period* (Copenhagen, 1951) 48–9; Travlos, *Athens* fig. 411; T. Hölscher, *Griechische Historienbilder* (Würzburg, 1974) 102–4; S. Ensoli, *L'heróon di Dexileos nel ceramico di Atene* (Rome, 1987). Inscription: *IG* II² no. 6217. For the vases found in the cenotaph, see E. Vermeule *JDAI* 85 (1970) 94–111.

17. Marble funerary relief, found in the bed of the Ilissus river, Athens, *c.* 340–330 B.C. With the 'Ilissus' relief the great series of Athenian grave monuments is almost at an end, and the sculptor has taken the possibilities of the genre to their limits. A young hunter, a small club on his left arm and his dog at his feet, rests on a stele – his own grave – whilst a young slave boy sleeps and mourns by his side. The hunter gazes out beyond the framework of the composition and beyond the visitor who has come to mourn at the graveside. His father, leaning on his staff, right hand to bearded chin, seeks to understand the reason for his son's death. The carving is sure and bold, and the contrast between child, youth and old man is clearly stated. In 317 B.C. sculptured memorials were banned in Athens (Cic. *de legibus* II.26.64–6).

(Athens, National Museum 869. Height 1.68 m)

K.F. Johansen, *The Attic Grave Reliefs of the Classical Period* (Copenhagen, 1951) fig. 9; N. Himmelmann-Wildschütz, *Studien zum Ilissos-Relief* (Munich, 1956); J. Frel, *Les sculpteurs attiques anonymes* (Prague, 1969) 41–6; Stewart, *GS* 92–4.

18. Marble votive relief, found in the Artemis sanctuary at Brauron on the east coast of Attica, *c.* 410 B.C. Votive reliefs were of wood (e.g. the Pitsa plaques, see *Pls. to Vol. III*, pl. 323) or terracotta (e.g. the Ninnion plaque from Eleusis). Those in stone are mainly Athenian (see *Pls. to Vol. IV*, pls. 220–1 for Archaic pieces). The Classical versions are long and low and start about the same time as the funerary reliefs, i.e. *c.* 430 B.C. The 'relief of the gods' presents in high relief Zeus, Leto, Apollo and Artemis, all facing right, as they watch the approach of Iphigeneia with a deer. The carving is very Parthenonian in style.

(Brauron Museum 1180. Preserved length 1.08 m)

G. Neumann, *Probleme des griechischen Weihreliefs*
(Tübingen, 1979) 62, fig. 39a–b; L. Kahil, 'Le relief des
dieux du sanctuaire d'Artémis à Brauron: essai d'interpretation', in Jean-Paul Descoeudres (ed.), *Eumousia,
Ceramic and Iconographic Studies in Honour of Alexander
Cambitoglou* (Mediterranean Archaeology Supplement
1, Sydney, 1990) 113–17. On votive reliefs, see Robertson, *HGA* 373–8 and Ridgway, *FC* 130–44.

19. Marble record relief found on the Acropolis,
Athens, 403–402 B.C. Some Athenian inscribed
stelae recording treaties, decrees and such were
topped by figured slabs in low relief. They began
c. 425 B.C. The figures are usually deities or
personifications of the parties to an agreement.
19 shows the slab which topped the copy of an
Athenian decree (Cephisophon as secretary)
honouring the Samians who in 405 B.C. had
stood by Athens after Aegospotami. Hera,
Samos' patron goddess, holding a sceptre, clasps
the hand of Athena who grasps her spear: the
alliance is seen as a pact of *xenia* sealed with the
ritual handshake. The quality of the record reliefs
is generally poor.

(Athens, Acropolis Museum 1333. Width 56 cm)

R.E. Binnebössel, *Studien zu den attischen Urkundenre-
liefs des 5. und 4. Jahrhunderts* (Kalderkirchen, 1932) no.
22; Robertson, *HGA* 372–3; *LIMC* Athena no. 607;
Boardman, *GSCP* fig. 177. Inscription: *IG* I³ no. 127
and M–L, no. 94.

Free-standing Sculpture

20. Bronze statue of a charioteer, found at Delphi, 478 or 474 B.C. The charioteer was originally part of a group that included a chariot and four horses of which fragments remain. The group was a victory monument found below the Sacred Way, and its base with inscription is extant, showing it to have been set up for the owner of a winning team in the Pythian games: Polyzalus, tyrant of Gela in Sicily. The figure wears the usual charioteer's long robe with shoulder straps, and the victor's headband. The statue was hollow-cast by the direct method in which the original model was destroyed; it was also made piecemeal: head, upper and lower torso, arms and feet. The eyes were inlaid with glass and stone, the lips were copper-covered and the headband was silvered. In style the figure has Archaic traits (shape of head) but has an austerity of effect which is emphasized by the loss of the chariot which would have concealed the long, columnar skirt. The sculptor is not known, though Pythagoras, a Samian sculptor based at Rhegium in south Italy, has been suggested.

(Delphi Museum 3484 + 3540 (base block 3517). Height 1.80 m)
  Fouilles de Delphes IV.5 (Paris, 1955) 39–49 (F. Chamoux); C. Houser and D. Finn, *Greek Monumental Bronze Sculpture* (New York, 1983) 20–31; Mattusch, *GBS* 127–35. For the inscription, see Boardman, *GSCP* fig. 34.

21. Marble statue found at the site of Motya in western Sicily, *c.* 470–450 B.C. The site at which this statue was found was Carthaginian, and hence its interpretation is doubtful. The long dress and large breast band suggest a charioteer (cf. **20**), but the dress has also been thought to resemble that of a priest of the Phoenician god Melkart. The absence of the right arm makes it difficult to understand the action; the fingers of the left hand show the left arm was akimbo, the right arm was raised. The interplay between the fine, thin garment and the muscular body beneath is well managed. It is unclear where the statue was made or for what purpose.

(Motya, Whitaker Museum. Height 1.81 m)
  G. Pugliese Carratelli, *Sikanie: storia e civiltà della Sicilia greca* (Milan, 1985) figs. 239–42; V. Tusa, 'Il Giovane di Mozia', in Kyrieleis, *AKGP* II 1–11; N. Bonacasa and A. Buttitta (eds.), 'Le statua marmorea di Mozia e la scultura di stile severo in Sicilia', *Atti della Giornata di Studio, Marsala 1 June 1986* (*Studi e Materiali* 8, Rome, 1988).

20

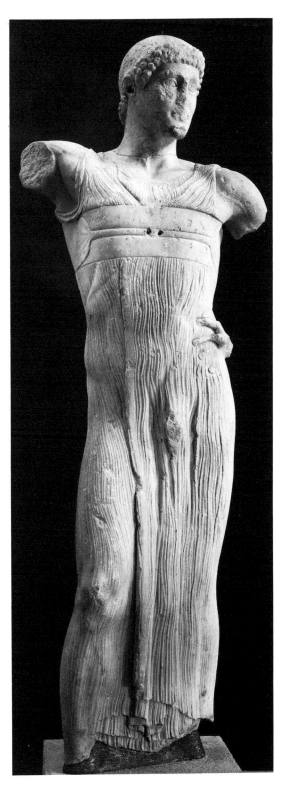

22. Bronze statues found in the sea off the south coast of Italy, near Riace Marina, *c.* 460–440 B.C. The 'Riace Bronzes' are two life-size naked and bearded male statues of warriors who carried shields and weapons. Statue A (**a**) may have worn a helmet and is in an aggressive stance; the more mature statue B (**b**) retains part of his helmet and is in quieter mood. Although a date in the middle of the fifth century has been doubted, it is now generally agreed that they were made in the same workshop not many years apart, most likely in Athens. The difference in their effect has been attributed to different bronzeworkers. They were hollow-cast by the indirect method and therefore retained their packing; their lips and nipples are copper-covered, and statue A has silver teeth. They were found without context, and whom they represent and where they were originally erected is still uncertain. The most widely publicized theory is that they were part of the Athenian dedication of 460 B.C. at Delphi for their victory at Marathon and that the sculptor was Phidias. They stand on the threshold of the Classical style: the soles of the feet of both bent and straight leg are still flat on the ground, but the treatment of their anatomy is more advanced than that of Early Classical work.

(Reggio Calabria, Museo Nazionale. Height of (**a**) 2.05 m, of (**b**) 1.97 m)

A. Busignani, *Gli Eroi di Riace* (Florence, 1981); W. Fuchs, *Boreas* 4 (1981) 25–8; C. Houser and D. Finn, *Greek Monumental Bronze Sculpture* (New York, 1983) 116–33; L.V. Borelli and P. Pelagatti (eds.), *Due Bronzi di Riace* (*Bollettino d'Arte Serie Speciale* 3 (1984)); Mattusch, *GBS* 200–8; B. Cohen, *Hesperia* 60 (1991) 465–502.

23. Bronze statue of Zeus from the sea off Artemisium, northern Euboea, *c.* 460 B.C. The statue of Zeus was found in the sea together with the Hellenistic bronze jockey (*Pls. to Vol. VII. 1*, pl. 189). The god levels his thunderbolt (missing) in his right hand as he strides forward with the effortless power and authority he wields. There are still Archaic and Early Classical traits in the figure: braided hair and locks, single viewpoint, but the rhythm of the movement is bold and well caught. The heaviness of the figure recalls the protagonists of the east pediment of the Zeus temple at Olympia (see **1**). The original location of the bronze foundry and the sanctuary in which the figure stood are unknown, as is the name of the sculptor. Names suggested include Onatas and Calamis.

(Athens, National Museum Br. 15161. Height 2.09 m)
  Ridgway, *SS* 62–4; R. Wünsche, *JDAI* 94 (1979) 77–111; C. Houser and D. Finn, *Greek Monumental Bronze Sculpture* (New York, 1983) 76–85; Mattusch, *GBS* 150–3.

24. Marble copy of an original bronze statue of *c.* 460–450 B.C. The copying and adaptation of Greek bronze statues in marble was a popular industry in the Roman period (*c.* 100 B.C. to the second century A.D.), and the Romans were mainly interested in statuary from the Early Classical period onwards. The peplos was the preferred garment for Early Classical statues of women and goddesses (see the temple of Zeus at Olympia, **1**), and a number of copies of Early Classical *peplophoroi* have survived. **24**, which has been named 'Amelung's Goddess' from the scholar who reconstructed the type from different versions of the head and body, is a fair example of the type. The figure is heavily swathed in a cloak which covers the peplos. The identity of the figure has been debated, but on the basis of a figure on a late-fifth-century calyx-crater it seems likely that it represents Europa; a small headless version of the figure in New York carries the name of Europa on the base. Finds of a statuette from Hama in Damascus and of a full-size copy from Baiae have proved the correctness of Amelung's reconstruction. The origin of the original workshop and the identity of the bronzeworker are unknown.

(Photograph of cast in Oxford, Ashmolean Museum, from Berlin, Staatliche Museen K 166 and 167 (605 and 1158). Height 1.97 m)

Ridgway, *SS* 65–9; Robertson, *HGA* 192–4; R. Tölle-Kastenbein, *Frühklassische Peplosfiguren: Originale* (Mainz, 1980) and *APl* 20 (1986); *LIMC* Aphrodite no. 148. For the identity of the figure, see M. Robertson, *Journal of the Warburg and Courtauld Institute* 20 (1957) 1–3. For Roman copies, see M. Bieber, *Ancient Copies* (New York, 1977) and B.S. Ridgway, *Roman Copies of Greek Sculpture* (Ann Arbor, 1984).

25. Bronze head found with other fragments off the toe of Italy at Porticello in the straits of Messina, *c.* 460–450 B.C. 'Il Filosofo', as this head has been dubbed, has thin head hair and heavy beard, together with individual features (thin lips, hooked nose). In general style the head fits best in the Early Classical period. The identity of the head is unclear, certainly it is no deity; it may be an heroic or human figure, but a centaur head (of Chiron?) has also been suggested. The ship from which this head and other bronze fragments were lost, may have sunk towards the end of the fifth century B.C., though some would place the wreck and the head later (*c.* 400 B.C.).

(Reggio Calabria, Museo Nazionale. Height 42 cm)

B.S. Ridgway, 'The Bronzes from the Porticello Wreck', in Kyrieleis, *AKGP* II, 59–69; C.J. Eiseman and B.S. Ridgway, *The Porticello Shipwreck. A Mediterranean Merchant Vessel of 415–385 B.C.* (Texas, 1987); Mattusch, *GBS* 198–200. On the date of the wreck, see D.W.J. Gill, *International Journal of Nautical Archaeology* 16 (1987) 31–3.

26a. Marble copy of the head of an original bronze portrait statue of Themistocles of *c.* 460 B.C. It was common practice for the Roman copyists of Greek full-length portrait statues to copy only the head and fashion them into busts or herms (as **26a**), adding an identifying inscription below. The Themistocles herm raises a number of questions – the head shows characteristics of the Early Classical period (e.g. the hair), whereas other details are more advanced, particularly the specificity of features (but cf. **25**). It is generally considered a copy of an original made shortly after Themistocles' death in 462 B.C. We are told that there was a small statue in the temple of Artemis Aristoboule in Athens which had been built by Themistocles near his house in Melite (Plut. *Themistokles* 22.1–2) and that there was a monument in the market-place in Magnesia where he fled in exile (Thuc. 1.138.5);

mention is also made of a statue or statues there (Nepos, *Themistocles* 10.3). Some scholars consider the herm head a clever pastiche of much later date. The beginnings of Greek portraiture can be glimpsed in some of the fringe areas of the Greek world, and the Themistocles head may point in that direction.

(Ostia, Museo Ostiense 85, from Ostia. Height of head 26 cm)
   A. Linfert, *APl* 7 (1967) 87–94; Ridgway, *SS* 99–100; D. Metzler, *Porträt und Gesellschaft* (Münster, 1971) 182–207; M. Robertson, *HGA* 187–8; Richter, *Portraits* 210–12. On the shrine of Artemis Aristoboule, see Travlos, *Athens* 121–3.

26b. Marble copy of the head of an original bronze portrait statue of Pericles of *c.* 425 B.C. Cresilas is said to have made a portrait of 'Olympian' Pericles (Pliny, *NH* XXXIV.74), most likely after his death in 429 B.C., and one was seen by Pausanias (1.25.1 and 28.2) on the Athenian Acropolis. The two have usually been identified, and the copies of the head of Pericles which are extant are usually connected with the Cresilas/Acropolis figure. The original was a full-length bronze like the Riace statues (**22**) and like them naked apart from defensive and offensive wea-

pons. We have no means of knowing how far or whether the features resembled those of Pericles – the statue was a 'role' portrait of the *strategos* type.

(London, British Museum 549, from Tivoli. Height of head 48 cm)

D. Pandermalis, *Untersuchungen zu den klassischen Strategenköpfen* (Freiburg, 1969); D. Metzler, *Porträt und Gesellschaft* (Münster, 1971) 213–22; Richter, *Portraits* 173–5; B. Cohen, *Hesperia* 60 (1991) 465–502.

26c. Marble copy of the head of an original bronze portrait statue of Socrates of *c.* 340–330 B.C. In the fourth century the range and number of 'role-types' of portraits increased and included tragedians and philosophers; of the latter that of Socrates has always been of interest. Two versions are extant, one perhaps of the early fourth century (Type A) and one after the middle of the century (Type B, **26c**). Both showed a bearded face with broad flat features and balding head. Interest in naturalism and individuality was increasing in the fourth century, and the literary comparison to a *silenos* (Plato, *Symp.* 215; Xen. *Symp.* 5.4–7) may have given the craftsmen a base from which to work. The second portrait

is likely to have been the one by Lysippus that the Athenians voted to erect in the Pompeion (Diogenes Laertius, II.43). The copy may reproduce some of the elements of Lysippus' version; the sculptor seems to have imparted a visionary look to the philosopher. But the individual style of the sculptor would have been affected by the opinion of the time and by the posthumous fame that Socrates had gained by that time.

(Rome, Museo Nazionale Romano (Terme) 1236, from Rome. Height 35.5 cm)

Robertson, *HGA* 509–10; E. Voutiras, *Studien zu Interpretation und Stil griechischer Porträts des 5. und frühen 4. Jahrhunderts* (diss., Bonn, 1980) 172–93; Richter, *Portraits* 198–204.

27. Marble copy of an original bronze statue of the Discus-thrower by Myron of *c.* 450 B.C. Myron of Eleutherae (on the borders of Attica) was noted for the rhythm and proportion of his figures and for the novelty of the poses in which he set them. Although his most famous statue in antiquity was a realistic bronze cow on the Athenian Acropolis, his best known work today is his *Diskobolos* or Discus-thrower. It was much copied in Roman times, the most accurate

version being the Lancelotti (**27**). It shows a moment of stillness in a continuous action. There are still Archaic features (e.g. the hair) and the viewpoint is single, but the pose unambiguously demonstrates the possibilities of the medium of bronze. The statue was presumably a victor monument, but there is no evidence for its location.

(Rome, Museo Nazionale Romano (Terme) 126371, from Rome. Height 1.55 m)

Robertson, *HGA* 340–1; F. Haskell and N. Penny, *Taste and the Antique* (New Haven and London, 1981) 199–202; Mattusch, *GBS* 144–50. On Myron, see Ridgway, *SS* 84–6 and 89 and Stewart, *GS* 255–7.

28. Marble copy of an original bronze statue of Apollo of *c.* 460–450 B.C. The conventional label 'Apollo' given to copies of original bronze statues of the Early Classical period may mark genuine Apollos or mask victor figures. The Kassel Apollo is certainly an Apollo, shown by his long hair and by the bow in his left and the branch in his right hand (both now missing). The soles of both feet are still flat on the ground (cf. the Riace Bronzes **22**). Some scholars connect the Kassel Apollo with the Apollo Parnopius on the Athenian Acropolis, said to be by Phidias (Paus. 1.24.8).

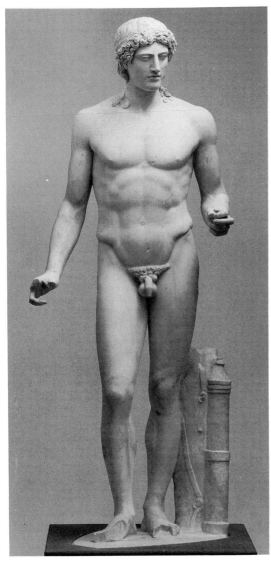

(Kassel, Staatlichen Kunstsammlungen 3. Height 1.97 m)

E.M. Schmidt, *APl* 5 (Berlin, 1966); Ridgway, *FC* 184–5; *LIMC* Apollon no. 295 = Apollo no. 41. For a selection of copies of 'Apollos', including the Kassel, see Boardman, *GSCP* figs. 65–9.

29. Marble copy of an original bronze statue of the Spearbearer of Polyclitus of *c.* 440 B.C. For the Romans Polyclitus of Argos was, together with Phidias, the most famous name in Classical Greek sculpture, and of his many works the *Doryphoros* or Spearbearer was the most popular, being frequently copied in whole or part. The sculptor was noted for his *symmetria* or commensurability and is said to have written a treatise on proportion, entitled *Kanon* (Pliny, *NH* xxxiv.55–6). For some the rules he was laying down were explicitly exemplified in the Spearbearer. The original was of bronze and showed a spear-carrying hero (Achilles?), left leg bent and loose, toes on the ground, right leg straight and tense. The movement is chiastically changed for the arms, right straight but loose, left bent but carrying the spear. Polyclitus' career seems to have stretched for thirty years, from *c.* 450 B.C., and he was considered the leading exponent of the Peloponnesian school of sculpture. For a copy of another of his works, the *Diadoumenos*, see *Pls. to Vol.* VII. *1*, pl. 147, found on Delos.

(Naples, Museo Nazionale Archeologico 6146, from the Palaestra, Pompeii. Height 2.12 m)

H. von Steuben, *Der Kanon des Polyklet* (Tübingen, 1973); Robertson, *HGA* 329–31; A. Stewart, *JHS* 98 (1978) 122–31; Mattusch, *GBS* 162–6; Stewart, *GS* 263–6; D. Kreikenboom (ed.), *Polyklet, der Bildhauer der griechischen Plastik* (Mainz, 1990) 135–98 and nos. 41–58. On Polyclitus and his school, see Ridgway, *FC* 201–6 and A. Griffin, *Sikyon* (Oxford, 1982) 120–32.

30. Marble copy of an original bronze statue of an Amazon of *c.* 430 B.C. The story of the competition between the most famous sculptors of the later fifth century to make a statue of an Amazon for the temple of Artemis at Ephesus is well known. The sculptors named by Pliny (*NH* xxxiv.53) are Polyclitus, Phidias, Cresilas, Cydon (usually counted a mistake for 'the Cydonian', referring to Cresilas) and Phradmon. All the other sculptors voted Polyclitus' statue second to their own. The competition itself has been doubted, as have the number and names of the contestants. However, there are many copies of what may be a set of Amazon statues that are of

29

30

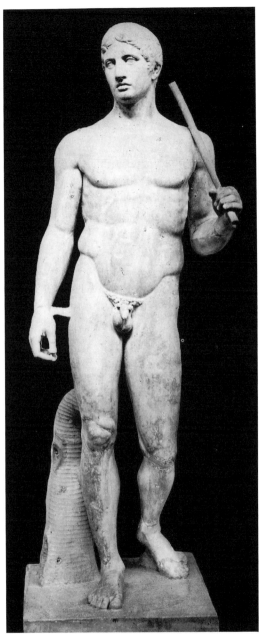

opinion exists for apportioning the copy types to individual sculptors. Fragments of the New York type have been found in the Baiae copyist's workshop.

(New York, Metropolitan Museum of Art 32.11.4, Rogers Fund. Height 2.03 m)

Robertson, *HGA* 334–5, 338–9; M. Weber *JDAI* 91 (1976) 28–96; *LIMC* Amazones nos. 602–605a; E. Harrison, 'Two Pheidian Heads: Nike and Amazon', in D. Kurtz and B. Sparkes (eds.), *The Eye of Greece* (Cambridge, 1982) 65–88; C. Landwehr, *Die antiken Gipsabgüsse aus Baiae* (Berlin, 1985) 60–76, nos. 29–41; Stewart, *GS* 262. For an unorthodox view, see B.S. Ridgway, *AJA* 78 (1974) 1–17; her belt, J. Boardman, *AJA* 84 (1980) 181–2.

similar size and dress, and copy works of the same date. All or some of these have been connected with the Ephesus dedication, and it is suggested that it was an Athenian thank-offering for a victory over, or peace concluded with, Persia. The New York copy (**30**) shows the Amazon wounded below her left breast and conveys pathos and exhaustion. No consensus of

31. Marble statue of winged Victory of Paionius at Olympia, *c.* 420 B.C. Statues of winged victories are known from the Nike made by Archermus of Chios and dedicated by Micciades on Delos *c.* 550 B.C. The inscription below Paionius' statue explains that the dedication was made by the Messenians and their Naupactian colonists from the spoils of their enemies (*apo ton polemion*), doubtless their success with the Athenians at Naupactus in 425 B.C. (Paus. v.26.1). Paionius was from Mende in northern Greece, an Athe-nian ally. The statue was set on a triangular pillar, 9 metres high, and was conceived as flying down to earth; Zeus' eagle spreads its wings beneath the figure's feet. The drapery is blown against Victory's body; originally her wings and cloak framed the composition. It is a virtuoso exercise in carving and was made from one block.

(Olympia, Museum 46–8. Height 1.98 m)
   T. Hölscher, *JDAI* 89 (1974) 70–111; E. Harrison, 'Two Pheidian Heads: Nike and Amazon', in D. Kurtz and B. Sparkes (eds.), *The Eye of Greece* (Cambridge, 1982) 53–65; Stewart, *GS* 89–92. For the inscription, see Boardman, *GSCP* fig. 129 and Stewart, *GS* 271, T 81. On Nikai, see Ridgway, *SS* 36–7 and *FC* 108–11.

32. Marble and limestone statue of a goddess, *c.* 400 B.C. There are a number of Sicilian and South Italian statues (both free-standing and architec-tural) that combine marble and other materials (wood, limestone, cf. **2**). For this reason the 'Getty goddess', which has a limestone body and garment with lines running diagonally across the legs, and a marble head inserted, has been con-sidered to come from Sicily or South Italy. The statue most likely represents Aphrodite and would have been furnished with added hair and adornment. The size of the statue suggests that it was a cult statue. There are traces of pigment.

(Malibu, The J. Paul Getty Museum 88.AA.76. Height 2.37 m)
   The J. Paul Getty Museum Journal 17 (1989) 110, no. 11; R.R. Holloway, *The Archaeology of Sicily* (London, 1991) 107–9. For acrolithic heads, see E. Langlotz and M. Hirmer, *The Art of Magna Graecia* (London, 1965) pls. 62–3, 86–7 and 118–19, and Ridgway, *SS* 121–3, 125 and 129.

33. Marble copy of an original bronze statue of Peace carrying Wealth by Cephisodotus of *c.* 370 B.C. The bronze original of the statue of Peace carrying the child Wealth was set up in the Athenian Agora (Paus. 1.8.3; IX.16.1). It is likely to have been commissioned by the *demos* of Athens as a cult statue to mark the 'universal peace' (*koine eirene*) agreed between Athens and Sparta in 371 B.C. Eirene's official cult was established in 374 B.C. The sculptor was the Athenian Cephisodotus, the father of Praxiteles, and the connexion between this group and the Hermes and Dionysus has often been noted. The intimacy of the group is new in sculpture and accords with other emotional aspects of fourth-century sculpture. Personifications were also

31

proliferating: Tyche, Demos, Democratia, etc. The finds from the copyist's workshop at Baiae include fragments of the cast of the Wealth.

(Munich, Staatliche Antikensammlung und Glyptothek 219, from Rome. Height 2.01 m)

Robertson, *HGA* 384–7; H. Jung, *JDAI* 91 (1976) 97–134; B. Vierneisel-Schlörb, *Glyptothek München, Katalog der Skulpturen. 2. Klassische Skulpturen des 5. und 4 Jahrh. v. Chr.* (Munich, 1979) 255–66; C. Landwehr, *Die antiken Gipsabgüsse aus Baiae* (Berlin, 1985) 103, no. 63; *LIMC* Eirene no. 8; Stewart, *GS* 173–4 and 275–6. For the Panathenaic amphorae that include the group on a pillar beside Athena, see N. Eschbach, *Statuen auf Panathenäischen Preisamphoren des 4 Jhs v. Chr.* (Mainz, 1986) 58–70 (year 360/359 B.C.) cat. nos. 38–45, pls. 16–19.

34. Bronze statue of Athena, found in the Piraeus, *c.* 350 B.C. The Piraeus Athena was found in a hoard of the early first century B.C. along with two fourth-century bronze statues of Artemis and an Archaic bronze Apollo (see *Pls. to Vol. IV,* pl. 133). The combination of deities has suggested that the statues had been looted from the sanctuary on Delos, perhaps by Mithridates. The goddess held a spear in her left hand and either an owl or a Victory on her right. The sculptor is unknown, but the names of both Cephisodotus and Euphranor have been suggested; the fourth-century date has been doubted and the figure has been placed in the late Hellenistic period. It seems to have been adapted by a Roman copyist who carved the 'Mattei' Athena. The fifth-century masculine goddess has been transformed into a benevolent and more sympathetic divinity.

(Piraeus Museum. Height 2.35 m)

G.B. Waywell, *BSA* 66 (1971) 373–82; O. Palagia, *Euphranor* (Leiden, 1980) 21–3; G. Dontas, *AK* 25 (1982) 15–34; C. Houser and D. Finn, *Greek Monumental Bronze Sculpture* (London, 1983) 58–61; *LIMC* Athena no. 254 (Mattei no. 255).

35. Marble copy of the original marble statue of Aphrodite of Cnidus by Praxiteles, of *c.* 350–340 B.C. The stories attaching to Praxiteles' Aphro-

dite Euploia, both political and erotic, are well known (Pliny, *NH* xxxvi.20–1). She was the first naked cult statue, and although her original setting is unknown, she was later housed in a specially constructed round temple. She is shown bathing, and therefore a reason is given for her to have set aside her clothes. This was a new manner of presenting divinity by teasing the observers with an erotic display, and Praxiteles began a vogue for naked female statues in monumental sculpture. The copies of this particular statue, which can be matched with coin types from Cnidus, and of the many later works give little indication of the quality of the originals.

(Reconstruction in Munich, based on Vatican inv. 812. Height 2.04 m)

Robertson, *HGA* 390–3; F. Haskell and N. Penny, *Taste and the Antique* (New Haven and London, 1981) 330–1; *LIMC* Aphrodite no. 391; Stewart, *GS* 177–8 and 279–80; R.R.R. Smith, *Hellenistic Sculpture* (London, 1991) 79–83. For the location of the sculpture, see I. Love, *AJA* 76 (1972) 61–76, 393–405.

36. Marble head of a statue ('The Aberdeen Head'), from Greece, *c.* 350–330 B.C. 'The Aberdeen Head' has always been considered 'Praxite-

35

36

lean', and some scholars would attribute it to Praxiteles himself, noting the greater subtlety of modelling and sensitivity in the surface of the skin than that found on the group of Hermes and Dionysus at Olympia which is now generally considered a Hellenistic copy. The head has deep set eyes, an expressive mouth, tousled hair and a withdrawn look. There are holes for a metal crown in his hair. It is not known whom it is meant to represent; Heracles and Hermes have been suggested.

(London, British Museum 1600. Height 29.2 cm)

A. Stewart, *Skopas of Paros* (Park Ridge, 1977) 105 (young Heracles); R.M. Cook, 'The Aberdeen Head and the Hermes of Olympia', in U. Höckmann and A. Krug (eds.), *Festschrift für Frank Brommer* (Mainz, 1977) 77; W. Geominy, *Die florentiner Niobiden* (Bonn, 1984) 246–7, 269–70. For the downdating of the Olympia group, see S. Adam, *The Technique of Greek Sculpture in the Archaic and Classical Periods* (London, 1966) 124–8 and K. Dohan Morrow, *Greek Footwear and the Dating of Sculpture* (University of Wisconsin, 1985) 83–4.

37. Bronze head of a 'Berber', from Cyrene, *c.* 330 B.C. The increase in portrait-like features, noted under **11** and **26** and linked to the peripheries of the Greek world and non-Greek subjects, is seen also in this bronze head of a young Libyan with high cheekbones and drooping eyebrows. The bone structure and skin texture are well conveyed and individuality is given by the beard and moustache. The teeth are silver (cf. **22**). Some scholars date the head to the third century.

(London, British Museum 268. Height 30 cm)
Robertson, *HGA* 517 and pl. 159a.

38. Bronze statue of a youth, from the sea off Anticythera, *c.* 350–330 B.C. The Polyclitan chiastic stance is here maintained, but the features are more intense. The original source and location are unknown, nor is it certain whether this is a victor statue or a mythological

37

34

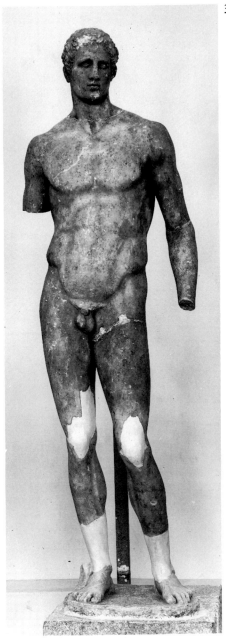

figure – Perseus holding the Gorgon head and Paris with the apple have been suggested.

(Athens, National Museum Br. 13396. Height 1.94 m)
    D. Arnold, *JDAI* Ergänzungsheft 25 (1969); P.C. Bol, *Ath. Mitt.* Beiheft 2 (1972) 18–24; C. Houser and D. Finn, *Greek Monumental Bronze Sculpture* (London, 1983) 92–9.

39. Marble statue of Agias, set up at Delphi, *c.* 338–336 B.C. About 340 B.C. Lysippus of Sicyon was commissioned by Daochus, tetrarch of Thessaly, to make a bronze statue of Agias, a victor in the pancratium and an ancestor of Daochus. The statue was to be erected in his home town of Pharsalus, in Thessaly. Daochus was a delegate to the Amphictyonic Council and its president 336–332, and in the 330s a group of marble statues of Daochus' family, including Agias, was erected in a hall to the north east of the temple of Apollo in the sanctuary at Delphi. The statues, which include athletes and non-athletes, survive in parts, as do their inscriptions. They were set in a line and resembled a three-dimensional panel painting. The Agias seems to copy the Lysippus original with its lean body, slim hips and small head; others recall earlier styles of figure.

(Delphi, Museum 369. Height 2.00 m)
    T. Dohrn, *APl* 8 (1968) 33–53; J.J. Pollitt, *Art in the Hellenistic Age* (Cambridge, 1986) 47–58; B.S. Ridgway, *Hellenistic Sculpture I The Styles of ca. 323–200* B.C. (Madison, 1990) 46–50. For Lysippus and his school, see A. Griffin, *Sikyon* (Oxford, 1982) 133–46. For the setting, see *Fouilles de Delphes* II (1960): J. Pouilloux, 'Le région nord du sanctuaire', 67–80, pls. 33–8, plans 11–12 and fig. 4.

40. Marble copy of an original bronze statue of Apollo ('Belvedere'), of *c.* 330–320 B.C. Leochares of Athens is usually thought to be the sculptor of the original on which the Belvedere version is loosely based. He made an Apollo Pythius (a type of Apollo as archer) that stood in front of the Apollo Patrous temple in the Athenian Agora (Paus. 1.3.4). Apollo Belvedere originally held a bow in his left hand and maybe carried arrows in his right. The effect of the statue is theatrical – Apollo appears, as it were, on stage and looks ready to depart. Fragments of a cast of the statue were found in the copyist's workshop at Baiae.

(Rome, Vatican inv. 1015, from Rome. Height 2.24 m)
    O.R. Deubner, *JDAI* 94 (1979) 223–44; F. Haskell and N. Penny, *Taste and the Antique* (New Haven and London, 1981) 148–51; *LIMC* Apollon no. 79 = Apollo no. 57. For the Baiae fragments, see C. Landwehr, *Die antiken Gipsabgüsse aus Baiae* (Berlin, 1985) 104–11, nos. 64–76.

Painting and Mosaic

41. Athenian red-figure volute-crater, found at Numana (south of Ancona), *c.* 460 B.C. In the second quarter of the fifth century B.C. Athenian vase-painters were attracted by subjects and styles that were currently being used for panel-paintings that were attached to the interior walls of public buildings in the centre of Athens. The Theseum, for instance, was adorned with scenes of Amazon and centaur battles (Paus. 1.17.2–6). Both these scenes are to be found on the Numana crater. The Amazon battle on the body is fought on uneven ground, with overlapping and fore-shortened figures and some that are partially hidden by the landscape. The centaur battle on the neck is taking place at the feast and includes an 'axe man' seen to relate to the Aristogeiton of the Tyrannicides group (see *Pls. to Vol. IV*, pl. 141) and to the Theseus of the west pediment of

the Zeus temple at Olympia (see **1b**). The borrowing by vase-painters of the styles and compositions suggested by descriptions of the panel-paintings is certain but is general, not particular.

(New York, Metropolitan Museum of Art 07.286.84 (Rogers Fund 1907). Height (without volutes) 63.5 cm; maximum width 58 cm)

ARV 613, no. 1, attributed to the Painter of the Woolly Satyrs; *Para* 397; *Add²* 268–9; D. von Bothmer, *Amazons in Greek Art* (Oxford, 1957) ch. 10, no. 7, pp. 167–9; M. Robertson, *Greek Painting* (Geneva, 1959) 123; J.P. Barron, *JHS* 92 (1972) 20–45. On Classical and fourth-century vase-painting, see Boardman, *ARFV* II.

42. Athenian white-ground covered cup, found at Vari (Attica), *c.* 460 B.C. The white-ground cups of the middle of the fifth century were special commissions, most likely for the grave. The Boston cup is unusual in shape, having the tondo painted on a surface that encloses the bowl of the cup. Apollo is shown standing on broken ground, as he reveals himself in his majesty to a seated Muse; the Muse holds her hand to her chin, as if puzzled. The colours and the arrangement of the figures (one seated, one standing)

have suggested connexions with panel-paintings of the time, especially those of Polygnotus.

(Boston, Museum of Fine Arts 00.356 (lost?). Diameter of bowl 16.5 cm; diameter of scene 11 cm)

ARV 741, below, resembles the later work of the Carlsruhe Painter; *Para* 413; *Add²* 283; M. Robertson, *Greek Painting* (Geneva, 1959) 132; J. Mertens, *Metropolitan Museum of Art Journal* 9 (1974) 91–108; I. Wehgartner, *Attisch Weissgrundige Keramik* (Mainz, 1983) 162, no. 2 and pl. III; *LIMC* Apollon no. 689a.

43. Athenian white-ground lekythos, from Oropus (Attica), *c.* 440–430 B.C. By the third quarter of the fifth century the proportion of white-ground vases was heavily weighted towards funerary lekythoi. The major painter was the Achilles Painter; his pupil, the Phiale Painter, who also painted white-ground calyx-craters, was more expressive in his treatment of the funerary subjects. A seated Hermes, the conductor of dead souls, waits while a woman, standing by her own tombstone, adorns herself before setting out for Hades. The seated/standing composition develops that of **42**.

42

(Munich, Staatliche Antikensammlung 2797 (inv. 6248). Height of lekythos 35.9 cm)

ARV 1022, 138, attributed to the Phiale Painter; *Para* 441; *Add*² 316; Simon–Hirmer, pls. XLVI–XLVII; J.H. Oakley, *The Phiale Painter* (Mainz, 1990) no. 138, pl. 109. For white-ground lekythoi, see D.C. Kurtz (ed.), *Greek Vases, Lectures by J.D. Beazley* (Oxford, 1989) 26–38 and D.C. Kurtz, *Athenian White Lekythoi, Patterns and Painters* (Oxford, 1975).

44. Athenian red-figure epinetron (onos), found in a grave at Eretria, *c.* 430 B.C. In the latter part of the fifth century vase shapes and scenes began to show a bias in favour of the life of women (pyxis, lekanis, epinetron; marriage, family life). Sometimes the reference is direct, sometimes what appears to be a direct reference is heightened by giving figures mythological names. On

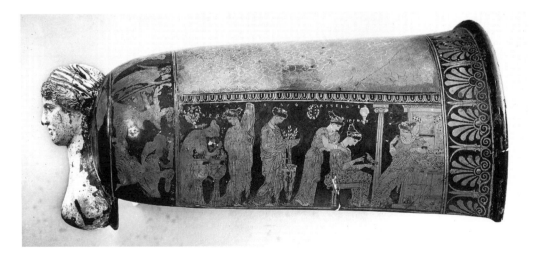

44, doubtless a wedding or funeral gift, the bridal scene is raised to the mythological level by the name of the bride, Alcestis, and by the significant names given to her friends, e.g. Asterope, Charis, and on the other side of the object there are Aphrodite and Eros, with Peitho, Hebe, Harmonia and such. The myth of Peleus and Thetis (cf. **47**) is set at right angles to the other scenes. The pretty, rather fussy style of painting points forward to the rich style of the late fifth century.

(Athens, National Museum 1629 (CC 1528). Length 29 cm)

ARV 1250, 34, attributed to the Eretria Painter; Para 469; Add² 354; LIMC Alkestis no. 3; Simon–Hirmer, pl. 216; A. Lezzi-Hafter, Der Eretria-maler, Werke und Weggefährten (Mainz, 1988) no. 257, pls. 168–9.

45. Athenian red-figure volute-crater, c. 400 B.C. There are many small vases in the late fifth century and some large and imposing ones, such as the hydriae of the Meidias Painter and his circle. The Getty volute-crater is one of the clearest examples of the elaboration in potting and painting that will be developed by the potters and painters of South Italy who learned their skills from immigrant craftsmen from Athens. The ornate neck and handles, the ribbing and the elaborately moulded stand are all elements that will recur in South Italian. The subjects of the decoration centre round Adonis, a popular figure of the time, particularly with women who celebrated a festival in honour of him. The Meleager Painter decorated cups, stemlesses and craters.

(Malibu, The J. Paul Getty Museum, 87.AE.93. Height of crater 54.2 cm; height of stand 16.4 cm)

L. Burn, GV Getty 5 (1991) 107–30. On Adonis, see W. Atallah, Adonis dans la littérature et l'art grecs (Paris, 1966) and LIMC Adonis.

46. Athenian red-figure squat lekythos with relief figures, from Kerch, South Russia (anc. Panticapaeum), *c.* 400–380 B.C. Late-fifth-century elaboration and richness are sometimes found on vases that have relief clay added to the surface of the vase. Xenophantos' lekythos is a particularly clear example of this. The floral decoration and certain of the supernumerary figures are painted in red-figure; the principal figures on the main scene of a hunt are added in appliqué. There is a small frieze of Persians on the shoulder, also in relief. Above that the potter has added his name and his origin: Xenophantos the Athenian. The decision to build up scenes in relief clay, which is popular at this time, was doubtless prompted by the popularity of relief scenes on metal vases (see **56**).

(St Petersburg, Hermitage St. 1790. Height 38.5 cm)

ARV 1407, attributed to the Xenophantos Painter; *Para* 488. E.A. Zervoudaki, *Ath. Mitt.* 83 (1968) 1–88 (see 26, no. 35); G. Kopcke, *AA* 1969, 545–551. For relief vases generally, see F. Courby, *Les vases grecs à reliefs* (Paris, 1922), esp. ch. 10.

47. Athenian red-figure pelike, found in a grave at Camirus, Rhodes, *c.* 340 B.C. Kerch (anc. Panticapaeum) is a site in the eastern Crimea where a great number of Athenian red-figure vases of the middle and later fourth century have been found. The name 'Kerch' has been given to the style of decoration in which the excavated vases were painted: much colour, relief and gilding, and a certain freedom of draughtsmanship. The myth of Peleus and Thetis was suitable both as a wedding and as a funerary gift, as the story could be interpreted for both occasions (cf. **44**).

(London, British Museum E 424. Height 42.5 cm)

ARV 1475, 4, attributed to the Marsyas Painter; *Para* 495; *Add²* 381; Simon–Hirmer, pl. LII. On Peleus and Thetis, see X. Krieger, *Das Kampf zwischen Peleus und Thetis in der griechischen Vasenmalerei* (Münster, 1973).

48. Apulian red-figure calyx-crater, *c.* 350–340 B.C. By the middle of the fourth century B.C. the schools of vase-painting that had developed from the immigration of Athenian potters and painters into South Italy and Sicily had split into distinct groups, and of the styles of painting and composition Apulian craftsmanship was the most flamboyant. Here Dionysus embraces Ariadne in the presence of a maenad and a satyr. A young Eros flies in to crown the couple, and the mask of a bearded satyr lies on the ground. South Italian and Sicilian potters borrowed Athenian shapes but also decorated native shapes with red-figure scenes. For other South Italian, see *Pls. to Vol. VII. 1*, pls. 95 and 190–1.

(Basel, Antikenmuseum BS 648.)

RVAp II 480, no. 18/13, attributed to the Hippolyte Painter. See also A.D. Trendall, 'Farce and Tragedy in South Italian Vase-painting', in T. Rasmussen and N. Spivey (eds.), *Looking at Greek Vases* (Cambridge, 1991) 151–82.

49. Detail from a wall-painting in tomb II beneath the Great Tumulus at Vergina, Macedonia, *c.* 350 B.C. Wall- and panel-painting of the fourth century was highly rated in antiquity. All is now lost, but one or two specimens of tomb-painting have survived. Chief of these are two painted tombs now recovered at Vergina (anc. Aegae), cf. **50.** A small rectangular tomb was discovered under the Great Tumulus; it had been robbed of its funerary offerings, but the wall-paintings are still preserved. The myth concerns Pluto and his rape of Persephone. One wall shows Pluto carrying off Persephone in his chariot, and the girl desperately stretches out her arms to the companion she is leaving behind. Another wall depicts Persephone's mother Demeter seated on the stone of sadness. The painting is deftly executed, with quick brush strokes and impressionistic lines. Several names have been suggested as the painter, chiefly Nicomachus, but there is too little evidence to decide.

(Vergina, in situ. Length of wall 3.5 m)

M. Andronikos, *Vergina* (Athens, 1984) 86–95. For another tomb painting of the fourth century, at Leucadia, near Naoussa, see Ph. Petsas, *Ho Taphos ton Leukadion* (Athens, 1966) and *Pls. to Vol. VII. I*, pls. 67 and 247.

50. Detail from a wall-painting on the front of 'Philip's' tomb under the Great Tumulus at Vergina, Macedonia, *c.* 340–330 B.C. The tomb, which is generally considered to be that of Philip II, has a Doric façade with a continuous frieze above. The frieze is decorated with a painting that depicts a hunt in a forest: huntsmen and hunting dogs, wild animals (deer, boars and a lion), trees, rocks and a stele. The figures are small in comparison with the landscape. Philip and Alexander (**50**) have both been recognized amongst the figures in the hunt. Comparisons have been made with the Naples mosaic from Pompeii which copies an original painting of Alexander versus Darius at the Battle of the Issus (333 B.C.). The name of Philoxenus of Eretria has been mentioned as the painter, but there is too little evidence on which to base a verdict.

(Drawing from the original in situ, Vergina. Length of frieze 5.60 m)

M. Andronikos, *Vergina* (Athens, 1984) 106–19. For the Naples mosaic, see Robertson, *HGA* 497–503, pl. 155.

51. Pebble mosaic, found at Pella, Macedonia, late fourth century. Greek mosaic as a means of covering the floors of the main rooms of private houses with patterned designs (floral and figured) begins in the late fifth century. The technique used natural pebbles, mainly black and white. By the later fourth century the figures were more three dimensional with other colours added (red, pink, brown, grey) and the occasional use of clay or lead strips to emphasize detail and contour. There is also shading, foreshortening and chiaroscuro. The prime examples have been found at Pella, on large floors of peristyle houses (see *Pls. to Vol, VII. 1*, pl. 66). Here Dionysus rides a panther (for another, see *ibid.*, pl. 139). One bears a signature: 'Gnosis made'.

(Pella, Museum. Height 2.65 m; width 2.70 m)

M. Robertson, *JHS* 85 (1965) 72–89, *JHS* 87 (1967) 133–6, and 'Early Greek Mosaic', in B. Barr Sharrar and E.N. Borza (eds), *Macedonia and Greece in Late Classical and Early Hellenistic Times* (Studies in the History of Art 10, National Gallery of Art, Washington, 1982) 240–9; Ph. Petsas, *Pella, Alexander the Great's Capital* (Thessaloniki, 1978) 83–114.

Luxury and Minor Arts

52. Bronze support for an incense-burner, found under the Sacred Way at Delphi, *c.* 470 B.C. It was a commonplace to shape handles in the form of the human figure; the best preserved Greek examples are those fashioned as handles for bronze mirrors. The solid-cast bronze figure from Delphi supports a hemispherical bronze bowl, raised from a single sheet of metal. The base to which the statuette was attached is missing, and the pierced and dome-shaped cover is not shown. The figure is similar to other peplos figures of the same period, cf. **1a** and **24**. The origin of the figure has been much disputed; suggestions range from Athens to Paros, from Sicyon to Syracuse.

(Delphi, Museum inv. 7723. Total preserved height 26 cm; height of figure 16 cm)
   Fouilles de Delphes v (1969) 155–60, no. 199 and pls.

44–7 (C. Rolley); E. Walter-Karydi, *JDAI* 91 (1976) 1–27; R. Tölle-Kastenbein, *Frühklassische Peplosfiguren* (Mainz, 1980) no. 28a, pls. 117b–118 (Syracusan). For mirror supports, see L.O. Keene Congdon, *Caryatid Mirrors of Ancient Greece* (Mainz, 1981).

53. Bronze head of Victory, found in the Athenian Agora, *c.* 420 B.C. 'Golden Nikai (Victories)' are known from ancient authors and inscriptions as statues which from the Periclean period onwards preserved the state's gold reserves. The head of half life-size, found behind the Stoa of Zeus in the Athenian Agora, has been thought to be the remains of one such. Grooves, of two separate dates, mark the places where the sheet silver and gold were fastened over the bronze base; small fragments of precious metal remain in the channels. The eyes and earrings are missing, as is the top-knot of hair which was made separately; parallels for the hair style can be found in contemporary vase-painting. Venus rings mark the neck.

(Athens, Agora Museum B 30. Height 20 cm)
   H.A. Thompson *Harvard Studies in Classical Philology*, Supplement 1 (1940) 183–210; D.B. Thompson, *Hesperia* 13 (1944) 173–209; Ridgway, *FC* 123–4; Mattusch, *GBS* 172–6.

53

2

54

54. Incised silver-gilt stemless cup, found in a tomb in the Bashova Mound at Duvanli (Bulgaria), late fifth century. Most silver and gilt objects have been found in contexts on the fringes of the Greek areas and beyond (Macedonia, Thrace, Scythia), as it was in those areas that objects in precious metal were deposited in graves and thus have been preserved. Many of the vase shapes are similar to those which survive in great numbers in clay; influence from one to the other is obvious. The stemless cup **54** is close in shape to the Athenian stemlesses of the late fifth century B.C., and the incised scene in gilt of Selene on a horse may be compared for style and composition with Athenian red-figure tondos. The cup may therefore have been made in Athens. The stemless carries an incised inscription in Greek letters on the rim: DADALEME.

(Plovdiv, Archaeological Museum 1516. Diameter of cup 13 cm; weight 220 g)

B.D. Filow, *Die Grabhügelnekropole bei Duvanlij in Südbulgarien* (Sofia, 1934) 5–7, 209–10 and pl. V; D.W.J. Gill, 'Classical Greek Fictile Imitations of Precious Metal Vases', in *Pots and Pans, a Colloquium on Precious Metals and Ceramics* (Oxford Series in Islamic Art 3, 1986) 9–30. For a general survey of plate, see D.E. Strong, *Greek and Roman Gold and Silver Plate*

(London, 1966). For Duvanli, see R.F. Hoddinott, *Bulgaria in Antiquity* (London and Tonbridge, 1975) 58–69.

55. Silver-gilt roundel, found at Galaxidi (anc. Oiantheia in Locris), late fifth century. This small roundel with gold figure on silver is all that remains of a stemless cup. The technique of the

55

48

figures is in relief, raised from the background surface (cf. **56**). Vase-painters and decorators copied the technique by using added clay (cf. **46**). The scene shows Eros assisting Aphrodite from the waves and has been thought to reflect the composition on the gold-figured base of the chryselephantine statue of Zeus at Olympia (Paus. v.11.8). The late-fifth-century date for the roundel has been doubted; it has also been thought to be Roman imperial.

(Paris, Louvre MNB 1290 (Bj 15). Diameter 3 cm)

E. Simon, *Die Geburt der Aphrodite* (Berlin, 1959) 43, fig. 26; Robertson, *HGA* 318–19, pl. 120d; *LIMC* Aphrodite no. 1173 (cf. no. 1172). For the throne of Zeus, see J. Fink, *Der Thron des Zeus in Olympia: Bildwelt und Weltbild* (Munich, 1967).

56. Silver-gilt bowl with relief scene, found at Rogozen, Bulgaria, fourth century B.C. This silver-gilt bowl has a scene in high relief. A masterful Heracles reclines on a rock and pulls a cowering Auge towards him. The inscriptions read: *AΥTH* and *ΔHΛAΔH* (='of course', i.e. ?Heracles). Gold is used for the hair, lionskin, quiver, etc. Pricked out on the rim of the bowl in Greek letters is the Thracian personal name DIDYKAIMO. The Rogozen treasure contained no fewer than 165 pieces of silver and silver-gilt, some native Thracian, some as the Auge bowl Greek, maybe Athenian.

(Sofia, Archaeological Museum inv. no. 22304. Diameter of bowl 13.6 cm; weight 182.83 g)

A. Fol, B. Nikolov and R.F. Hoddinott, *The New*

56

Thracian Treasure from Rogozen, Bulgaria (London, 1986) no. 4; B.B. Shefton, 'The Auge Bowl', in B.F. Cook (ed.), *The Rogozen Treasure, Papers of the Anglo-Bulgarian Conference 12 March 1987* (London, 1989) 82–90 and for the inscription, see 38–9 (Hind); *LIMC* Auge, and Herakles no. 2797.

57. Gemstones, fifth/fourth centuries B.C. The technique of gem-cutting re-emerged in Greece in the seventh century B.C. In the Classical period the development of styles in this miniature art parallels those in major works. Subjects range from mythological scenes (as Danae on **a**) to contemporary figures (as **b**) and from natural life (animals, insects, birds (**c**)) to political references (as Nike decking a trophy on **d**). Some gems are signed, as **b** and **c** which carry the signature of Dexamenus as maker, from Chios. The stones from which they were carved are various; **a** and **b** are red and white jasper scaraboids, **c** and **d** are blue chalcedony scaraboids. The nearest parallel in size and designs is to be found on coins.

57a

57c

57b

57d

(a Boston, Museum of Fine Arts 98.716, from Greece. Length 17 cm; b Boston, Museum of Fine Arts, from Kara (Attica). Length 20cm; c St Petersburg, Hermitage, from Kerch. Length 20 cm; d London, British Museum 601. Length 33 cm)

J. Boardman, *Greek Gems and Finger Rings* (London, 1970) pls. 449, 467, 468 and 590.

58. Incised ivory fragments from the covering of a box, from Kul Oba, near Kerch, fourth century B.C. Ivory was used for covering wooden boxes and was sometimes decorated with scenes which were incised and stained. **58** shows part of the fragmentary remains of ivory veneer of a wooden coffin found in a stone vault inside a Scythian tomb barrow at Kul Oba, some 6 kilometres west of ancient Panticapaeum in the Crimea. There were various scenes: Pelops and Oinomaus' chariot race, the rape of the daughters of Leucippus and the Judgement of Paris. The part illustrated shows Aphrodite turning towards Eros at her shoulder.

(St Petersburg, Hermitage KO 116.974A. Height of detail 8.5 cm; height of whole piece 21.5 cm)

E.H. Minns, *Scythians and Greeks* (Cambridge, 1913) 195–206 and figs. 100–3; N. Himmelmann-Wildschütz, *Zur Eigenart des klassischen Göttesbildes* (Munich, 1959) fig. 5a–b; M.I. Artamonov, *Treasures from Scythian Tombs in the Hermitage Museum* (London, 1969) fig. 257–62; G. Sokolov, *Antique Art on the Northern Black Sea Coast* (Leningrad, 1974) nos. 27–8; *LIMC* Aphrodite no. 1419, cf. Athena no. 419. For the Judgement of Paris, see I. Raab, *Zu den Darstellungen des Parisurteils in der griechischen Kunst* (Frankfurt, 1972) 183, B 54. For ivory from Vergina, see M. Andronikos, *Vergina* (Athens, 1984) 123–40 and 206–8.

59. Gold objects and cloth from 'Philip's, tomb under the Great Tumulus at Vergina, Macedonia, 340–330 B.C. The tomb of 'Philip' under the Great Tumulus at Vergina (anc. Aegae) has produced a plethora of gold objects. Two gold caskets served as ash urns; **59a** from the main chamber has lion's paw feet, a star design on the lid and attached rosettes on the sides inlaid with paste. The gold gorytus (**59b**), found in the antechamber, was a metal covering for a leather quiver and was essentially a Scythian object. A fragmentary piece from the same mould has been found in the Kuban. The scene shows a battle with men duelling and women fleeing with babies, perhaps the Trojan War. One edge is decorated with flying geese, and one with a guilloche; one prong has a single figure of a warrior. Jewellery was found in both chambers. That from the antechamber (**59c**) was found in the second gold casket. It comprises stalks and stems, leaves and flowers. Textile rarely survives, so the purple and gold cloth (**59d**) from the second casket is precious evidence for the technique and the designs, but also together with the much less preserved evidence for cloth in the first casket, it adds another element to the picture of burial practices being conducted in Macedonia that the Greeks had abandoned but knew from Homer (*Il.* XXIV.791–6).

58

59a

(Thessaloniki, Archaeological Museum. **a** (casket) Dimensions 20.7 × 41 × 34 cm; **b** (gorytus) Length 46.5 cm; **c** (diadem) Diam. 27cm; **d** (cloth) width 61.5 cm)

General: M. Andronikos, *Vergina* (Athens, 1984). Gorytus: V. Schlitz, *Revue archéologique* 1979, 305–10.

Diadem: R.A. Higgins, 'Macedonian Royal Jewellery', in B. Barr Sharrar and E.N. Borza (eds.), *Macedonia and Greece in Late Classical and Early Hellenistic Times* (Studies in the History of Art 10, National Gallery of Art, Washington, 1982) 141–51.

59b

59c

60. Bronze volute-crater, from tomb B 1 at Derveni, near Thessaloniki, *c.* 330 B.C. The Derveni crater was found in 1962 eleven kilometres north west of Thessaloniki. It had served as an ash urn for a man, the bones had been wrapped in a cloth (cf. **59**) together with a gold ring, three gold pins and a gold coin of Philip II. The upper part of the crater was covered with a cloth and a gold olive wreath placed on top of the strainer lid. An inscription in silver lettering round the rim says '(I am the crater) of Astion the son of Anaxagoras from Larissa'. The crater weighs 40 kilograms. Handles, base and shoulder figures were cast separately. The relief scene on the body of the crater concerns Dionysus and Ariadne, with maenads and satyrs. One figure wears only one sandal and has been identified as Lycurgus, king of Thrace, an opponent of Dionysus.

(Thessaloniki, Archaeological Museum, Derveni B 1. Height 85 cm)

M. Robertson, 'Monokrepis', *Greek, Roman and Byzantine Studies* 13 (1972) 39–48; Robertson, *HGA* 482–4; E. Jiouri, *Ο Κρατήρας τοῦ Δερβενίου* (Athens, 1978); B. Barr-Sharrar, 'Macedonian Metal Vases in Perspective: some observations on context and tradition', in B. Barr-Sharrar and E.N. Borza (eds.), *Macedonia and Greece in Late Classical and Early Hellenistic Times* (Studies in the History of Art 10, National Gallery of Art, Washington, 1982) 123–38.

2. CITIES AND ARCHITECTURE

J. J. COULTON

Greek architecture began to develop its characteristic features in the eighth century B.C., in connexion with the newly burgeoning sanctuaries. Temples were distinguished from houses by their length (sometimes about 100 feet), by their retention of a simple, free-standing plan, when contemporary houses were becoming more complex and crowded, and in some cases by a surrounding portico of posts. During the seventh century the characteristic methods of construction were introduced, with walls of large, well-jointed blocks of stone and tiled roofs, and at the same time the distinctive forms of the Doric order were developed (or invented), giving the impression of a traditional wooden structure turned to stone, which the archaeological evidence belies. The Ionic order developed more freely in the sixth century, although its origins may go back to the seventh, and initially the two orders were geographically separated.

By the beginning of the Classical period the orders, the monumental stone construction (see **65**), and the temple plan with surrounding portico (e.g. **64**) were firmly established, and the same forms and techniques were occasionally applied to other buildings in sanctuaries and civic centres. It is partly because the conventions were firmly established that it is possible to understand the developments, variations and refinements in Classical architecture.

The most important public buildings in the fifth and fourth centuries B.C. continued to be temples and similar cult buildings (**61–73**), but there was increasing attention now to the secondary buildings of a sanctuary and to the planning of the sanctuary as a whole (**75–78**). Obviously related to the latter was a greater development of town planning, particularly (but not only) in newly founded cities where existing buildings exercised no constraints (**79–81**). At the same time a growing range of civic buildings (**82–6**) appears, especially at Athens (the influence of democracy?); and although in the fifth century these are often built to lower standards than contemporary temples, by the fourth century the difference has almost disappeared.

GENERAL BIBLIOGRAPHY

A.W. Lawrence, *Greek Architecture* (4th edn, rev. R.A. Tomlinson, Harmondsworth, 1983); J.J. Coulton, *Greek Architects at Work* (London, 1977); *CAH* v² chs. 8*b*, *c* (R.E. Wycherley).

61. Paestum, second temple of Hera (= temple of Neptune) (**a**) view from north west; (**b**) view in colonnade. Down to the end of the Archaic period the Doric temples of the western Greek colonies maintained a distinctive style and a considerable degree of variation, while their contemporaries on the Greek mainland embodied by the late sixth century a more rigorous and severe canon. This canon, which continued into the second quarter of the fifth century, heavily influenced the temples of Victory at Himera and of Athena at Syracuse, built after Gelon's victory over the Carthaginians in 480 B.C., and much the same stage is represented by the second temple of Hera at Paestum (traditionally known as the temple of Neptune), which was probably built around 470–460 B.C. Because of its excellent state of preservation, it gives the best general impression of the kind of Doric temple built in the early Classical period.

The column height of this temple is twice the axial spacing, as in the temple of Zeus at Olympia (*c.* 470–457 B.C.), and the capitals have the stiff profile found in mainland Greek temples rather than the softer, more elaborate design of the earlier Doric temples at Paestum. Local style remains, however, in the details of the grooved triglyphs in the frieze, and the design of the front and back porches shows uncertainty in handling the new system. For the porch columns, although set on a substantial step, match the size

of the outer ones, with the result that there is insufficient space between them and the ceiling for a properly proportioned architrave and frieze; the frieze in particular is very low, with tiny triglyphs between elongated metopes.

In the cella, the main room of the temple where the cult statue once stood, two-storeyed colonnades helped to support the main roof beams, as in many other temples. Although the cella walls have been almost completely destroyed, the inner colonnades are unusually well preserved. A small doorway in one served a stairway to the roof space above the ceiling, a feature found in many other West Greek temples.

(F. Krauss, *Paestum, die griechische Tempel* (3rd edn, Berlin 1976) 46–65; J.J. Coulton, *JHS* 94 (1974) 13–24; D. Mertens, *Der Tempel von Segesta* (Mainz, 1984) 55–65; Berve–Gruben–Hirmer, 413–15 (**a** = pl. 116; **b** = pl. 121)).

62. Athens, the Parthenon seen from the Propylaea. The Parthenon, the most important temple of the Periclean construction programme, is remarkable in many ways. It was the first major mainland Greek temple to be built entirely of marble, and the only large temple to have all the metopes of its outer frieze filled with reliefs, both characteristics which link it with earlier treasuries rather than temples. The continuous frieze which runs all round the inner building is taken from the Cycladic version of the Ionic order, and this introduction of Ionic elements into the Doric order is typical of Periclean architecture. Cycladic masons, long experienced in marble working, are likely to have been brought in to work on the spectacular new building, and the mixture of styles would also have suited Pericles' view of Athens as combining the best of the Ionian and Dorian characters. The temple also embodies all the 'refinements' (variations from the expected straight lines and verticals), which are found in many of the more important Classical temples (see **63**).

The Parthenon stands on a platform built for an earlier temple which was begun probably in the 480s and never finished, and it took over a number of features from this predecessor. However, the east and west façades of the new temple had eight columns, not six, so the platform had to be extended northwards. Perhaps to counteract the additional breadth, the columns were made higher in relation to their spacing, and the capitals more compact, than its rival, the temple of Zeus at Olympia, which has the usual six columns (compare **61a**).

The additional breadth of the Parthenon is all given to the cella, providing a more spacious setting for the great gold and ivory statue of Athena (see **4** for reconstruction), and this may indeed have been the motive for the change in the exterior. Presumably also to improve the statue's setting, the inner columns are not in two straight rows, but continue behind the statue (contrast **61b**), and it is now known that the cella was lit by two large windows.

62

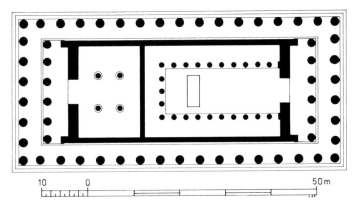

10   0   50m

The fragmentary accounts covering the Parthenon's construction show that it was begun in 447 B.C. and effectively complete in 438 B.C. They record the materials bought and wages paid only in summary form, and their fragmentary state means that no complete cost can be extracted, but calculations based on temples for which more detailed accounts survive suggest a total of between 500 and 800 talents, or roughly 3–5 million man/days.

A.K. Orlandos, *I Architektoniki tou Parthenonos* (Athens, 1978); Travlos, *Athens* 444–57 (**62** = fig. 566).

63. Architectural refinements; (**a**) imaginary temple with exaggerated refinements; (**b**) drawing for setting out entasis in a column of the temple of Apollo at Didyma near Miletus. The exterior of a major Greek temple consisted in principle of a series of uniform vertical columns standing on a horizontal platform and carrying a horizontal superstructure (the entablature). In many cases, however, a number of slight modifications were introduced of which the chief are shown here in exaggerated form. The stylobate on which the columns stand is not horizontal, but curves upwards (by 105 mm in 69.5 m on the long sides of the Parthenon), and the entablature repeats the curve; the columns have a curving taper or entasis (the deviation from a straight taper is 17 mm in a height of 10.43 m in the Parthenon), and lean slightly inwards (59 mm in

the Parthenon); and the corner columns are slightly thicker than the others (43 mm in the Parthenon). The purpose of these variations is much disputed, but the ancient written evidence strongly suggests that they were intended to counter optical effects which would make a truly regular building seem irregular.

Incised drawings on the lower walls of the temple of Apollo at Didyma show how the entasis was set out (**b**). The parallel lines, a dactyl ($\frac{1}{16}$th foot) apart, correspond in number to the number of feet in the height of the column shaft. The intended upper and lower radii of the column were set out from the vertical line at the right along the top and bottom lines, and the arc of a circle (radius *c.* 3.17 m) was drawn to join them. The column radius required at, say, 6 feet up is then the interval between the vertical line and the curve, measured along the sixth of the parallel lines, the radius at 12 feet is the interval measured along the twelfth line, and so on, so that the actual column shaft has the same width but sixteen times the height of the drawing. The effect is to stretch the conspicuous circular arc into a barely perceptible elliptical one. A similar system may have been used for the slight horizontal curvature described above.

(**a**) J.J. Coulton, *Ancient Greek Architects at Work* (London, 1977) 108–11, fig. 44. (**b**) L. Haselberger, *Ist. Mitt.* 30 (1980) 191–215; L. Haselberger, H. Seybold, *AA* 1991, 165–88.

63a

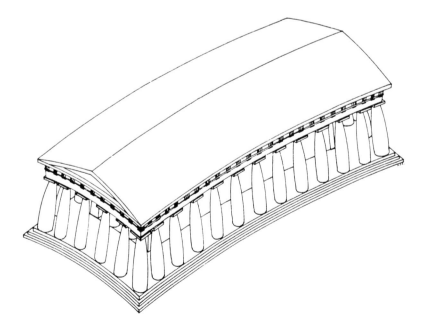

0.843

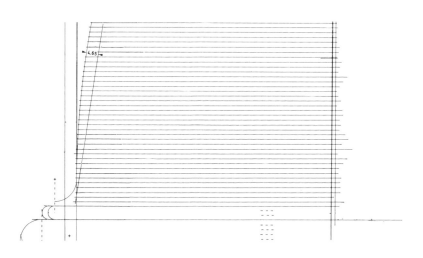

4.65

64. Athens, Hephaesteum, (**a**) view from the south west; (**b**) plan. The temple of Hephaestus, above the west side of the Athenian Agora, is less accurately dated than the Parthenon, but was begun around 450 B.C. and finished some twenty years later. It has the more slender columns, more compact capitals, and lighter entablature characteristic of Periclean architecture (compare

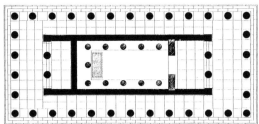

64b

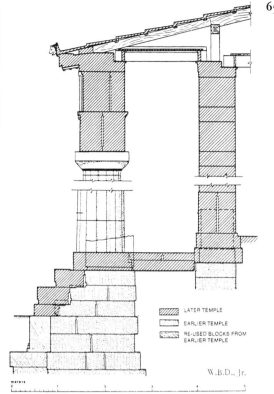

65

LATER TEMPLE

EARLIER TEMPLE

RE-USED BLOCKS FROM
EARLIER TEMPLE

W.B.D., Jr.

(a) with **61a**), and various features of sculpture and architecture, such as the inner colonnades around three sides of the cella, suggest influence from the Parthenon. The Hephaesteum is the work of an unnamed architect, to whom some scholars, but not all, attribute three other Attic temples, including that of Poseidon at Sunium (**65**) of which a notable feature is the continuous Ionic frieze, which runs across the front porch (pronaos) and on to meet the outer entablature.

W.H. Plommer, *BSA* 45 (1950) 67–78; H. Koch, *Studien zum Theseustempel in Athen* (Berlin, 1955); Berve–Gruben–Hirmer, 391–4 ((**a**) = pl. 32; (**b**) = fig. 67; Travlos, *Athens* 261–73).

65. Sunium, temple of Poseidon, (**a**) partial cross section, showing incorporation of earlier material; (**b**) cutaway isometric drawing, showing interior and system of construction. The temple of Poseidon at Sunium, crowning the southeasternmost point of Attica, forms part of the Periclean programme of rebuilding temples destroyed by the Persians, and its walls and colonnade stand on the foundations of its predecessor, with the new marble step blocks concealing the limestone of the old building (**a**). It was probably built around 440 B.C., perhaps by the same architect as the Hephaesteum. The cutaway reconstruction drawing (**b**) shows how the Ionic frieze above the pronaos extends across the whole building, as in the Hephaesteum, and the marble ceiling above is set at the same high level. The unusual arrangement of the frieze defines the front portico as a distinct area, and marks a

65b

growing interest in the management of architectural space, as well as solid volumes.

The characteristic construction of monumental Greek buildings can also be seen in (**b**). Large blocks of stone (here a local marble) are closely jointed together and held in place not by mortar, but by their own weight assisted by metal clamps and dowels. The columns are built up from separate drums, which would be fluted only after the building was structurally complete (cf. **69**). Marble ceilings, used earlier in the Cyclades, became accepted in Attica from the middle of the fifth century, and from there spread to other parts of the Greek mainland.

W.H. Plommer, *BSA* 45 (1950) 78–94, ((**b**)=pl. 8); W.B. Dinsmoor Jr., *Sounion* (Keramos Guides, Athens 1974) ((**a**)=p. 11); Travlos, *Attika* 404–15.

66. Athens, Acropolis, Propylaea, (**a**) plan; (**b**) west façade and Pinakotheke seen from Nike sanctuary. The Propylaea, or gate complex of the Acropolis, was begun in 437 B.C., after the Parthenon was virtually complete, and work on it stopped, probably in 432 B.C., before it was quite finished. A different architect, Mnesicles, was responsible for the Propylaea, so the close similarities in form with the Parthenon presumably result from the employment of the Parthenon work force. The Propylaea is unusually complex for a Classical Greek building, with a large central gate-building and smaller wings projecting westward on either side of the broad approach ramp; two wings to the east were also planned, but not built. As built, the Propylaea is not symmetrical, although it would appear so to an approaching visitor. Some scholars suppose that a grand symmetrical plan fell foul of the objections of a conservative priesthood, but it is equally possible that the asymmetrical plan is an intentional response to the limitations and requirements of a difficult site.

Along the west front, the wings and central building all rise from the same four-stepped platform, but the bottom step beneath the wings is built of dark grey limestone so that only three steps count visually below the smaller columns, but four below the larger ones. The central block has a shallow east portico, a door wall with five graduated doors, and a deep west porch with a marvellous marble ceiling supported on Ionic columns, which were by convention slenderer than Doric ones, and so could reach up beyond the outer Doric columns. The central span of the main façades is made wider than normal, with

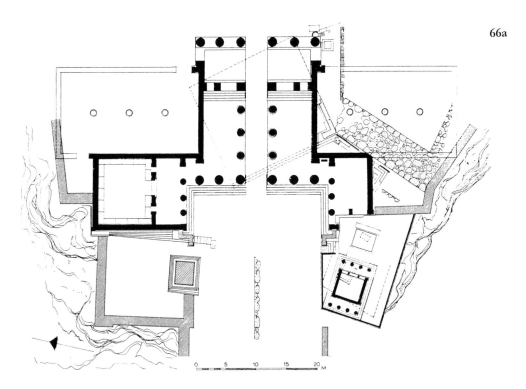

66a

three metopes instead of two in its frieze, so as to allow more space for the processional way up to the Acropolis. The columns of each façade vary slightly in height so that the entablature curves upwards, although the stepped platform, broken by the roadway, is horizontal.

J.A. Bundgaard, *Mnesicles: a Greek architect at work* (Copenhagen, 1957); Travlos, *Athens* 482–93 ((**a**) = fig. 614); Berve–Gruben–Hirmer, 379–84 ((**b**) = pl. 5).

67. Athens, Acropolis, temple of Athena Nike, seen from the east. The temple of Athena Nike stands on a narrow bastion which continues the platform of the Propylaea, so that the visible temple cannot be earlier than the 430s. Its style suggests construction around 425 B.C., possibly to celebrate victory over the Spartans at Sphacteria, for which the choice of the Ionic order would be particularly appropriate. The restricted site made a normal surrounding portico impossible, but since the west façade was a landmark for all approaching the Acropolis, the back of the temple was given equal treatment with the front.

The forms of the Ionic order are characteristic of Athens in the fifth century, following the Cycladic version with continuous sculptured frieze but no dentils. The capitals are more compact than Archaic ones, and similar to those of the Propylaea, where the Ionic architrave also has three horizontal bands (fasciae) instead of the earlier plain face. But the most important feature is the Ionic base, with convex, concave and convex elements, for this Attic form, at this stage simply one of several variants, later became almost universal.

The style and plan of the temple of Athena Nike connect it closely with a temple, now lost, which once stood by the river Ilissus, and less closely with the Doric temple built by the Athenians at Delos and the Erechtheum. An inscription naming Callicrates as architect for a new temple of Athena Nike has suggested that he was responsible for all four buildings, and he is also known to have worked on the Parthenon and the Middle Long Wall from Athens to the Piraeus. The inscription has usually been dated in the 440s in which case it would not be directly connected with the visible temple of Athena Nike, but this dating is now less secure.

I.M. Shear, *Hesperia* 32 (1963) 375–428; Travlos, *Athens* 148–57 (**67** = fig. 206).

68. Athens, Acropolis, the Erechtheum seen from the west. The starting date for the Erechtheum is unknown, but detailed accounts survive for its completion between 410 and 405 B.C. The work was generally divided into small contracts for, say, fluting one column or carving one figure, but some, like sawing wood, was paid at piece rates. Citizens, metics and slaves were employed side by side, and skilled craftsmen of all classes were paid a drachma per day. The architect, paid at the same rate, was changed annually, and was obviously responsible for the execution rather than the design of the building.

The Erechtheum, housing the ancient statue of Athena Polias, the most sacred in Attica, probably replaced the Archaic temple to the south west. No artificial platform could be allowed to interfere with the sacred features of the new site, however, so the north and west sides of the temple rise from a lower ground level than the east and south sides, giving it an unusually irregular design. The choice of the

Ionic order may have had symbolic value here too, but the richly decorated forms also make an effective contrast with the larger but soberer Doric of the Parthenon to the south. The Attic Ionic column bases are the first completely canonical ones of the type. Above the three-banded architrave, the dark stone frieze of the east, west and north porches (to which white marble figures were originally fastened) follows the Cycladic version of Ionic, but above the famous Caryatids of the south porch, the visual load is lightened by replacing the frieze with blocklike dentils, in the Asiatic manner.

L.D. Caskey *et al., The Erechtheum* (Cambridge, Mass., 1927); Travlos, *Athens* 213–27 (**68** = fig. 284).

69. Segesta, view of the unfinished temple from the north. Segesta in western Sicily was an Elymian city, but the temple is in a fully Greek style. It was probably begun around 420 B.C., and was still unfinished when the Carthaginians occupied Segesta in 409–405 B.C. The stepped platform had a rising curve, for which some of the setting out marks have survived (compare **63**), but the temple lacks the obvious Ionic features of the Parthenon or Hephaesteum, and has more in common with Sicilian temples of the

second quarter of the fifth century than with those of Periclean Athens.

The unfinished state of the temple makes it particularly interesting. Excavation has proved that a cella building was intended, so that the present state simply illustrates the normal Doric practice of building the outer colonnade ahead of the inner building. The entablature lacks only the final smoothing, but the columns are still unfluted and the knobs (for manoeuvring the blocks) and projecting panels have yet to be worked off the step blocks. These jobs were left to a late stage partly to avoid damage to fragile edges, but also because discontinuities in carving could be more easily avoided if the fluting and final blocks surfaces were cut when the columns, walls and steps were complete.

Mertens, *op. cit* (**61**); Berve–Gruben–Hirmer, 442–3.

70. Delphi, Tholos in the sanctuary of Athena Pronaea (**a**) plan; (**b**) restored elevation. The Tholos, which consists of a circular cella within a ring of columns, like a round version of a temple, was probably erected in the first quarter of the fourth century B.C. There was an Archaic forerunner in the sanctuary of Apollo, and two or three fourth-century followers (cf. **72**). Its func-

69

tion is disputed, but others are associated with deified or heroized mortals. Their elevation gives much the same effect as the front view of a normal temple, but unless there are fewer than sixteen columns (here there are twenty), a circu-

lar building will appear wider than the normal six-columned façade. To avoid a squat effect the architect, Theodorus of Phocaea (or Phocis?), made the columns taller than usual, and his book on the building may have inspired the lighter proportions found in most later fourth-century temples. The roof was pyramidal not conical, since a cone cannot be covered with uniform tiles. Just touching the inner wall surface are columns with Corinthian capitals closely related to those at the temple of Apollo at Bassae (cf. CAH v² 193, fig. 1b). The new capital type, and the use of an internal colonnade for decoration rather than to reduce the roof span (as also at Bassae) are characteristic of Peloponnesian architecture in the fourth century.

J. Charbonneaux, K. Gottlob, *Fouilles de Delphes, Le sanctuaire d'Athéna Pronaia: la Tholos*; F. Seiler, *Die griechische Tholos* (Mainz, 1986) 56–71; ((a) = fig. 27; (b) = fig. 29).

70a

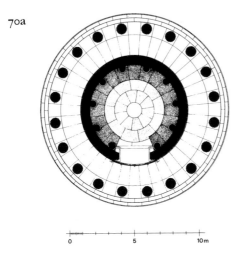

0   5   10 m

70b

0   1   2   3   4   5 m

71. Tegea, temple of Athena Alea, (**a**) plan; (**b**) restored drawing of interior. The Archaic temple of Athena was burnt in 394 B.C., but the new temple was not begun for some thirty years. Fourth-century temples often had only twelve columns on the long sides, but this has fourteen, and it is also unusual in having a secondary door in the north long wall; both features may have derived from its predecessor. Although the architect is said to be the sculptor Scopas, a Parian, the interior is typically Peloponnesian, with Corinthian half-columns along the walls with bases of non-standard profile. The capitals are more richly vegetable than earlier ones, (perhaps the sculptor's contribution), but have not yet reached the canonical form.

C. Dugas, J. Berchmans, M. Clemmensen, *Le Sanctuaire d'Athéna Aléa à Tegée* (Paris, 1924); N. Norman, *AJA* 88 (1984) 169–94 ((**a**) = ill. 9); (**b**) = Stewart, *GS* fig. 541, © Candace H. Smith 1990).

72. Epidaurus, Tholos in the sanctuary of Asclepius (**a**) restored cross-section; (**b**) unfinished Corinthian capital found nearby. The Tholos was the second major building in the new development of the sanctuary of Asclepius at Epidaurus, probably begun in the 360s, soon after the completion of the temple of Asclepius, but not finished for about thirty years. It probably commemorated Asclepius as hero, while the temple honoured him as god, but it is the Tholos which is the more elaborate, with magnificent

71a

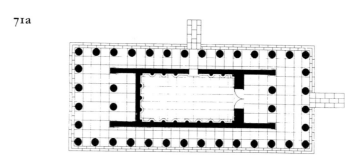

71b

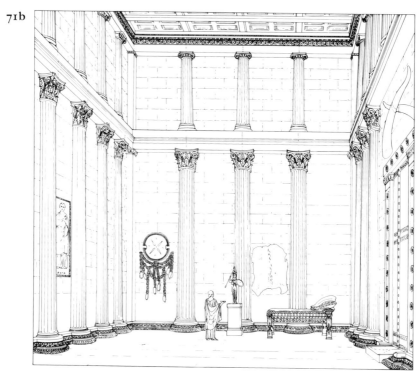

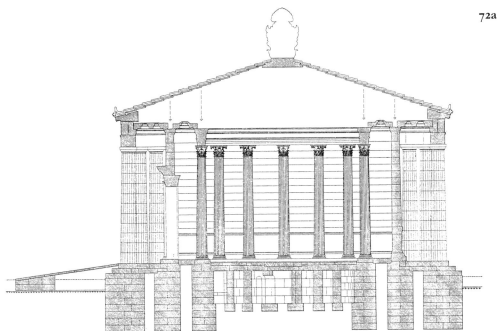

coffered marble ceilings, and beautiful Corinthian interior capitals (here on free-standing columns). The separate foundation rings for the outer and inner colonnades and for the cella wall are found also in rectangular temples. The narrow inner 'foundations' carried no superstructure, but defined a series of connected concentric passages beneath the floor, probably associated with the rituals in honour of the dead hero.

The Corinthian capitals of the Tholos come closest of any in the fourth century to the standard form so popular in the Roman period: two rows of spiky acanthus leaves occupying about half the capital height, then two pairs of spiral tendrils below the concave-sided abacus; in each pair, one spiral turns outward to support the abacus, while the other turns inward to meet its counterpart beneath a central flower. It is only the capital which is distinctively Corinthian in Classical Greek architecture; the remainder of the order is normal Ionic. Although of the same size and very similar design to the capitals of the Tholos, the capital shown in **b** was not used in the building, but found buried nearby. The roughly stippled surface shows that it was never finished, and one inner spiral was broken. The probable explanation is that it was intended as a specimen capital. For a complex piece such as a capital, a specimen was normally made at full size and in the intended material, and the masons would carefully copy it the required number of times. Usually the specimen would be used in the building, but in this case the undercutting of the spirals was apparently over-ambitious, and a slightly modified, more practical, design was produced.

G. Roux, *L'Architecture de l'Argolide aux IV et III siècles av. J.-C.* (Paris, 1961) 131–200 ((**a**) = pl. 39; (**b**) = pl. 48.2); Seiler, *op. cit.* (**70**), 72–89.

73a

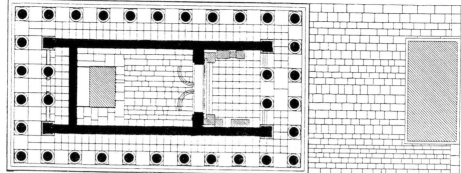

73b

1   0   3 M

73. Priene, temple of Athena (**a**) plan; (**b**) Ionic order. Architecture had flourished in Ionia in the sixth century, but very little has survived from the century and a half following the Persian suppression of the Ionian revolt in 494 B.C. From the middle of the fourth century on the situation changes. After the burning down of the temple of Artemis at Ephesus in 356 B.C. a new temple was begun, which adapted the forms of its Archaic predecessor rather than following the developments which had affected the Ionic order in Athens and the Peloponnese in the preceding hundred years. The same spirit of Ionian revival is visible in the temple of Athena on the new site

of Priene (cf. **81** below), begun soon after the city's re-foundation in 353/2 B.C. Its bases are of the Ephesian type, with a double concave element on a square plinth, and the entablature has dentils instead of a continuous frieze (contrast **67**). Only the three-stepped platform and the shallow rear porch are perhaps taken from mainland architecture.

The architect of this temple, Pytheus, was another who wrote about his work, and the design of his Ionic capitals was influential. The plan too was probably intended as the embodiment of a rational idea which could be followed by others, for it is based on a simple square grid.

68

The columns all stand on plinths 6 Ionic feet square and 6 feet apart, so that the axial span is 12 feet, and the centres of the corner columns form a rectangle 60 × 120 feet. The antae which end the cella walls are 4 feet across, and are aligned with the columns of the fronts and sides, so that the inner building is 40 × 100 feet; the interior length of the cella is 50 feet.

T. Wiegand, H. Schrader, *Priene* (Berlin, 1904) 81–119 ((**a**) = part of pl. 10; (**b**) = figs. 57 and 74 combined); M. Schede, *Die Ruinen von Priene* (2nd edn, G. Kleiner, W. Kleiss, Berlin, 1964) 25–47; W. Koenigs, *Ist. Mitt.* 33 (1983) 134–76.

74. Halicarnassus, restored model of the Mausoleum. The monumental tomb which Mausolus, satrap of Caria, had built for himself was one of the wonders of the ancient world. It was begun before his death in 353 B.C., but work continued into the 340s. Its form was derived from a variety of sources including Lycian pillar tombs, Greek temples and Egyptian pyramids, but the architects were Greek: Pytheus who designed the temple of Athena at Priene, and Satyrus from Paros; and so too were the sculptors who worked on its decoration and (to judge from their handiwork) the masons who built it. In this it illustrates the growing influence of Greek culture over non-Greek in Asia Minor.

Little of the building remains in place, and the description in the Elder Pliny's *Natural History* has given rise to a large number of rival reconstructions. Recent Danish work on the site has now limited the possibilities considerably, and it is clear that the building consisted of a tall podium carrying a colonnade of nine by eleven Ionic columns, above which a pyramid of twenty-four steps rose to a pedestal for the chariot group on the apex. The whole, according to Pliny, was 140 feet high. A sculptured frieze crowned the podium and another probably decorated the wall within the colonnade, but the main decoration was of free-standing sculpture, which probably stood on ledges on the podium, between the columns, and on the pyramidal roof (see **11**). The Ionic order is, not surprisingly,

very close to that at Priene, with the same Ephesian base profile, similar capital proportions, and blocklike dentils in place of the frieze.

K. Jeppesen, *JDAI* 107 (1992) 59–102 (**74** = pl. 30.1).

75. Delphi, sanctuary of Apollo (**a**) plan; (**b**) restored drawing of the Stoa of the Athenians with the temple of Apollo behind. The oracle of Apollo at Delphi was at its most influential in the Archaic period, and the sanctuary took its basic shape then (*Pls. to Vol. III*, pls. 309a–b), so that it

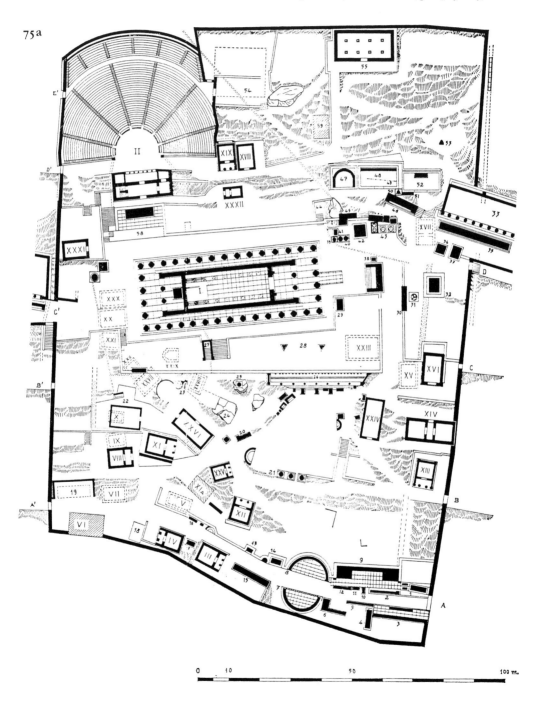

75a

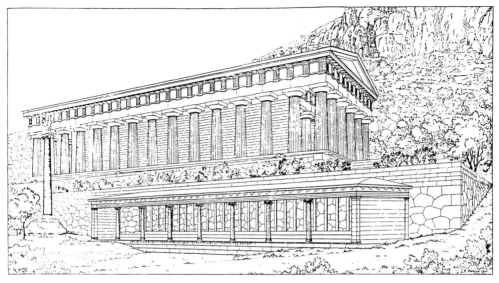

represents the kind of pre-existing background into which Classical buildings might be inserted. The buildings are arranged along the Sacred Way which zigzags up the steeply sloping site to the terrace on which the temple of Apollo stands, dominating the sanctuary by its size and central position. The altar, built by the people of Chios in the first half of the fifth century B.C., lies roughly, but not exactly, on the axis of the temple, but the other buildings are on various orientations, depending on the nature of the ground and the most advantageous direction for display.

The numerous small buildings with two-columned porches are treasuries, set up by individual cities as a mark of their piety and a display of their wealth. They could house the city's more valuable dedications and sacrificial equipment, and were often very richly decorated. Among the Classical examples are those of the Thebans (**a** VI; *c.* 370 B.C.) and the Cyreneans (**a** XIII; middle of the fourth century B.C.).

Another popular building type in sanctuaries was the stoa, a long, narrow portico which could be used both to shelter visitors and to protect and display dedications. At Delphi the Stoa of the Athenians below the temple terrace (**b**) faces onto an important ritual area, and was perhaps intended to provide important visitors with a sheltered viewing stand. It is notably small and irregular, but these features are a sign of the limited space available here, rather than of early date. The temple of Apollo shown dominating it on the terrace above is the one built by the Alcmaeonids in the late sixth century, but it was rebuilt to virtually the same plan after an earthquake disaster in 375 B.C.

A monumental inscription on the upper step of the Stoa of the Athenians shows that, like several other buildings in the sanctuary of Apollo, it was built to display naval trophies. The enemy is not named, which probably means that they were Greeks, not Persians. The choice of Ionic columns, rarely seen at Delphi, may indicate a victory of the Delian League. The column bases do not yet have the Attic profile (see **67**), and the style of the architecture and lettering suggests a date in the 460s.

The main post-Classical buildings on the plan **a** are the stoas to the east and west, and the theatre (II) to the north west.

Fouilles de Delphes II, Architecture et Topographie: many fascicles; G. Roux, *Delphes, son oracles et ses dieux* (Paris, 1976) (**a** = plan at end); P. Amandry, *Fouilles de Delphes II, La Colonne des Naxiens et le portique des Athéniens* (Paris, 1953) (**b** = fig. 7); G. Kuhn, *JDAI* 100 (1985) 269–87.

76. Restored elevation of the sanctuary of Hera outside Argos. Like the sanctuary of Apollo at Delphi, the sanctuary of Argive Hera was built on a steeply sloping site, and its first buildings belong to the Archaic period: a very early temple on the upper terrace (visible to the right of the later temple in the centre of the illustration), with a stoa and other buildings below it. However, unlike Delphi, the Argive sanctuary was approached by monumental stairways running straight up the hill, rather than by a winding roadway, a difference which became particularly clear after the extension of the sanctuary which took place in the fifth century B.C.

The old temple of Hera was burnt down in 423 B.C., but preparations for a new temple of Hera had already been begun about forty years earlier. First a broad terrace was created in front of the existing buildings, and another stoa was backed against it (the lowest building in the illustration). In the middle of the new terrace the temple itself was built, much taller than its predecessor, and incorporating several features from the style of Periclean Athens, although its architect was an Argive, Eupolemus. A broad staircase ran in front of the stoa and continued on to occupy the full width of the terrace, so as to provide monumental access to the temple.

The Archaic buildings had been roughly parallel to each other, following the natural contours of the hillside, but the Classical terracing was more consciously organized, with the new South Stoa set parallel to the Archaic North Stoa, and the temple on the same alignment between them. This arrangement provided a more orderly setting for the temple, and a display of parallel colonnaded façades rising above each other up the hillside, which must have been intended to impress pilgrims approaching the sanctuary across the flat Argive plain.

C. Waldstein, *Argive Heraeum* I (Boston, 1902) 105–36, pl. 6; P. Amandry, *Hesperia* 21 (1952) 222–74; J.J. Coulton, *BSA* 68 (1973) 65–85; P. Amandry in *Etudes Argiennes* (*BCH Suppl.* 6, 1980) 234–44.

77. Brauron, restored plan of the sanctuary of Artemis. The temple of Artemis at Brauron, built in the late sixth century B.C., stood beside a spring on a low terrace at the foot of a hill, with other structures to the south east. The full plan of the sanctuary is not yet excavated, but a major change in its arrangement must have resulted from the decision, taken in about 425 B.C., to enclose the area north east of the temple by building a large stoa around three sides of it. In the event the east and west sides were not completed, but the idea of providing such a

76

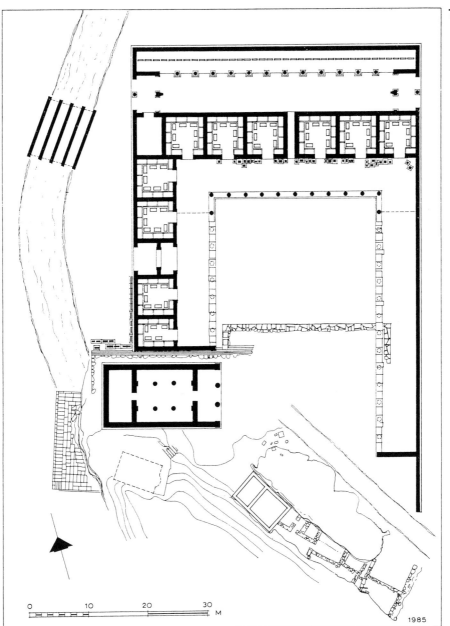

1985

regular colonnaded frame for a sanctuary was a novelty.

The Doric colonnade of the stoa is the earliest known to have three metopes above all its intercolumniations, and was also one of the first to require an internal angle. Here difficulties with the design led to a frieze with sharply reduced metopes, and a cornice with no mutules. Behind the north and west porticoes was a series of rooms. One on the west served as an entrance to the courtyard within, and a small room at the north-west corner probably controlled entrance to the narrow court behind; but the majority of the rooms were dining rooms, each equipped with eleven couches, so arranged that the feet rather than the head of a diner would be in the corner of the room; the two couches in each corner shared a table. Formal dining facilities of this kind were regularly provided at sanctuaries, although rarely on such a scale. The building may well be associated with the activities of the *arktoi*, young girls in the service of Artemis, but it is not the *amphipoleion* in which they lived, for that was two-storeyed.

Ch. Bouras, *I Anastelosis tis Stoas tis Brauronos* (Athens, 1967); Travlos, *Attika* 55–77 (**77** = fig. 58).

78. Olympia, model of the Altis, viewed from the west. The buildings in the sanctuary of Zeus at Olympia (the Altis) were already organized in the Archaic period, for the treasuries set up by various cities were all arranged in a row at the foot of the hill of Kronos (*Pls. to Vol. III*, pl. 304). In the fifth century the focus of the sanctuary moved southwards with the construction (*c.* 470–457 B.C.) of the temple of Zeus, clearly seen in the middle of the model (cf. *CAH* v² 194, fig. 17). It is roughly parallel to the older temple of Hera (which Zeus previously shared), but the most striking reorganization of the space of the sanctuary occurred in the middle of the fourth century. The stadium, which had previously extended much further west, was moved eastwards, and was now separated from the sanctuary proper by a large stoa, the Echo Stoa. This was not completed before the Roman period, but the intention is clear: it was to provide a colonnaded boundary to the sanctuary along the east side, and its axis is as nearly as possible parallel to the façades of the two main temples (a third temple in honour of the Mother of the Gods faced more southwards). At the same time retaining walls at right angles to the Echo Stoa were built behind and in front of the Treasury terrace, and the southern boundary wall was also built on the same axis, so that on three sides the sanctuary space was regularly defined and brought into relation with the main buildings.

Other Classical buildings visible in the model are the South-east Building to the left of the Echo Stoa (middle of the fourth century); the South Stoa, along the left side of the model, which was of similar date, and probably served as a viewing stand for processions approaching the sanctuary; the Leonidaeum, in the upper left corner, which was built by the wealthy Leonidas of Naxos in the last quarter of the fourth century and provided accommodation for important visitors, arranged around a spacious internal court; and in the upper right corner of the Altis proper, the circular Philippeum, begun after 338 B.C. by Philip of Macedon to hold statues of the Macedonian royal family, and completed by Alexander.

J.J. Coulton, *Architectural Development of the Greek Stoa*, (Oxford, 1976) 48–50 (**78** = pl. 3); I.D. Kontis, *To Hieron tes Olympias kata ton D p.Ch. Aiona* (Athens, 1958).

78

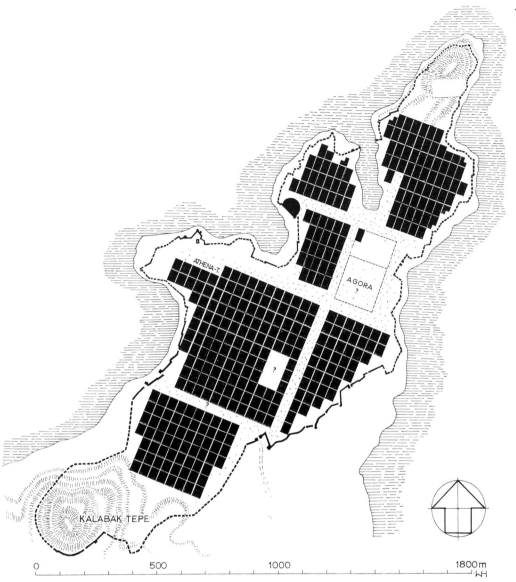

79. Miletus, plan of the new city. The Archaic city of Miletus was destroyed by the Persians in 494 B.C., and a new city, based on a regular grid plan, was laid out after the liberation of Ionia in 478 B.C. The periphery of the new city, as usual in both planned and unplanned Greek cities, was irregular, allowing the fortification walls to follow the most convenient defensive line. As in some earlier foundations, public spaces were set aside from the start. However, architectural development of these extensive areas did not seriously begin before the late fourth century B.C. It is to these areas that most excavation has been devoted, and the domestic areas of Miletus are largely unknown.

However, enough has been found to show that the city blocks at Miletus are of two different shapes following slightly different orientations; each part centres on, and probably took its orientation from, an important sanctuary: Apollo Delphinios to the north and Athena to the south. Earlier research restored the northern house blocks as only half the size of those to the south, suggesting a social differentiation, but it has recently been more plausibly argued that the block size was the same in both areas, with each type holding six identical house plots of the same size and shape, but differently arranged.

The replanning of Miletus has been connected with Hippodamus of Miletus, the most famous Greek city planner, who was certainly involved in the laying out of Piraeus in the 470s B.C., Thurii in 444/3 B.C., and, implausibly, Rhodes in 408 B.C. Hippodamus was credited by Aristotle with the invention of the grid plan, but excavation has shown that it was already used in Archaic colonies, presumably because it allowed a visibly fair distribution of property. His interests were perhaps rather in the best arrangement of such plans to allow for their proper social functioning, with house blocks of convenient size and shape, and sufficient public spaces in suitable positions.

Haus und Stadt 7–11, 247–53 (**79** = fig. 7).

80. Himera, air view of the excavated houses of the upper city, seen from the north west. Himera was founded in 648 B.C., but in the early fifth century, probably in connexion with the refoundation of the city as a Doric colony by Theron in 476 B.C., the irregular Archaic city was overlaid by a new street system consisting of parallel streets 5.70 to 6.00 m wide, which run east–west across the plateau which forms the main city. Presumably these were linked by a north–south street in the unexcavated area at the top left of the picture, but in any case the house blocks were *c.* 32.5 m (100 feet) wide, but up to 160 m long, more comparable to those of Olynthus (see **126**) than to the squarish blocks at Miletus (**79**).

Each long block was divided by a narrow drainage space into two rows of house plots accessible from the streets on either side. Each house plot originally measured about 16 m square (again very similar to Olynthus), but there was a good deal of redevelopment during the

80

short life of the city (destroyed in 409 B.C.), so that this egalitarian ideal did not last long. The surviving remains suggest considerable variation in house plans, but it seems that the main rooms were most commonly arranged along the street front, with a courtyard area in the inner part of the house. This meant that (unlike the arrangement at Olynthus where all houses faced southwards) the houses in the northern half of each block at Himera faced south onto their courtyards, while those in the southern half faced north.

Most of the excavated area at Himera consists of housing, but an Archaic sanctuary in the north-east corner of the city was allowed to survive the redevelopment, and retained its orientation without regard to the regularity of the new plan. No agora or civic buildings have yet been found.

J.W. Graham, *AJA* 76 (1972) 300–1; N. Allegro *et al.*, *Himera* II; *Campagne di Scavo 1966–1973* (1976) (**80** = pl. 2); *Haus und Stadt* 4–6.

81. Priene, perspective reconstruction of the city *c.* 300 B.C. Priene, one of the smaller Ionian cities, was moved to a new site in the middle of the

fourth century B.C., probably because the old site was affected by silting of the river Meander. The new city on a sloping site above the river plain (?) has the main east–west street *c.* 7.10 m wide, while the north–south ones, running up the slope, varied from 3.5 m to 5.9 m wide. The fact that many of the north–south streets, and even at one point the main east–west street, were stepped, has sometimes been taken as a failure of the planners in applying a rigid grid system to an unsuitably steep site; rather it reflects the importance of pack animals over wheeled vehicles in ancient transport.

The drawing shows the city at an early stage in its development, but rectangular areas within the network of regular city blocks have been set aside for the agora in the centre, for the most important sanctuary, of Athena (see **73**), on the shoulder above it, and for the sanctuary of Zeus (to the right of the agora). These temples were among the earliest public buildings in the new city, but attention was also given to the agora, and the frame of porticoes which later almost enclosed it had already been begun. Another early public project, vital for the security of the city, was the circuit of fortifications; defensibility

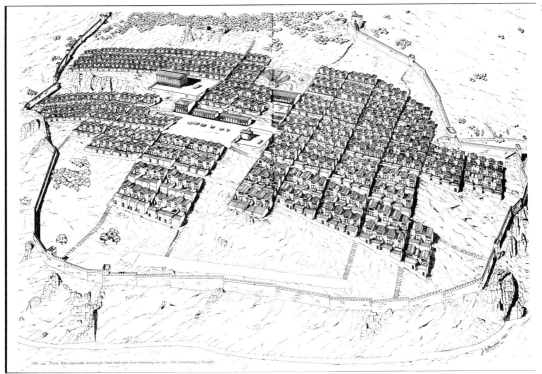

Abb. 144 Priene: Rekonstruierte Ansicht der Stadt bald nach ihrer Gründung um 300 v. Chr. (Zeichnung: J. Wendel)

was an important consideration in choosing a new city site, and, as at Miletus, the fortifications were not affected by the regularity of the city plan, but followed a naturally strong line, within which the city buildings fitted quite loosely.

As at Olynthus (see **126**) the residential blocks at Priene were divided into uniform house plots, but the blocks are less elongated (35.4 × 47.1 m) and the eight house plots run north–south. As at Olynthus, the houses were centred on a court, with the main rooms to the north, and were roughly uniform although not identical. However, the pattern of rooms at Priene, found also in the houses of other Ionian cities or colonies, is different, perhaps reflecting a social difference between Ionians and mainland Greeks.

Wiegand *et al.*, *op. cit.* (**73**) 35–328; *Haus und Stadt* 141–86, fig. 144.

82. Athens, Agora (**a**) restored drawing of the west side; (**b**) plan and restored elevation of the Stoa of Zeus; (**c**) plan of the Tholos and bouleuteria. Although there were certainly some civic buildings in the Archaic period, rather few are known, and even in the fifth century we know little about the centres of most major Greek cities such as Corinth, Argos, Miletus or Syracuse. The Agora at Athens therefore provides the best picture of Classical civic building, yet given Athens' unique constitution, it is probably not typical. By the end of the fifth century a number of public buildings lined the south, west (**a**) and north sides of an irregular open area which had been defined by stone marker posts by *c.* 500 B.C.

Several of these were stoas, whose use in sanctuaries is seen above (**75–8**); those shown in

the drawing are the small Royal Stoa (late sixth century but much rebuilt), which was the seat of the *archon basileus*, and beside it the Stoa of Zeus (*c.* 420 B.C.), with its elegant projecting wings. In the latter (**b**) the wings have their Doric columns set rather close, as in most temples, whereas the central part has a wider spacing with three metopes in the frieze above each span, which was more suitable to the scale and function of stoas, and later became a convention. The plan shows also how the inner columns (Ionic here, as usual), which carry the wooden ridge beam, are set twice as far apart as the outer ones which carry the marble architrave and frieze.

To the left in (**a**) are the circular Tholos with a conical roof, and the old bouleuterion (council chamber) built *c.* 460 and 500 B.C. (**c**). Behind the latter is the new bouleuterion, built around the end of the fifth century, when the old one became a record office. Both council chambers were designed with banks of seats round three sides of the room, a type which was widely adopted elsewhere. The Tholos, where the prytaneis, the fifty councillors on duty at the time, ate and slept, is not obviously adapted to its purpose, although various arrangements of couches within it have been proposed; perhaps the circular shape was chosen more for a symbolic than a practical reason. Unlike the Stoa of Zeus, which was a fine marble building, the Tholos and the two bouleuteria were sturdy but simple, with little external elaboration other than their tiled roofs.

J.M. Camp, *The Athenian Agora* (London, 1986) ((**a**) = fig. 71); Travlos, *Athens* 1–27, 191–5, 527–33, 553–61, 557–80, (**b**) = fig. 666, (**c**) = plan by R.C. Anderson, 1992); *CAH* v² 209–15 (R.E. Wycherley).

82a

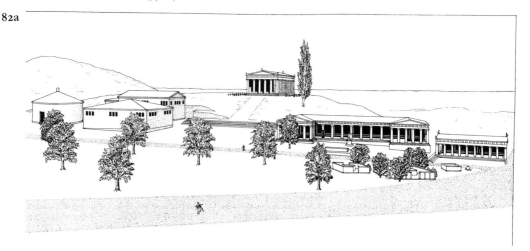

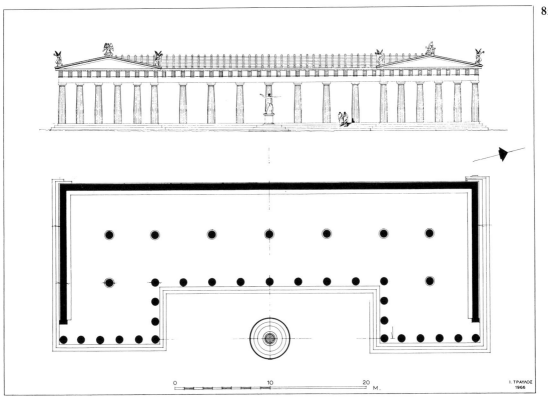

82b

0   10   20
M.

Ι. ΤΡΑΥΛΟΣ
1966

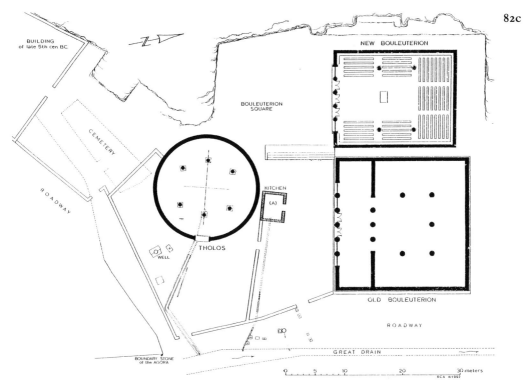

82c

BUILDING
of late 5th cen B.C.

NEW BOULEUTERION

BOULEUTERION
SQUARE

CEMETERY

ROADWAY

KITCHEN
(A)

THOLOS

WELL

OLD BOULEUTERION

ROADWAY

BOUNDARY STONE
of the AGORA

GREAT DRAIN

0   5   10   20   30 meters

RCA 4/1992

79

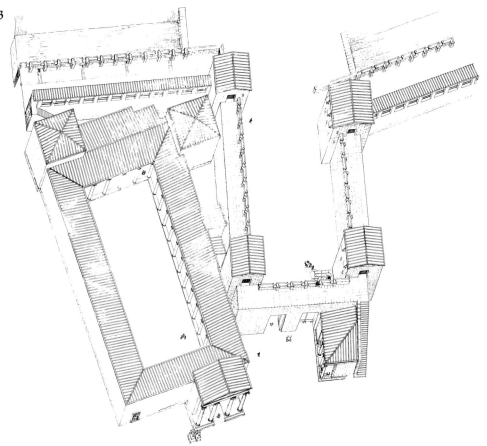

83. Athens, Pompeion and Dipylon Gate, axonometric reconstruction, looking north west. Processions were an important part of Greek public religion, and in Athens perhaps the most important was the procession of the Great Panathenaea, which every four years wound its way from the Dipylon Gate through the Agora to the Acropolis. The mustering area was just within the fifth-century fortifications, between the Dipylon and Sacred Gates, and at the end of the century a substantial building was constructed to house these preparations. The main element was a large court surrounded by porticoes (a common element in many later civic buildings), which offered a convenient combination of shelter and unobstructed space. The court was entered by small propylon (columned gateway) which, like the much grander entrance to the Acropolis (**66**), had a ramp passing through the middle, and other rooms, perhaps dining rooms, opened off the north and west porticoes.

The propylon was not in the centre of the east side but near the north-east corner, and the rooms to the north and west varied in size to fit the space available between the court and the fortifications, so that the Pompeion gives the impression of a series of distinct elements efficiently fitted into an awkward space, rather than a co-ordinated complex. Although the porch and court had Ionic columns, the materials and construction were noticeably less ambitious than contemporary temples; the walls were of mud brick on a dressed stone socle; the columns were unfluted, and the beams they carried were probably of wood rather than stone.

W. Hoepfner, *Kerameikos* x, *Das Pompeion und seine Nachfolgerbauten* (Berlin, 1976) fig. 147.

84. Piraeus, Arsenal of Philo, (**a**) marble stele with specifications; (**b**) perspective reconstruction. Philo of Eleusis is better known to us than any other Classical Greek architect. He was rich

```
ᴸ ᴼ
. Υ Ν Γ Ρ Α Φ Α Ι Τ Η Σ Σ Κ Ε Υ Ο Θ Η Κ Η Σ Τ Η Σ Λ Ι Θ Ι Ν Η Σ Τ Ο Ι Σ Κ Ρ Ε Μ Α Σ Τ Ο Ι Σ Σ Κ Ε Υ Ε Σ Ι Ν
Ε Υ Θ Υ Δ Ο Μ Ο Υ Δ Η Μ Η Τ Ρ Ι Ο Υ Μ Ε Λ Ι Τ Ε Ω Σ Φ Ι Λ Ω Ν Ο Σ Ε Ξ Η Κ Ε Σ Τ Ι Δ Ο Υ Ε Λ Ε Υ Σ Ι Ν Ι Ο Υ
Σ Κ Ε Υ Ο Θ Η Κ Η Ν Ο Ι Κ Ο Δ Ο Μ Η Σ Α Ι Τ Ο Ι Σ Κ Ρ Ε Μ Α Σ Τ Ο Ι Σ Σ Κ Ε Υ Ε Σ Ι Ν Ε Ν Σ Ε Ι Α Ι Α Ρ Ξ Α
Μ Ε Ν Ο Ν Α Π Ο Τ Ο Υ Γ Ρ Ο Γ Υ Λ Λ Ι Ο Υ Τ Ο Υ Ε Σ Α Γ Ο Ρ Α Σ Γ Ρ Ο Σ Ι Ο Ν Τ Ι Ε Κ Τ Ο Υ Ο Γ Ι Σ Θ Ε Ν Τ Ω Ν Ν    5
Ε Ω Σ Ο Ι Κ Ω Ν Τ Ω Ν Ο Μ Ο Τ Ε Γ Ω Ν Μ Η Κ Ο Σ Τ Ε Τ Τ Α Ρ Ω Ν Γ Λ Ε Ο Ρ Ω Ν Γ Λ Α Τ Ο Σ Γ Ε Ν Τ Η Κ Ο Ν Τ Α Γ
Ο Δ Ω Ν Κ Α Ι Γ Ε Ν Τ Ε Σ Υ Ν Τ Ο Ι Σ Τ Ο Ι Χ Ο Ι Σ
```

[Θ]εο[ί].

[σ]ΥΝΓΡΑΦΑὶ ΤᾶC CΚΕΥΟΘΗΚΗC ΤᾶC ΛΙΘΙΝΗC ΤΟῖC ΚΡΕΜΑCΤΟῖC CΚΕΎΕCΙΝ
ΕΥ̓ΘΥΔΌΜΟΥ ΔΗΜΗΤΡΊΟΥ ΜΕΛΙΤΈΩC, ΦΊΛΩΝΟC Ἐ ΞΗΚΕCΤΊΔΟΥˑ Ἐ ΛΕΥCΙΝΊΟΥ.
CΚΕΥΟΘΉΚΗΝ ΟἰΚΟΔΟΜῆCΑΙ ΤΟῖC ΚΡΕΜΑCΤΟῖC CΚΕΎΕCΙΝ ἐΝ ΖΕΊΑΙ ἀΡΞΑ-
ΜΕΝΟΝ ἀΠὸ ΤΟΥ̓ ΠΡΟΠΥΛΛΊΟΥ ΤΟΥ̓ ἐΞ ἀΓΟΡᾶC ΠΡΟCΙΌΝΤΙ ἐΚ ΤΟΥ̓ ὄΠΙCΘΕΝ ΤῶΝ Ν-   5
ΕΩCΟΊΚΩΝ ΤῶΝ ὀΜΟΤΕΓῶΝ, Μ̄ΑΚΟC ΤΕΤΤΆΡΩΝ ΠΛΈΘΡΩΝ, ΠΛΆΤΟC ΠΕΝΤΉΚΟΝΤΑ Π-
ΟΔῶΝ ΚΑὶ ΠΈΝΤΕ CὺΝ ΤΟῖC ΤΟΊΧΟΙC.

Lines 1–7
The gods
Specifications of the stone arsenal for the loose tackle, by Euthydomus,
son of Demetrius of Melite and Philo, son of Exekestides of Eleusis.
Build an arsenal for loose tackle in Zea, beginning by the gateway from
the agora as one approaches from behind the shipsheds with a common
roof, 400 ft in length, 55 ft in width, including the walls.

```
                Ε Π Ι Δ Ε Τ Ο Υ Ο Ρ Θ Ο Σ Τ Α Τ Ο Υ Γ Λ Ι Ν Θ Ο Ι Σ Ι Ν Ο Ι Κ Ο Δ Ο Μ Η Σ Ε Ι Τ Ο Υ Σ Τ
Ο Ι Χ Ο Υ Σ Μ Η Κ Ο Σ Τ Ε Τ Ρ Α Γ Ο Σ Ι Ν Γ Λ Α Τ Ο Σ Γ Ε Ν Τ Ε Η Μ Ι Γ Ο Δ Ι Ω Ν Ε Γ Ι Δ Ε Τ Α Ι Σ Γ Ω Ν Ι
Α Ι Σ Μ Η Κ Ο Σ Ε Κ Τ Ο Υ Μ Ε Τ Ρ Ο Υ Τ Ω Ν Τ Ρ Ι Γ Λ Υ Φ Ω Ν Γ Α Χ Ο Σ Τ Ρ Ι Η Μ Ι Γ Ο Δ Ι Ο Ι Σ Υ Ψ Ο Σ Δ
Ε Γ Ο Ι Η Σ Ε Ι Τ Ω Ν Τ Ο Ι Χ Ω Ν Α Γ Ο Τ Η Σ Ε Υ Θ Υ Ν Τ Η Ρ Ι Α Σ Ε Γ Τ Α Κ Α Ι Ε Ι Κ Ο Σ Ι Γ Ο Δ Ω Ν Σ Υ
Ν Τ Η Ι Τ Ρ Ι Γ Λ Υ Φ Ω Ι Υ Γ Ο Τ Ο Γ Ε Ι Σ Ο Ν                                            30
```

ἐΠὶ Δὲ ΤΟΥ̓ ὀΡΘΟCΤΆΤΟΥ ΠΛΙΝΘΊCΙΝ ΟἰΚΟΔΟΜΉCΕΙ ΤΟὺC Τ-
ΟΊΧΟΥC, Μ̄ΑΚΟC ΤΕΤΡΆΠΟCΙΝ, ΠΛΆΤΟC ΠΈΝΤΕ ἡΜΙΠΟΔΊΩΝ, ἐΠὶ Δὲ ΤΑῖC ΓΩΝΙ-
ΑΙC Μ̄ΑΚΟC ἐΚ ΤΟΥ̓ ΜΈΤΡΟΥ ΤῶΝ ΤΡΙΓΛΎΦΩΝ, ΠΆΧΟC ΤΡΙΗΜΙΠΟΔΊΟΙC. Ὕ ΟC Δ-
ὲ ΠΟΙΉCΕΙ ΤῶΝ ΤΟΊΧΩΝ ἀΠὸ ΤᾶC ΕΥ̓ΘΥΝΤΗΡΊΑC ἐΠΤὰ ΚΑὶ ΕἴΚΟCΙ ΠΟΔῶΝ CὺΝ ΤΑῖΙ ΤΡΙΓΛΎΦΩΙ Ὑ Πὸ Τὸ ΓΕῖCΟΝ,   30

Lines 26–30
And on the orthostates he will build the walls with ashlar blocks, length 4
ft, width 2½ ft (but for the corner blocks the length will depend on the size
of the triglyphs), height 1½ ft. And he will make the height of the walls
from the levelling course 27 ft, including the triglyphs beneath the
cornice.

enough to undertake a shared liturgy (in this case
the annual maintenance of a trireme) and the
speech he made giving an account of his Arsenal
(or tackle shed) at Piraeus was a masterpiece (Cic.
De Orat. I.62). He also built the massive portico
in front of the Hall of the Mysteries at Eleusis
(Vitr. VII pr. 17), of which remains survive.

However, the fullest knowledge of his work is
provided by the specifications (syngraphai) for the
Arsenal (c. 340 B.C.), which were inscribed on a
marble stele (IG II–III² 1668). We know that
syngraphai were prepared for other (all?) public
buildings, but these, drawn up by Philo with
Euthydomus of Melite, are the only ones to
survive virtually intact. They give a careful
description of the building from the foundations
to the roof, and (although this is disputed
ground) they may have formed the complete

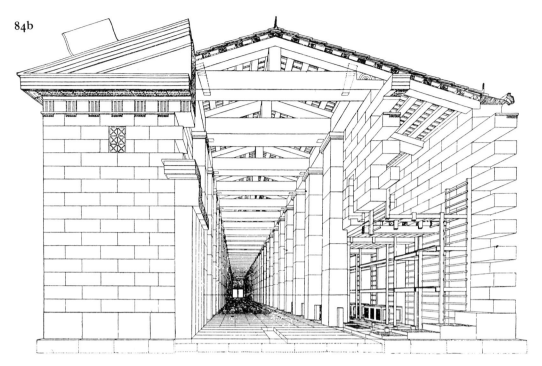

84b

official design of the building without accompanying plans and elevations drawn to scale. Certainly no such drawings are mentioned in the text, although there was a *paradeigma* or specimen of a tackle chest, probably made at full scale for eventual use in the building (cf. **72b**). The lower parts of the building are described in great detail, but there are some puzzling omissions, particularly in the upper parts; there was certainly to be a Doric frieze, for example, but no instructions are given for its design. It was perhaps accepted that these could be fully worked out as the work proceeded.

Recently found remains may solve some of these problems, but a pretty clear picture of the intended building emerges from the specifications alone. It was to be 400 Attic feet (132 m) long and 55 feet (16.3 m) wide, with double doors at each end leading into a spacious central aisle 20 feet wide and 30 feet high, separated by stone pillars from the two side aisles which were divided into two low storeys holding the chests and shelves for the naval tackle. Unlike the Tholos and Pompeion of the fifth century (**82–3**), the walls were of dressed limestone, and crowned by a Doric frieze and cornice; this was no mere utilitarian building, and the specifications describe the central aisle as 'for the people to pass through'.

V. Marstrand, *Arsenalet i Piraeus* (Copenhagen, 1922) ((**a**) = pl. 1.6, (**b**) = fig. 88); K. Jeppesen, *Paradeigmata* (Aarhus, 1958) 69–101; *Archaeological Reports for 1988–89*, 15.

85. Athens, reconstruction drawing of the fountain by the Dipylon Gate. Fountain buildings are among the earliest public buildings attested in both archaeological and literary sources. At Athens the Enneakrounos (nine-spouted fountain) was built in the south-east corner of the Agora by Pisistratus or his sons. The fountain built just inside the Dipylon Gate at the end of the fourth

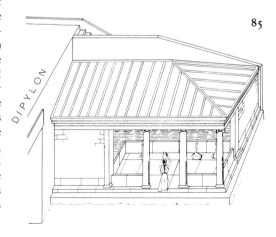

85

century B.C. (cf. **83**) illustrates a typical general arrangement. A reservoir at the back of the building receives a constant flow of water which can be drawn by users leaning over a thin stone partition, or (if not used) can overflow through spouts onto the paved floor in front. A roof protecting the reservoir, supported by a small colonnade, provided a well-lit and pleasantly sheltered space where those using the fountain could wait their turn.

G. Gruben, *AA* 1969, 39; U. Knigge, *Der Kerameikos von Athen, Führung durch Ausgrabung und Geschichte* (Athens, 1988) 73–5, fig. 66.

86. Megalopolis, plan of the Thersilium. Megalopolis in Arcadia was established in the 360s B.C. by the Boeotian Epaminondas to be a centre for the Arcadian League and a counter to Spartan power, and the great meeting hall for the league assembly, called the Thersilium after its donor, probably belongs to the years soon after the foundation of the city.

The Thersilium, entered by a large columned porch to the south, measured 52.5 × 66.5 m, and as in any large roofed hall like this, the main problem for the architect was to provide support for the roof. Greek roofs were based on a simple structure of vertical supports and horizontal (or slightly sloping) beams, not on complex trusses, and although the central span of the Parthenon was over 10 m, in most buildings the roof spans were *c.* 5 to 7 m, so a large hall meant a forest of columns. In most such halls the columns were arranged in simple grid pattern, which gave poor visibility from many parts of the room. This is much improved in the Thersilium by arranging the columns in lines radiating from a point near the centre of the hall where the speaker stood, so that uninterrupted avenues of space extended from this point all the way to the outer walls. The disadvantage of this scheme was that the spans increased in each succeeding ring of columns, until an additional column was needed, and it is indicative of the roofing problem that in the third ring of columns, which originally had the widest spans (*c.* 10 m), additional columns had to be added later, reducing the spans to 5 m. Very large

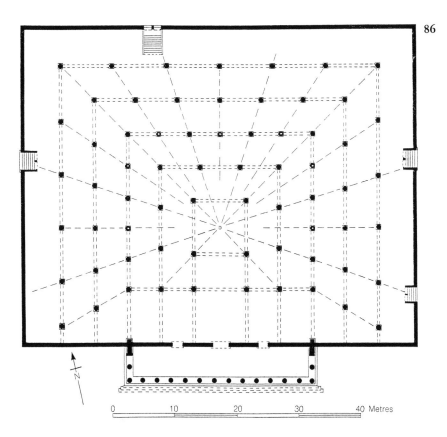

86

0   10   20   30   40 Metres

3. THE ECONOMY AND TRADE

ROBIN OSBORNE

The economy of the Classical Greek world, both the Greek mainland and the wider Greek world extending from the Black Sea to Sicily and North Africa, was firmly based on agriculture. Most Greek cities expected to be able to feed most of their inhabitants most of the time with most of the produce of their own land. But since climatic conditions meant that no city could be sure that it could survive without importing foodstuffs, there was a constant movement of agricultural produce from one part of the Greek world to another.

There is no doubt that agriculture was profitable, for the large landowner at least. The grain trade was the only trade with which cities regularly expected to interfere, and the only trade where city regulations extended beyond the prevention of swindling in the market place. Cities did not intervene to keep up the price of grain for farmers in years of glut, but might prevent farmers exporting grain to cities where the price was higher, just as they might prevent merchants based in them from freely taking grain elsewhere. Such regulations worked periodically both for and against the same farmers, and, coupled with relatively poor communications and the cost of bulk transport, helped to ensure that, even in areas where the soil was poor, the larger farmer who was involved in the market stood to make handsome profits out of the unpredictability of the weather. Land remained the backbone of the wealth of the upper classes in all Greek cities.

But land was by no means the only source of wealth. Enormous fortunes were certainly being made (and less certainly also lost) in the Athenian silver mines during the fourth century, and quite probably during the fifth also. We know of rich individuals at Athens who had no capital tied up in land at all, but operated as large-scale credit agencies and/or owned slave-run craft workshops. Much sea-borne trade depended on such credit agencies, and those who owned and manned ships seem to have been less likely to

make great profits than those who provided them with the capital to buy a cargo. Traders seem generally, from both literary and archaeological evidence, not to have specialized, either in particular goods or in a particular market, and the bulk of traders tramped from one port to another, with a final destination more or less in mind but taking and putting off cargoes as they went according to what the market offered, and often ending up with highly diverse cargoes. Archaeologically this has the advantage in enabling the distribution of non-perishable goods, particularly pottery, to be taken to be surrogates for perishable staples and signs of wider trade links.

The market was shaped in important ways by the availability of raw materials. The opening up, or closing down, of mines, particularly mines of silver and gold, had a big effect. On a shorter timespan the local effects of climate were also important. And although direct political interference with trade was very limited, political factors also affected the market. This can be seen in the case of the Athenian Empire of the fifth century, which transformed the Aegean both by clearing it of pirates and by creating a very much heightened demand at the centre.

While the political imposition of tribute by one city on another must certainly have had an impact, even if historians and archaeologists cannot yet agree on whether or not they can recognize it, the economic impact within a city of direct and indirect taxation has been little investigated. Similarly, it is not yet clear to what extent a city's decision to mint coinage was either dictated by or affected the market, and the political significance of coinage can be more easily traced than its economic impact. This is in part because neither literary nor archaeological sources lend themselves to straightforward quantification, and this prevents any diachronic account of the economy being written that is more than simply impressionistic. For this reason it is not realistic

85

to treat the Classical Greek economy as distinct from the economy of the Archaic or Hellenistic Greek world, and the reader is advised that the sections on Industry in *Pls. to Vol. IV* and *Pls. to Vol. VII.I* contain much that is equally relevant to the period covered by this volume, and those volumes should be consulted further to flesh out the picture presented here.

This section attempts to illustrate the Classical Greek economy through its surviving traces. The staple crops on which the economy was based have disappeared, but some at least of the agricultural installations created to produce those staples have survived. The exploitation of mineral resources left very physical marks on the landscape, and some at least of the end products have escaped decay or the melting pot. Clay beds do not retain their traces of working in the same way, but the final products which they produced survive in very large numbers. The economic significance of such pottery can be overestimated, but the images painted upon it provide invaluable evidence for the society's self-projection, a self-projection in which we might note

that the only economic activity of any kind to play a significant part is that involving the oldest service industry of all.

GENERAL BIBLIOGRAPHY

P. Cloché, *Les classes, les métiers, le trafic* (Paris, 1931), useful collection of images; M.I. Finley, *The Ancient Economy* (London, 1973; 2nd edn 1985); P.D.A. Garnsey, K. Hopkins, C.R. Whittaker, *Trade in the Ancient Economy* (London, 1983); R.G. Osborne, *Classical Landscape with Figures. The Ancient Greek City and its Countryside* (London, 1987).

87–95. Agriculture:

87. Classical farm complex at Hagia Photini in the Charaka valley (southern Attica). A large number of building complexes featuring the foundations of towers have been found in southern Attica. They show a clear preference for the better soils in this rather barren area, and there is little doubt that most, if not all, were centres of agricultural activity, even if some were also linked to mining works (below **96–9**). Work by

87a

sufficient to put this rather poor land into production, and a security problem sufficient to require the construction of secure tower buildings. The German archaeologist who has worked most in the area, however, suggests that such establishments were equally to be found in other areas of Attica.

((a) model; (b) photograph of tower foundations)

H. Lohmann, *Jahrbuch Ruhr-Universität Bochum* 1985, 71–96; H. Lohmann, 'Agriculture and country life in classical Attica', in B. Wells (ed.), *Agriculture in Ancient Greece* (Athens, 1992) 29–57; J. Young, *Hesperia* 25 (1956) 122–46; M. Waelkens, *Miscellanea Graeca* 5 (1982) 149–62; J. Wickens, *Hesperia* 52 (1983) 96–9; R. Osborne, *Demos: the Discovery of Attika* (Cambridge, 1985) 29–36.

German archaeologists in the Charaka valley, at the south-west tip of Attica, has revealed associated extensive terracing, threshing floors, olive press beds and rock-cut boundary inscriptions, while a similar complex, known as the Cliff Tower in the Agrileza valley to the east, has a field wall and threshing floor but also a rock-cut inscription marking a burial and recording a calendar of cult activities. Together these finds indicate the production of cereals and oil by workers resident on the land, in circumstances of considerable pressure on landed resources.

Although dating evidence is not abundant, it appears to be the case that the buildings belong to the fifth and fourth centuries B.C., and some scholars suggest that it may have been increased activities in the silver mines, and in particular the employment there of very large numbers of slaves, which created a demand for foodstuffs

88. Tower at Aspropyrgos on Siphnos. As well as being found in Attica, towers, sometimes with and sometimes without associated buildings or other constructions, have been found unevenly distributed over the rest of mainland Greece and the islands. Towers are few on the mainland except in Attica and the Argolid; among the islands they are particularly to be found on Kea (Ceos), Thasos and Siphnos. The towers vary very considerably in form and manner of construction, and it is clear that even in their original state they reached very different heights.

Some fifty-five ancient towers have been discovered on the island of Siphnos. The round tower at Aspropyrgos on Siphnos is a particu-

88a

88b

larly large and well built example, divided internally and with a water cistern excavated beneath it. A broken olive press-bed was found within it, making a role as an agricultural centre likely. The latest archaeological investigation suggests, on the basis of pottery finds, that it was constructed in the late sixth century, and may have been at first primarily a watch-tower and only later primarily agricultural, but even the earliest pottery includes fragments of storage jars.

R. Osborne, *Dossiers d'Archéologie* 172 (1992) 42–51; J.F. Cherry, J.L. Davis and E. Mantzourani, 'The towers of northwest Keos', in J.F. Cherry, J.L. Davis

89

and E. Mantzourani, *Landscape Archaeology as Long-term History. Northern Keos in the Cycladic Islands* (Los Angeles, 1991) 285–98; H. Hohmann, *Antike Welt* 14 (1983) 27–38; N.G. Ashton with E. Th. Pantazoglou, *Siphnos: Ancient towers B.C.* (Athens, 1991) 132–5.

89. Classical terraced landscape near Glyphada in Attica: terracing, in use or recently abandoned, covers a large part of the modern Greek landscape, and there can be no doubt that extensive terracing existed in Classical times. But ancient literary sources make almost no mention of the existence, building, or maintenance of terracing, and it is difficult to prove archaeologically that any given terracing is Classical in date. Association with Classical building complexes can assist (see **87** above), but otherwise the archaeologist is dependent on finds of pottery associated with terrace walls. One of the most convincing cases for a Classical terracing system was made by John Bradford for these terraces on the foothills of Hymettus (now under modern housing) which he detected as regular marks on these wartime air photographs and then dated by the pottery found on the ground.

Attica has a reputation for thin soils in Classical literature, and one reason for this may be that population pressure had made it worthwhile for the Athenians to terrace and exploit thin soils like these and like those of the Charaka valley (**87**).

J.P.S. Bradford, *Ancient Landscapes* (London, 1957) 29–34; O. Rackham and J.A. Moody, 'Terraces', in B. Wells (ed.), *Agriculture in Ancient Greece* (Athens, 1992) 123–30.

90. Attic red-figure chous with donkey being chased from threshing floor. Scenes of agricultural activity of any kind are very rare in Classical iconography, whether on painted pottery or in sculpture, just as descriptions of agricultural activity are very rare in Classical literary sources. Occasionally, however, agricultural scenes do appear on vases, sometimes, it seems, for their comic effect, as is perhaps the case here, where we see a bearded figure, stripped to the waist, wielding a blunt wooden instrument, perhaps a pestle used for pounding grain, at an ass whose rear feet are on a pile of grain and who appears to have been enjoying too much of the grain his feet have been helping to thresh. Between the figure and the ass is written an inscription that appears to mean 'Rogue!' or 'You are asking to be beaten!' Asses, sometimes accompanied by satyrs with whom they have some affinity, are curiously common on this particular shape of pot.

(Hamburg, Museum für Kunst und Gewerbe 1962.124)
  H. Hoffmann, *Antidoron Jürgen Thimme* (1983) 61–73.

91. Attic red-figure cup with scenes of animal husbandry. The scenes on this cup follow the meat cycle through its stages, with insemination and grazing on the exterior and a scene of a boy holding a piece of meat on the interior. The interest of these scenes to the symposiasts who used the cup perhaps lay in comparing and contrasting the meat cycle with the human life cycle.

(Bologna, Musee Civico 366)
  ARV 412, 9.

92. Rock-cut olive presses in northern Kea (Ceos). Olive press-beds are one of the few items of agricultural equipment which survive at all well from Classical antiquity. They needed to be heavy and stable, and their weight tends to mean that they do not move very far and are often found *in situ* (compare **88**). In some cases, as in this example, the press-bed is actually carved into the rock. The distribution of press-beds suggests that it was normal for farmers to press their olives at the production centre rather than transporting olives to some central place to be pressed. This is one clear archaeological sign of the independence of farming units and the reluctance of farmers to rely on others even when such reliance might reduce the capital costs of the farming enterprise. The provision of a double press-bed in this case suggests that this site, which was equipped with a tower, was the centre of olive oil production on some considerable scale. These particular press-beds are probably of late-Classical or Hellenistic date. A saddle quern and a hopper mill were also found on this site.

J.F. Cherry, J.L. Davis, E. Mantzourani, *Landscape Archaeology as Long-term History. Northern Keos in the Cycladic Islands* (Los Angeles, 1991) 83–4, fig. 5.18; H. Blümner, *Technologie et Terminologie der Gewerbe und Künste bei Griechen und Römern* (Leipzig and Berlin, 1912) 328–55; J. Boardman, *Phil. Trans. Royal Society London* B 275 (1976) 187–96; S. Isager and J. Skydsgaard, *Ancient Greek Agriculture: An Introduction* (London, 1992) 57–66.

93. Ceramic beehives. Since they were first recognized as such by the archaeologists who cleaned the Vari House on the south slopes of Hymettus in Attica, fragments of ceramic beehives have been found in excavation and surface survey work all over Greece, and it has become clear that bee-keeping was a ubiquitous activity. The ceramic finds indicate that coarse-ware pots with the interior deliberately roughened by combing were, at least from Classical times onwards, provided for hives. These pots could be extended with additional rings and had a ceramic lid, perforated for the bees to get in and out. Such hives could be repeatedly used.

The drawing (**a**) shows a reconstruction of such a beehive, modelled on the finds at the Vari House. The photograph (**b**) shows fragments turned up by deep ploughing at Vraona in eastern Attica.

J.E. Jones, A.J. Graham, L.H. Sackett, *BSA* 68 (1973) 355–452; J.E. Jones, *Archaeology* 29 (1976) 80–91; E. Crane and A.J. Graham, *Bee Hives of the Ancient World* (Gerrards Cross, 1985).

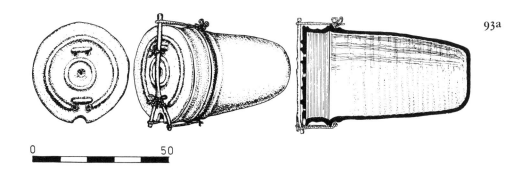

93a

0   50

93b

94. Making bread. Finds of grinding stones in domestic contexts, notably at Olynthus, suggest that many households ground their own grain and produced their own bread. Bread- and cake-making figures in terracotta figurines from Tanagra and in some images on painted pottery. On this lekythos various stages of the process of making bread appear to be shown – the removal of the husks from the grain, the grinding of the flour or the kneading of the dough (a similar action is used for each and it is not clear what the figure standing on the stool is engaged in), and the cooking of the loaves in a simple oven.

(Boeotian black-figure lekythos, sixth century B.C.; Vlasto Collection, now National Museum, Athens)

B.A. Sparkes, *JHS* 82 (1962) 121–37; B.A. Sparkes, *JHS* 85 (1965) 162–3; L.A. Moritz, *Grain-mills and Flour in Classical Antiquity* (Oxford, 1958).

95. Gardening was primarily a productive occupation, not a means of creating delightful leisure space, in Classical antiquity. It is clear from Theophrastus' botanical works that there was a considerable market for garden products, particularly those employed in making wreaths, and we know of one rose garden in Attica, almost certainly a commercial enterprise. But both the symbolic value of garden plants and the decorative possibilities of growing flowers were appreciated. Excavations ·in the 1930s around the Hephaesteum in Athens revealed that, at least in the post-Classical period, there were shrubs

planted close to the temple in a regular pattern, and similar examples of temple gardens have been traced elsewhere more recently. Pots were used for the so-called 'Gardens of Adonis', whose rapid growth and premature decease seem to have been in the image of the narrative of Adonis himself. More mundanely, finds from domestic areas in Olynthus, such as the flower pot illustrated in this drawing, suggest that houseplants were a feature of at least some family residences there.

(After *Olynthus* XIII (1950) pl. 250, 1036. Height 0.84 m)

D.B. Thompson and R.E. Griswold, *Garden Lore of Ancient Athens* (Princeton, 1963); D.B. Thompson, *Hesperia* 6 (1937) 396–425; D.M. Robinson, *Olynthus* XIII; R.G. Osborne, 'Classical Greek gardens: between farm and paradise', in J.D. Hunt (ed.), *Garden History. Issues, Approaches, Methods* (Washington DC, 1992) 373–91; M. Detienne, *The Gardens of Adonis* (Hassocks, 1977).

96–108. Non-agricultural production:

96. The extent of silver mining in southern Attica. The mining of silver in southern Attica can be traced back at Thorikos at least into the early Bronze Age, and there are signs of activity on a significant scale both in the late Bronze Age and, more surprisingly, in the Protogeometric period. But there seems to have been a subsequent lull in activity before the scale of exploitation markedly increased at the end of the sixth century.

Geologically the silver in southern Attica is found in pockets between layers of marble and of schist. Silver is found at every junction of schist and marble but primarily where a layer of schist is above a layer of marble. One such junction, known as the first contact, actually issues from the sides of hills; but the richest such junction, the third contact, is only accessible through mining, and it is thought that it may have been the discovery of this rich layer, about 500 B.C., that led to the expansion in exploitation during the Classical period.

This map shows the extent of ancient mine workings in southern Attica. The galleries in the northern section exploit the first contact, those of the southern section the third contact, and it is in the southern section that extremely dense surface remains of installations for the processing of the mineral mined, lead as well as silver, are to be found today. In addition to the surface remains inscribed records of the leasing out of mining concessions during the fourth century by officials known as the *poletai* have been recovered from the Athenian Agora. These describe in detail the location of individual concessions and, although it is not easy to link the descriptions in these documents to the remains on the ground, further support the claim that during the middle of the fourth century, at least, a very large amount of mining was going on. References to mining cases in extant law-court speeches further suggest that individuals made an enormous profit from mining activities at this time.

C. Conophagos, *Le Laurium antique et la technique grecque de la production de l'argent* (Athens, 1980); *The Athenian Agora* XIX (Princeton, 1991) II. Poletai records by M.K. Langdon, 53–142; R.J. Hopper, *BSA* 48 (1953) 200–54; R. Osborne, *Demos: The Discovery of Classical Attika* (Cambridge, 1985) 111–26.

97. Laurium silver processing site. The processing of the silver-rich ore took place at the site of the mines. It involved two basic stages: separating the mineral-rich material from the rest of the material mined, and then reducing it to more or less pure minerals, in particular silver and lead. The former activity was accomplished by processes of grinding, which employed grinding stones similar to those used for grinding grain, and washing, by which the heavy mineral was separated from the lighter substances through the action of jets of water. While the technology used for grinding was basic and relatively mobile, the technology used for washing was specialized and involved the construction both of large cisterns to store the water and of special tanks, channels and sorting surfaces on which the grading of the material could take place. This plate shows a general view of one industrial compound in the Sunium region, excavated by the British School at Athens in the late 1970s and early 1980s in the Agrileza valley. The compound included a washery of particularly large dimensions, although normal in type, with a long stand-tank, fed from a large reservoir 11.2 m in diameter, and a large drying floor surrounded by water-channels and with two sedimentation tanks at the end furthest from the stand-tank. The area over the stand-tank was roofed, presumably to reduce evaporation losses, and to the east of the washery and of the reservoir were two courtyards surrounded by small rooms from which fragments of querns, of the lead oxide by-product of smelting the ore, and of domestic pottery were excavated.

J. Ellis Jones, *Archaeological Reports for 1984–5*, 106–23.

98. This washery in the Soureza area was excavated by C. Conophagos in 1976–8. The drying table, drainage channel and sedimentation basins can be clearly seen, and fragments of the stand-tank wall are visible to the bottom left.

C. Conophagos, *Le Laurium antique* (Athens, 1980) 375–89.

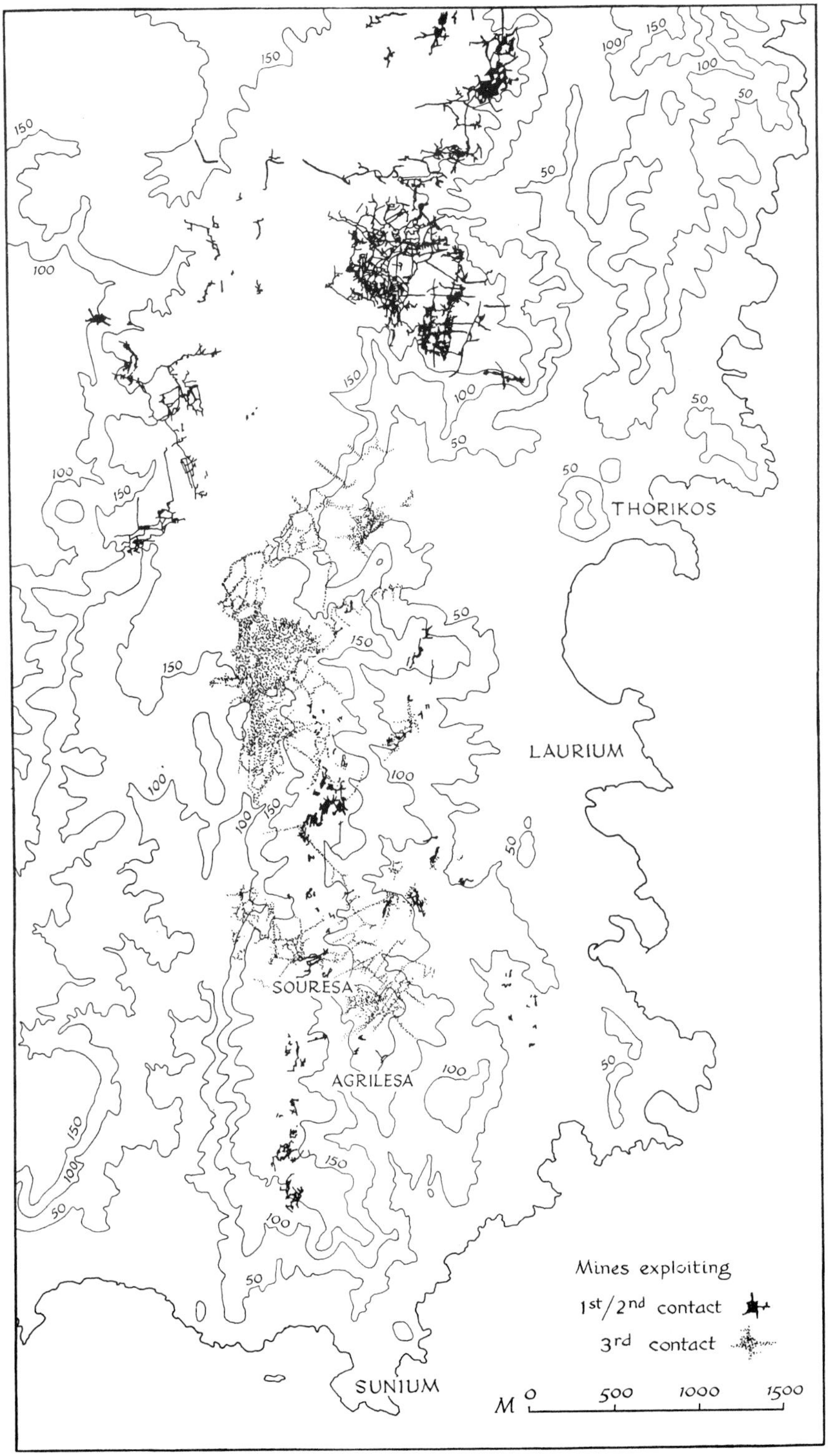

THORIKOS

LAURIUM

SOURESA

AGRILESA

SUNIUM

Mines exploiting

1st/2nd contact

3rd contact

M 0   500   1000   1500

99. The heavy demand for water with which to sort the ore in the washeries demanded the construction of a large number of cisterns. The example seen here is associated with one of three washeries to the north of that seen in **98** which were excavated in the 1980s.

100. Kean ruddle. Metals other than silver and gold tended either to be very widely distributed over Greece or not to be found there at all. Various minerals other than metals were highly localized, but few were in great demand. One mineral resource which, rather surprisingly, was

99

100a

in considerable demand was ruddle. Sometime around the middle of the fourth century the Athenians took advantage of their imperial control over Kea (Ceos) to insist that all ruddle mined in Kea was sent to Athens (*IG* II² 1128). This monopoly of ruddle has much puzzled historians since in general cities take little interest in trade in any goods other than foodstuffs. It would be clearer whether there were economic reasons for the Athenian interest in Kean ruddle if we had any good idea what the Athenians used ruddle for, but although we know of various uses

for ruddle (as a pigment, as a base for drugs, in caulking triremes) it is hard to see that Athens would find Kean ruddle indispensable to the survival of the city. It is possible that the regulation was in fact a gratuitous imposition intended to make Athenian political control felt, rather than a measure which made any significant economic difference to either Athens or the cities of Kea. These photographs show the probable site of the Kean ruddle mines.

Theophrastus, *On Stones* 54; M.N. Tod, *A Selection of Greek Historical Inscriptions* II (Oxford, 1948) no. 162; J.F. Cherry, J.L. Davis, E. Mantzourani, *Landscape Archaeology as Long-term History. Northern Keos in the Cycladic Islands* (Los Angeles, 1991) 299–303.

101. Quarrying of marble on Mount Pentelicum (Pendele). Unlike silver, stone was widely available and expensive to transport. As a result most individual sources of stone were exploited only occasionally and for particular building projects. A partial exception to this rule is provided by quarries of fine marble which came to supply an almost constant demand for stone suitable for sculpture, inscriptions and more or less standard architectural members. But the trade in Greek marbles only developed slowly and reached its height in the Roman period. During the Classical period even good marble sources were primarily employed locally. The quarries on Pendele (ancient Brilessos) seem hardly to have been

101a

97

exploited during the Archaic period (Attic sculpture seems generally to prefer island marbles when employing marble at all), and it was only with the various public building projects of the third and final quarters of the fifth century that extensive exploitation of Pentelic marble occurs. The surviving inscribed records of the building of the Parthenon include mention of payment to builders of roads, and traces of their construction (**a**) are still visible on the western slopes of Pendele, leading directly down from the Spelia quarries (**b**).

G.R. Lepsius, *Griechische Marmorstudien* (Berlin, 1890); R. Osborne, *Demos: The Discovery of Classical Attika* (Cambridge, 1985) 93–110.

102. Marble quarries at Manolates on the north coast of Samos. Recent work by German archaeologists has revealed that the column drums for the Second Dipteros at the Samian Heraeum, begun around 540 B.C. and whose construction continued into the fifth century, were quarried at a marble source in the north of the island. The quarry is small and the quality of the marble poor, suggesting that the builders of the temple were unable to afford higher quality marble from further afield. Although other marble quarries have at times been claimed on Samos itself, there is no sign that stone from them was ever used for building at the Heraeum. At times builders at the Heraeum brought in marble from quarries on the largest island of the Phournoi group, south west of Samos.

The way in which the drums have been quarried at Manolates is essentially identical to the way in which the drums for the fifth-century temple of Poseidon at Sunium in Attica were extracted from the Agrileza quarries a few kilometres to the north. In both cases the marble is somewhat brittle. Rather different remains from the quarrying of column drums (of limestone, not of marble) can be found in the quarries at Rocche di Cusa in western Sicily from which stone was taken for use in the Archaic temples at Selinus.

H.J. Kienast, *AA* 1992 171–214 at 206–14; G. Shipley, *A History of Samos 800–188 B.C.* (Oxford, 1987) 21 and Site Catalogue.

103. Quarrying of stone other than marble. Stones other than marble never commanded more than a local market in Classical Greece. In particular limestone was so widely available that even unusually coloured varieties hardly enjoyed much more than local use (there is some use of Eleusinian 'black' limestone as a colour contrast with Pentelic marble in Periclean buildings). Those building in limestone at all times looked for local stone and only when the local stone was unsuitable in the extreme was limestone imported from any distance, as happened with the fourth-century rebuilding of the temple of Apollo at Delphi. Limestone quarries therefore tend to be used for only a single project or only a single site, and in some cases the quarry site and the building site are actually identical. This is particularly the case with forts, which tend to be on rocky sites and where appearance is a secondary consideration, but it is also true of some whole settlements, notably the Piraeus where quarrying traces are virtually ubiquitous under Classical and Hellenistic housing.

The quality of stone quarried from such single-purpose quarries might be rather poor, with stones that were either softer or more brittle than would normally be acceptable being frequently employed if convenient. Such poor stone was perfectly acceptable, and regularly used, in foundations, but in some projects was used for the superstructure as well. The softness of the stone used for the Classical buildings in the sanctuary of Artemis at Brauron in east Attica can be seen in (**a**) from the way the quarries themselves have weathered. With large-scale building projects, however, the amount of stone which even a one-time quarry might produce was very large and the temporary employment afforded considerable. Something of the scale of the enterprise can

be gauged in (**b**) which shows a view of a limestone quarry on the Samian coast 2 km west of the Heraeum the blocks from which were used in the foundation to the outer peristasis of the Second Dipteros at the Samian Heraeum.

R. Osborne, *Classical Landscape with Figures. The Ancient Greek City and its Countryside* (London, 1987) 81–92; A. Dworakowska, *Quarries in Ancient Greece* (Warsaw, 1975); H.J. Kienast, *AA* 1992, 171–214, esp. 206–14.

104. Pottery manufacture. Modern scholars debate at length the economic importance of pottery manufacture in its own right, since preserved marks on ancient pots, although difficult to interpret, seem to indicate that ordinary, undecorated, fine-glazed pottery was extremely cheap. But while fine pottery was sold in its own right, transport amphorae were actually vital to the sale of various other secondary agricultural products, and in particular of wine and oil. Any city which desired to market its surplus oil and wine needed to produce the vessels in which they could be transported. Different cities developed slightly different shapes of transport amphorae, and these seem to have been a way of marking out the distinctive produce of that city (compare **132**). Some cities further individualized, and perhaps also indicated the date of, their amphorae by stamping the handles (see *Pls. to Vol. VII. 1*, pls. 127–8, and compare *Pls. to Vol. IV*, pl. 167). The scale of production required emerges not simply from the one shipping con-

tract preserved in the Athenian orators, where a single ship is contracted to put on board 3,000 jars of wine from Mende (Demosthenes 35.10), but from the large number of pottery establishments now known from all round the island of Thasos. The surface debris from one of those establishments, at Koukos on the south coast of the island, is shown here. On the basis of stamped amphora handles it has been suggested that this particular factory was in production from shortly after 340 until around 265 B.C.

Y. Garlan, 'Koukos. Données nouvelles pour une nouvelle interprétation des timbres amphoriques thasiens' in *Thasiaca* (*BCH* Supplément 5, 1979) 213–68; J.-Y. Empereur and Y. Garlan (eds.) *Recherches sur les amphores grecques* (*BCH* Supplément 13, 1986), especially Y. Garlan, 'Quelques nouveaux ateliers amphoriques à Thasos' 201–76; Y. Garlan, 'Les timbres amphoriques thasiens', *Annales Economies, sociétés, civilisations* 37 (1982) 837–46; D.W.J. Gill, *JHS* 101 (1991) 29–47.

105. Phidias' workshop. Remains of moulds. German excavations in the sanctuary at Olympia have uncovered, to the west of the temple of Zeus, the remains of the workshop in which Phidias, in around 430 B.C., constructed the chryselephantine cult statue of Zeus for the temple built there a quarter of a century earlier. Within the workshop were foundry remains – (**a**) shows the South Foundry – and fragments of

various moulds were recovered (**b, c**). Although the precise circumstances of use of the foundries are uncertain it seems very likely that they were connected with the construction of the workshop itself, and they therefore give us a rare

5b

5c

glimpse of some of the heavy industrial activity which was associated with any major building project.

A. Mallwitz and W. Schiering, *Die Werkstatt des Pheidias in Olympia. Olympische Forschungen* v (Berlin, 1964) 42–6.

106. Industrial activities in the Athenian Agora: the Keyhole foundry. Traces of considerable industrial activity, some of it involving significant amounts of pollution, have been found in and around the Athenian Agora, and a fourth-century house just outside the Agora has also yielded a curse-tablet cursing three bronze-workers. At least half a dozen metal-working establishments dating from the Archaic to Hellenistic period have been traced in the Agora itself. The Keyhole foundry illustrated here dates to the third quarter of the fourth century B.C. Numerous fragments of moulds indicate that the foundry was used for the production of a life-sized draped bronze statue, which was cast hollow by the lost-wax method. Although it is not clear whether the figure was male or female, clear fragments of moulds for arm, hand, and triangular overfold were found. The statue was cast in pieces and then joined after casting. The presence of pumice fragments indicates that the initial stages of cold-working the bronze also happened at this site.

C.C. Mattusch, *Hesperia* 46 (1977) 340–79; R.S. Young, *Hesperia* 20 (1951) 222–3.

107. Domestic industry: the working of wool. Although there is evidence for some wool-working in separate craft establishments, and fine fabrics in particular gained a reputation well beyond the confines of their city of production, it is clear that much wool-working was carried out at a domestic level. The wool basket is frequently used in vase-paintings, as also in literature, to allude to a domestic setting or to suggest domestic virtues, with undoubted overtones of sexual attraction. In this scene from the tondo of a cup by Douris, the exterior of which bears scenes of revelling, two elegantly attired women are shown. One is seated carding wool, separating the fibres with her long fingers and drawing them out across her knee, with a wool basket underneath her bare raised leg which is supported on a special support, known as a 'donkey'. The other woman lifts the tip of her garment in a gesture known as *anakalypsis* which is a gesture which often seems to have connotations of nubility. A second wool basket lies behind her on a couch. There is little reason to take this as a 'snapshot' of a typical domestic scene, but there is equally little reason to deny that this image gains much of its piquancy from having some

relationship to typical domestic scenes as well as some relationship to the way wool baskets and the motif of *anakalypsis* are used on other vases.

(Berlin, Staatliche Museen 2289)

ARV 435, 95; E. Keuls, 'Attic vase-painting and the home textile industry', in W.G. Moon (ed.), *Ancient Greek Art and Iconography* (Wisconsin, 1983) 209–30.

108. Shoe shop scene. Although the cobbler is in literary sources something of a symbol for the small craftsmen, cobblers make appearances on only three Athenian painted pots. The concentration in this scene seems to be on the craftsmanship, with a careful depiction of the cobbler's specialist tools, almost all of which can be paralleled in the leather-working tools used by traditional cobblers until very recent times.

(British Museum E.86)

ARV 786, 4; H. Blümner, *Technologie und Terminologie der Gewerbe und Kunste* vol. 1 (Leipzig, 1875) 280–6; *Classical Review* 56 (1942) 75–6, 116.

109–15 Exchange

109. Road remains. Although transport by sea was fundamental for long-distance transport of such bulky items as agricultural produce, most exchange involved some transport by land, and in some cases even long-distance land transportation seems to have been undertaken in preference to the risks and expensive transhipment involved in sea transport. Remains of Classical Greek roadways are in general known only for short stretches, through settlements or where particularly heavy transport required particularly substantial road building. But patient work by American archaeologists has recently traced virtually in its entirety the land route leading from the Spercheus valley, that is, effectively from the Gulf of Malia and the Aegean, to the Gulf of Corinth. This road is constructed with extreme care through mountainous countryside with skilful grading, sections where the roadway divided into an 'up' route and a 'down' route,

109

and sections constructed with gentle steps. Here are seen two sections of the road in the vicinity of modern Frakoula, showing the construction of the artificial road terrace and the use of 'ladder' construction in one of the steepest sections.

E.W. Kase, G.J. Szemler, P.W. Wallace and N.C. Wilkie (eds.), *The Great Isthmus Corridor Route* (Minneapolis, 1991); J. Young, *Antiquity* 30 (1956) 94–7.

110. Loaded donkey. This fragment of a cup by the Antiphon Painter, of around 480 B.C., shows a she-ass carrying her tail high, bridled and equipped with a wooden saddle over a tassled saddlecloth. The saddle is fastened with two narrow straps front and back and a broader girth strap. Upon the saddle is a doubled-up pack of striped material with elaborate scolloped flaps over its openings. The legs of the donkey have stripes known in Greek as *mukloi*. There are two *kalos* inscriptions, 'Nikostratos kalos' and 'Laches kalos'. There was no decoration on the exterior of the cup, and it is quite unclear what the attraction of this everyday scene was to the artist or his customers.

(Boston, Museum of Fine Arts 10.199)
  ARV 337, 26.

110

111. Harbour of the Piraeus. The Piraeus which became the port of Athens in the early fifth century (earlier shipping seems to have preferred the beach just to the south at Phalerum) had three excellent natural harbours, the Zea and Mounychia harbours on the south side of the Acte Peninsula and the great harbour known as Kantharos on the north side. Shipsheds for almost

111

300 triremes have been traced on the shores of the two southern harbours, and the Kantharos was shared by naval and merchant shipping. The development of the Piraeus owed much to the expanded naval activities of imperial Athens in the fifth century, and it was in the middle of the century that the settlement was replanned on a regular grid pattern. Even in the depressed years immediately after the Peloponnesian War it seems that goods worth approaching 2,000 talents a year moved into and out of this harbour. Control of the Piraeus became sufficiently politically important for the demarch of the Piraeus to be, exceptionally, selected centrally, and it was in the Piraeus that the movements began which led to the downfall of both the shortlived antidemocratic coups of 411 and 404.

R. Garland, *The Piraeus* (London, 1987); K.-V. von Eickstedt, *Beiträge zur Topographie des antiken Piräus* (Athens, 1991).

112. *Horoi.* Credit transactions do not naturally leave physical traces, but for about two centuries from the late fifth century on the Athenians seem regularly to have marked items of real estate which were pledged as security for loans by use of *horoi*, markers which declared themselves to be boundary stones of land, houses, gardens or other items of real estate which were security for a stated sum of money loaned by a named individual. The borrower of the money is not named, and it is clear that the debt went with the property which was security for it. Some *horoi* are dated, by archon name, but the majority are not. The wording of the *horoi* is formulaic but the transaction involved is described in a variety of ways: some *horoi* mark property which secured not a loan but a successful bid to manage an orphan estate or the value of a dowry received by the husband but repayable to the wife's kin in the event of divorce; *horoi* which secure loans describe those loans as *hypotheke* or 'sale upon redemption' (*prasis epi lusei*), but, as the example here illustrated suggests, there may be no legal difference between the two procedures.

This particular *horos* is one of some fifty-eight uncovered by the excavators of the Athenian Agora. It is inscribed twice with essentially the same inscription: 'This is the boundary marker of a house hypothecated upon redemption to Kallias of Euonymon'. One of the two inscriptions records an amount: 100 drachmae. Either this stone was used in two successive loan transactions, or the first shallow inscription was regarded as unsatisfactory and the stone was turned upside down and the same transaction recorded in deeper letters.

The Athenian Agora xix, Inscriptions (Princeton, 1991) 47, H 114; M.I. Finley, *Studies in Land and Credit in Ancient Athens 500–200 B.C. The Horos Inscriptions* with a new introduction by Paul Millett (New Brunswick and Oxford, 1985) xxiv, no. 80A, 81A with comment on p. xiv; P.C. Millett, *Lending and Borrowing in Ancient Athens* (Cambridge, 1991).

113. Sale of perfume. This self-referential pelike from the second quarter of the fifth century, compares and contrasts the context in which perfume is used and the context in which it is bought. On one side (**a**) it shows an interior scene in which one heavily draped long-haired young female figure hands over to, or receives from, another heavily draped seated woman with short hair an alabastron, a round-bottomed perfume flask held suspended on a string, which is to be filled, or has just been filled, from the pelike which stands between them. On the other side

(**b**) a heavily draped young woman hands over to, or takes from, an equally heavily draped seated woman an alabastron; the presence of a wool basket (see **107**) here behind the standing figure, and of a mirror upon the wall, suggests a domestic setting. Whether we reconstruct the story of a free woman in the house running out of perfume and sending out a sister or friend to purchase more, or the story of the purchase of perfume and its being brought back to a lady in the house, the artist has evidently chosen to emphasize the similarity between the commercial and the domestic settings, and between the seller of oil and the consumer of the oil, bringing out the modesty of all involved in the transaction by the universally heavy drapery and only offering any indication of status difference in the short and unadorned hair of the oil seller; modern commentators, by contrast, dwell on the gap in status between respectable women kept at home and women obliged to play a role in commerce which is indicated by our literary sources. It is notable that no money changes hands in this painting, and that women are never shown with money bags on pots (see **115**).

(Bern 12227)

H. Bloesch, *Antike Kunst in der Schweiz* (Zurich, 1943) 67–9, 172–3.

114. Sale of fish. Although fish were probably of limited importance in ancient Greek diets from the point of view of nutrition, they were an important source of variety in the diet, and came also to be a luxury good which marked out their purchasers as affecting a certain refined, and even undemocratic, life-style. But fish have little place in the imagery of Athenian painted pottery in the sixth or fifth centuries, except for some puzzling scenes in which fish appear to be being sacrificed. In the fourth century, however, plates decorated with fish, painted on a large scale and often of recognizable species, appear both in Attic and in various schools of South Italian red-figure. Nevertheless scenes of the sale of fish are rare. Here on a bell-crater we see a white-haired fishmonger, stripped to the waist, cutting the head (seen on the ground) and tail off a large fish for a bearded customer who displays his money in his hand. The grotesque heads here seem but one step removed from the hideous masks which appear on South Italian vases which show scenes of comic drama, and there is little doubt that this scene was intended to be humorous.

(Cefalù, Museo Mandralisca)

T.W. Gallant, *A Fisherman's Tale: An Analysis of the Potential Productivity of Fishing in the Ancient World* (Ghent, 1985); I. McPhee and A.D. Trendall, *Greek Red-figured Fish-plates* (*AK* Beiheft 14, 1987).

115. Prostitution. The exterior scenes on this early fifth-century red-figure cup by Makron show transactions being negotiated between men and women in a context which the presence of flowers in the hands of some of the women involved suggests is erotic. On one side of the cup (**a**) two empty-handed bearded men leaning on sticks negotiate with two women, one seated, wearing a *sakkos*, and with her himation fallen from her shoulder and gathered round her waist; on the other side (**b**) two similar women appear, but this time one of the men is beardless and both carry bags in their hands.

There is considerable modern debate as to whether such bags are to be interpreted as money bags or as containing knucklebones, and

107

whether such scenes as this are to be seen as respectable courtship of women by inviting them to share a game of knucklebones or as attempts to secure sexual favours from courtesans for payment. The occurrence of the bags first, in the late sixth century, in scenes where exchange of goods is clearly in question, and the fact that in a similar cup (Louvre G 143; *ARV* 469.148), also by Makron, one man has a bag in one hand and holds a coin in the other, both suggest that in the absence of other indications the bags would indeed be thought to indicate male purchasing power. Scenes where men with such bags make advances towards women include both scenes where they are clearly welcomed and scenes where they are equally clearly rejected.

Makron paints scenes similar to the one shown here on several cups, including one (Boston 89.272) where it is young men rather than women who are being courted, and one where, as rarely in scenes where women are present, one of the men is fully exposed (British Museum E61; *ARV* 468.145). In view of the contrast between the two sides of this cup, it is perhaps most attractive in this case to see the artist drawing attention to the similarity between the seduction of women where no money changes hands, the attractions presented to free women by the wealth of suitors, and the securing of the services of the prostitute.

(Toledo, Ohio Museum of Art 72.55)

E. Keuls, 'Attic vase-painting and the home textile industry', in W.G. Moon (ed.), *Ancient Greek Art and Iconography* (Wisconsin, 1983) 209–30; M. Meyer, *JDAI* 103 (1988) 87–125.

4. THE CIVIC LIFE OF ATHENS

JOHN McK. CAMP

116. Plan of the Agora in about 400 B.C. The Agora of Athens, like that of any Greek polis, was the focal point of civic life. A large open square, it was reserved for public meetings such as elections, ostracisms, festivals, athletic events, and market activity. Fountain houses and long colonnades (stoas) provided water and shelter to the crowds of people who visited the area every day. All public activities – administrative, legislative and judicial – are represented in the buildings which came to be built around its four sides. Administration: the highest magistrate, the eponymous archon, held office in the Prytaneum which lay several hundred metres to the east of the Agora, but most other magistrates were housed near the great square. Most prominent of these was the King Archon (*archon basileus*), who held office in the little stoa just at the north-west entrance to the square (**120**). Other officials were to be found in nearby buildings: the generals in the *strategeion* near the south-west corner; the *metronomoi*, in charge of official weights and measures, in South Stoa I; and the *poletai*, state auctioneers, somewhere near the Tholos. The archives were housed in the Metroon, which had formerly served as the bouleuterion, and public notices were displayed every day on the long base which carried statues of the eponymous heroes.

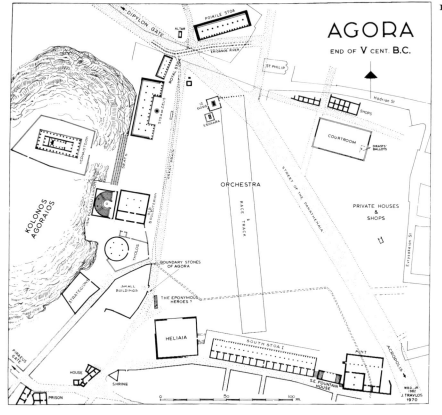

116

AGORA
END OF V CENT. B.C.

Legislation: law-making in Athens was in the hands of the Assembly (*ekklesia*) and the Council (*boule*). The Assembly met on the Pnyx (**117**) while the *boule* met in the Agora in the bouleuterion. A new bouleuterion was built at the end of the fifth century B.C. Here 500 councillors, fifty members from each of the ten tribes established by Cleisthenes, met every day except festival days to discuss and propose legislation to be referred to the full assembly. The executive committee of the Council was made up of each of the tribal contingents of fifty men serving in turn during the year. During their term in office these *prytaneis* were fed at public expense in the Tholos, a round building, which lay adjacent to the bouleuterion. In addition, at least a third of the *prytaneis* were expected to sleep in the Tholos so that there was an organ of government available for service twenty-four hours a day. Thus the Tholos/bouleuterion represents the functioning heart of the Athenian democracy. The symbolism was not lost on the Thirty Tyrants who used the Tholos as their headquarters (404 B.C.). Judicial: several of the law-courts of Athens are thought to have stood near the Agora. The north-east corner of the square was occupied by a succession of buildings in one of which a ballot box was discovered (**123**). In the south-west corner there is a large square enclosure of the sixth century B.C., less probably identified as the Heliaea, the largest of the courts of Athens.

The area of the ancient Agora has been under excavation since 1931 by the American School of Classical Studies at Athens.

(Plan by J. Travlos and W.B. Dinsmoor Jr)

For a general account see J. Camp, *The Athenian Agora* (London 1986) and for the ancient sources on the various buildings: R.E. Wycherley, *The Athenian Agora* III, *Literary and Epigraphical Testimonia* (Princeton 1957).

117. Set on the long ridge west of the Acropolis, the Pnyx was the meeting place of the full citizen body (the *ekklesia*) throughout much of the Classical period (Thuc. VIII.97.1 and Hyperides, *Contra Demosth.* 9.18ff.). The Assembly would meet about every ten days to consider legislation proposed by the Council of the 500 (*boule*). In theory, the Pnyx had to accommodate all the male citizens of Athens though its capacity never seems to have exceeded a maximum of 13,500, and for much of the time held only about 6,000. A large open-air meeting place set originally on a natural slope, the Pnyx apparently had three major building phases; the dates and interpretation of all three phases are still a matter of some controversy.

In phase I the seating area followed the natural slope of the east side of the ridge and a retaining wall was built to support a level area for the *bema* or speaker's platform. Little diagnostic pottery was found and the date of phase I is based on historical probability. The usual date given is about 500 B.C., to coincide with the democratic reforms of Cleisthenes, though recently some have preferred a date of about 460 B.C., and the reforms of Ephialtes. This phase of the Pnyx is the setting for several scenes in the plays of Aristophanes (*Acharnians*, *Knights*, *Wasps* and *Peace*). The second phase (Pnyx II) is dated to 404/3, a reconstruction of the Pnyx under the Thirty, attested by Plutarch: 'For this reason the Thirty afterwards turned the *bema* in the Pnyx, which was made to look at the sea, toward the land, because they thought that naval supremacy had been the origin of democracy, but that tillers of the soil were less ill-disposed toward oligarchy' (*Themistocles* 4). The excavators associated this passage with a large stepped retaining wall designed to create a seating area which no longer followed the natural slope and which had the *bema* to the west rather than east. The capacity in this phase is estimated between 6,500 and 8,000.

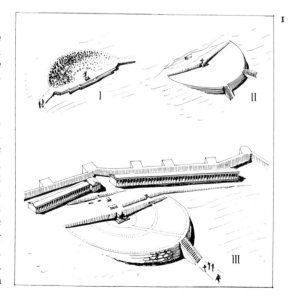

I

The third phase of the Pnyx represents a substantial enlargement of the seating area, up to 5550 m² accommodating about 10,000 to 13,000 people. A massive retaining wall was built of extraordinarily large blocks to hold the new, larger auditorium. To the south west, much of the bedrock was quarried down and a *bema* was fashioned out of the living rock. The date of this third phase is also a matter of controversy. A fair amount of Roman pottery found behind the retaining wall would seem to favour a late date. The style of the megalithic construction of the retaining wall is more appropriate, however, to a date in the fourth century B.C. There has also been some discussion as to how the people were seated in this phase of the Pnyx. Cuttings in the rocks for boundary stones or posts have been found, suggesting internal divisions, though there is no agreement as to whether the citizens sat by tribe, *trittys*, or in some other arrangement.

((a) Drawing by J. Travlos. (b) Model by C. Mammelis from plans by J. Travlos: Stoa of Attalos Museum, Athens)

The most recent excavations were carried out in 1930/1931 by K. Kourouniotes and H.A. Thompson (*Hesperia* (1932) 90–217). For more recent discussion see H.A. Thompson, *Hesperia* Supplement XIX (1982) 133–47.

118. Athenian political organization and the Monument of the Eponymous Heroes. The Monument reflects the political organization of Athens after the reforms of Cleisthenes in 508/7

B.C., when the four old Ionian tribes were replaced by ten new tribes. All the citizens were assigned to one of the tribes which were made up of members from each of the three geographical regions of Attica: city, coast and inland. All civic rights and many privileges depended on membership of one of the new tribes: citizens served in both the army and the Council in tribal

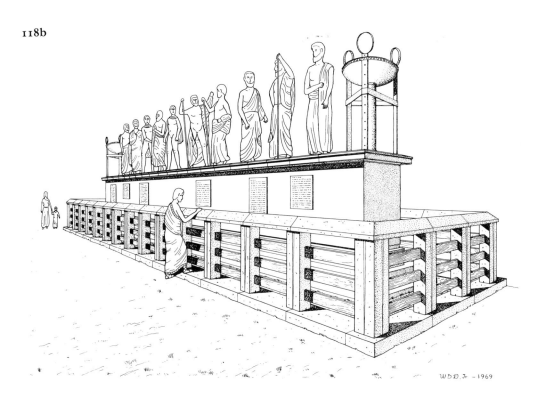

WDD.Jr -1969

contingents. The new bonds of loyalty thus forged replaced the old loyalties based on clans and geography and the tribal system should be seen as an essential feature of the Athenian democracy. Having created the ten tribes, Cleisthenes sent to Apollo's oracle at Delphi the names of 100 early Athenian heroes and the oracle chose ten, after whom the tribes were named. The Eponymous Heroes were Hippothoon, Antiochus, Aias, Leos, Erechtheus, Aigeus, Oineus, Acamas, Cecrops and Pandion. By the late fifth century a long statue base had been set up in the Agora carrying statues of all ten heroes. The monument was one of the few allowed to stand within the limits of the square, near the seat of government, as an embodiment of the tribal system. It served as a public notice-board, and announcements concerning members of the tribes would be hung on the front of the base beneath the appropriate tribal hero. Thus, a member of the tribe of Leontis would find relevant notices beneath the statue of Leos: lists for military conscription, public honours, upcoming court appearances, and the like. More general announcements were also posted; in particular legislation to be submitted to the *ekklesia* (Assembly) was displayed at the Epony-

mous Heroes for several days before the meeting so that citizens would have an opportunity to consider and discuss the proposals before voting. Set in its prominent location, the monument of the Eponymous Heroes was a crucial element in the dissemination of public information to the citizens of Athens and served also as the physical expression of the tribal system.

The monument is attested as early as the fifth century (Aristophanes, *Peace* 1183/4), though the remains in their present location date only to the third quarter of the fourth century B.C. At the end of the fourth century, when Athens fell under the control of the successors of Alexander the Great, Antigonus and Demetrius, the Athenians created two new tribes Antigonis and Demetrias, to honour their new overlords. The monument was extended and two new statues added to reflect the revised tribal system. The monument shows other changes reflecting further adjustments to the number and identity of the Eponymous Heroes as Athenian fortunes and foreign policy shifted in the Hellenistic and Roman periods.

(Drawing by W.B. Dinsmoor Jr)
T.L. Shear, *Hesperia* 39 (1970) 145–222.

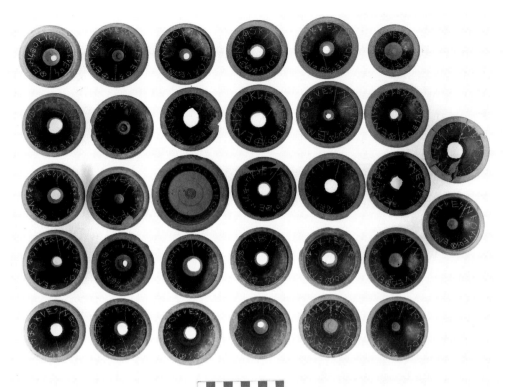

119. Soon after their victory at Marathon in 490 B.C., the Athenians instituted the practice of ostracism, a form of election designed to curb the power of any rising tyrant. They were no doubt inspired at least in part by the fact that their old tyrant Hippias, who had been thrown out years before, accompanied the Persian fleet, hoping to be reinstalled in power in Athens.

The procedure was relatively straightforward. Once a year the citizens met in the Agora and held a simple vote: was anyone becoming so powerful in the state that he represented a threat to the democracy? If a simple majority voted yes, they disbanded and met again two months later. On this second occasion the citizens brought with them a broken pot-sherd (*ostrakon*), on which they had inscribed the name of the man who was too powerful. These informal votes were counted and the man named on the most sherds lost. He was exiled for ten years and this was thought an effective way to prevent tyranny. Once cast, the *ostraka* were useless and were dumped in any convenient pit. Hundreds have come to light in the excavations of the Agora and the Ceramicus. They carry the names of all the well-known politicians of fifth-century Athens:

Aristides, Themistocles, Cimon, Pericles, Alcibiades, and scores of others. They shed light not only on the political history of the century but also on questions of literacy, orthography, and the pronunciation of Classical Greek.

A group of 190 *ostraka* found all together in a pit on the north slopes of the Acropolis provides a vivid glimpse into Athenian politics. (A selection is illustrated here.) They are all inscribed with the name Themistocles, architect of Athenian naval power and hero of the battle of Salamis, who was in fact ostracized. An analysis of the writing shows that all these *ostraka* were prepared by only thirteen people. The deposit thus apparently represents the left-overs of a plot to remove Themistocles, ready-made ballots for illiterate or uncommitted voters.

Ostracism as a system does not work particularly well, for if the first man in the state is powerful and popular enough, it can be used to eliminate a rival. During a period of strong opposition to his building programme on the Acropolis in the 440s, Pericles used an ostracism to remove his most vocal critic, Thucydides the son of Melesias, in 443 B.C.

In 417 B.C., when Nicias and Alcibiades were

deadlocked, another ostracism was held. In the days before public opinion polls, the outcome was uncertain; the two conspired together and a third man, Hyperbolus, was exiled instead. After such a distortion of the original intent of the law, ostracism at Athens was apparently abandoned.

(Stoa of Attalos Museum, Athens)
E. Vanderpool, *Lectures in Memory of Louise Taft Semple* (Oklahoma, 1973) 215–70.

120. The Royal Stoa (Stoa Basileios) occupies a prominent position at the north-west corner of the Agora just as one enters the square along the Panathenaic Way. With eight columns across the front and four down the middle it measures 18 metres long and 7.5 wide, surprisingly small for a stoa. It is also a modest building in its construction, made of limestone with a floor of packed clay. Nevertheless, it is one of the oldest and one of the most important civic buildings of Athens. Pottery from beneath its floor suggests that it was built *c.* 500 B.C., about the time of the Cleisthenic reforms. Its identification is based partly on the testimony of Pausanias: 'First on the right is the Royal Stoa, where sits the "king" when he holds the annual magistracy called "kingship"' (1.3.1–2). Two inscriptions found *in situ* on the steps of the building carry dedications of King Archons and thereby confirm the identification. Here, then, sat the King Archon (*basileus*) second-in-command of the Athenian state, a yearly elected magistrate responsible for religious matters and the laws. It was here in 399 B.C. that Socrates came to answer the charges of

impiety and importing new gods into the city: 'Now I must present myself at the stoa of the Basileus to meet the indictment of Meletus, which he has brought against me' (Plato, *Theaetetus* 210d; see also *Euthyphro* 2a). Here, too, were set up copies of the laws of Athens on marble stelae. The law code, based on the old laws of Draco (seventh century) and Solon (early sixth century), was drawn up in the late fifth century B.C. by a man called Nicomachus. A copy of Draco's law on homicide (about 621 B.C.?) was set up in 409/8 and carries this publication clause 'The law concerning homicide is to be inscribed by the scribes of the laws, after they have received it from the secretary of the *boule* for the prytany, on a stone stele, and placed in front of the Stoa Basileios' (*IG* I 115, lines 4–8). Other pieces of the Athenian constitution which stood originally in the Stoa have been found in the excavations. In addition the Stoa was the place where all incoming magistrates swore to uphold the laws. A large unworked limestone block lies just in front of the building, blocking access along almost a quarter of its length. Its prominent position suggests that it may well have been the oath-stone (*lithos*) referred to by Aristotle (*Ath.Pol.*7.1–2): 'The nine archons, taking an oath at the stone, declared that they would set up a golden statue if they transgressed any of the laws.'

The council of the Areopagus is known to have met in the building (Demosthenes xxv (v. Aristogeiton I) 23), and Aristophanes indicates that officials dined here: 'The herald will make proclamation that those from Section Beta shall

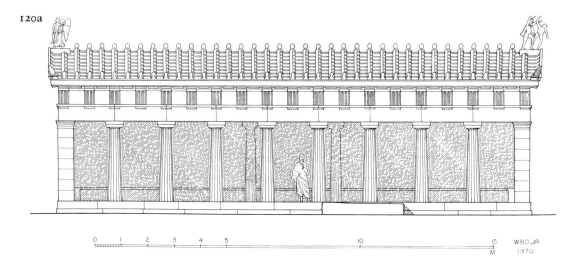

120a

0 1 2 3 4 5   10   15   W.B.D.,JR
                                        M   1970

follow to the Stoa Basileios to dine . . .' (*Eccl.*
684–5). That this is not just comic fantasy is
indicated by the discovery behind the building of
a large deposit of dining ware, much of it
inscribed with a ligature DE, for *demosion*, or
public property.

The Royal Stoa illustrates the variety of activities which took place in and around the civic
buildings of the Classical City. It was excavated
in 1969/1970.

(Drawing by W.B. Dinsmoor Jr)
  J. Camp, *The Athenian Agora* (London 1986) 53–7,
100–5.

121. Athenian laws and the Areopagus. Laws
(*nomoi*) in Classical Athens were usually passed by
a board of *nomothetai*, appointed by the *boule*
(Council) and *ekklesia* (Assembly) which also
passed their own decrees. They were then published on stone stelae and set up for public
display in some prominent place, usually near the
Agora. Many thousands of such inscriptions
have come to light, adding immeasurably to our
knowledge of Greek history when the literary
texts fail. Laws, treaties, public honours, lists of
officials, and the like were published regularly in
this fashion; a good example is the *Law against
Tyranny*. Passed in 337/6 B.C., a year after Philip

of Macedon's great victory over Athens and Thebes at Chaironea in Boeotia, the text reflects Athenian fears over the loss of autonomy, attempting to ensure there would be no collaboration if the power of the people were overthrown. It is crowned by a relief of Democracy crowning the seated Demos (people) of Athens. The text reads in part: 'If anyone rise up against the Demos [people] for tyranny or join in establishing the tyranny or overthrow the Demos of the Athenians or the democracy in Athens, whoever kills him who does any of these things shall be blameless. It shall not be permitted for anyone of the councillors of the Council of the Areopagus – if the Demos or the democracy in Athens has been overthrown – to go up into the Areopagus or sit in the Council or deliberate about anything. If anyone – the Demos or the democracy in Athens overthrown – of the councillors of the Areopagus goes up into the Areopagus or sits in the Council or deliberates about anything, both he and his progeny shall be deprived of civil rights and his substance shall be confiscated and a tenth given to the Goddess.'

The Areopagus was the old, traditional seat of authority, a council of elders. It took its name from the Hill of Ares (Areopagus) which lay just south of the Agora, where it assembled in early times. Somewhat like the House of Lords, the Areopagus was gradually stripped of much of its power over the years. Real political power was transferred to the *boule* (Council), *ekklesia* (Assembly), and *dikasteria* (the popular courts), though the Areopagus retained a certain measure of authority as is clear from the specific prohibitions against its meeting in the event of an overthrow of government. It was made up of former high officials, the nine archons, who took a seat on the Areopagus at the end of their magistracy. By the Classical period, it sat primarily as a court to hear cases of homicide, and it survived well into the Christian era as is clear from the address by St Paul to the Areopagites.

(Stoa of Attalos Museum, Athens, inv. I 6524.)

B.D. Meritt, *Hesperia* 21 (1952) 355–9; M. Ostwald, *Trans. Amer. Phil. Ass.* 86 (1955) 103–28; R. Wallace, *The Areopagos Council to 307 B.C.* (Baltimore, 1989).

122. Service as a juror on the law-courts of Athens was one of the duties and privileges of an Athenian citizen, and by the fourth century jurors were paid for jury duty. Plutarch (*Solon*

18.2) indicates that these popular courts wielded tremendous power in that they represented the final judgement of the *demos* and there was no further appeal beyond their decisions. The courts were accordingly large, with at least 201 jurors; Socrates was tried before 501 men, and courts of 1,000, 1,500, and 2,500 are not unheard of. An elaborate system of selection was used throughout the Classical period, using *pinakia* and *kleroteria*.

(**a**) Bronze *pinakion*. A juror's identification ticket, carrying his name (Demophanes), his father's name (Phil . . .), and the deme (and therefore tribe) to which he belonged (Kephisia). It also carried one or more official validating stamps which often followed Athenian coin types. Such *pinakia* were apparently of wood in later times. Some 200 bronze examples are known from Attica.

(**b**) *Kleroterion*. The allotment machine used to select juries and assign them to the courts. The rows of narrow slots were used to hold the jurors' *pinakia*. The magistrate in charge of the allotment procedure would take all the available *pinakia* of jurors from 'Tribe A' and put them in the first vertical row of slots, all those from 'Tribe B' in the second row, and so on until the machine was filled up or all the *pinakia* turned in had been placed. Along the side of the machine there was a hollow bronze tube, with a funnel at the top and a crank at the bottom. A mixture of black and white marbles would be poured into the funnel, lining up in the tube in random order.

A turn of the crank would produce a single ball. If it was white, the jurors whose *pinakia* were in the first horizontal row would be assigned to the jury for that day and would proceed at once into the court. If it was a black ball, all members in that row were dismissed. With the selection of ten jurors with each white ball, the procedure was repeated until the court was filled. The machine assured absolutely random selection, both in the order in which the *pinakia* were placed in the *kleroterion* and in the order in which black or white balls appeared. Thus there was no easy way to bribe an Athenian jury, made up as it was of at least 201 men chosen immediately before the court sat. At the same time, one member from each of the ten tribes was chosen with each white ball, ensuring equal tribal representation on every court. As much as any object left to us from antiquity, the *kleroterion* indicates the lengths to which the Athenians went in trying both to ensure equality and to forestall corruption in their governmental affairs.

This machine could also be used to appoint magistrates, simply by using a single white ball.

(Stoa of Attalos Museum, Athens (**a**) B 822, (**b**) I 3867)
Pinakia: J. Kroll, *Athenian Bronze Allotment Plates* (Cambridge, 1972). *Kleroterion*: S. Dow, *Harvard Studies in Classical Philology* 50 (1939) 1–34.

123. (**a**) *Klepsydra* (water-clock). Once an Athenian law-court was in session the proceedings followed certain rules of order. No trial took more than a single day; time was therefore allotted according to a set schedule and measured carefully by means of water-clocks: 'There are klepsydras which have small tubes for the overflow; into these they pour the water by which the lawsuits must be conducted' (Aristotle, *Ath.Pol.* 67.2). A single example has survived, dating to about 400 B.C. The replica depicted shows how it worked. The painted inscription indicates that it belongs to the tribe Antiochis, and the two XX's indicate the volume of water it held: 2 choes or 6.4 litres. It runs for only six minutes and thus represents a short speech. The preserved speeches of Demosthenes and other orators, whether on public or private matters, run much longer and there must have been larger vessels to time them. Testimony of witnesses and citation of legal documents did not count against one's speaking time, and there are numerous requests in the preserved speeches for the water to be stopped.

(**b**) Once the case had been heard the jurors voted by means of bronze ballots, several of which have been recovered in Athens, and the Piraeus. These take the form of round disks, carrying the inscription *psephos demosia* (public vote), with a central axle. A juror would be given two such ballots, one with a pierced axle, for guilty, and one with a solid axle, for acquittal. He would hold the ballots between thumb and forefinger, so that no one could see which way he was voting, and throw one into a container for valid votes, the other into one for discards. One such container has been found in a Classical building underneath the Stoa of Attalos in the north-east corner of the Agora. Two drain tiles were found set on end, forming a crude container or a support, and within them were found six bronze ballots. Less substantial methods, such as the vote by pebbles, are attested for earlier periods.

((**a**) Stoa of Attalos Museum, Athens, P2084)
R.S. Young, *Hesperia* 8 (1939) 274–84. J. Camp, *The Athenian Agora* (London 1986) 108–9.

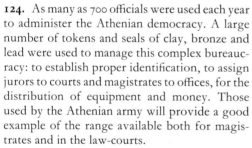

123b

124. As many as 700 officials were used each year to administer the Athenian democracy. A large number of tokens and seals of clay, bronze and lead were used to manage this complex bureaucracy: to establish proper identification, to assign jurors to courts and magistrates to offices, for the distribution of equipment and money. Those used by the Athenian army will provide a good example of the range available both for magistrates and in the law-courts.

(a) A series of lead tokens, third century B.C. Each carries a single letter (*A*, *Γ*, and *Δ* are attested) on one side, and a representation of a piece of armour (helmet, greave, breastplate, shield) on the other. These were evidently used in the distribution of such armour, owned by the state, to members of the army.

(b) Clay tokens of the cavalry commander Pheidon. Examples of some thirty disks, found in a well near the north-west corner of the Agora, stamped: 'Pheidon, the hipparch in Lemnos'. The hipparch was a cavalry officer and Lemnos an island dependency of Athens. In an extraordinary correlation between literary and archaeological evidence, a fragment of the comic poet Mnesimachus reads: 'Go forth, Manes, to the Agora, to the Hermes, the place frequented by the phylarchs [also cavalry officers], and to their handsome pupils whom Pheidon trains in mounting and dismounting.' (= Ath. *Deipnosophistae* 9.401). The tokens, which date to the fourth century B.C., must have been used in some official way, perhaps to establish the credentials of messengers.

(c) Terracotta token stamped with the name Xenocles of the deme of Perithoidae, with the title peripolarch. The peripolarch was the military officer responsible for frontier garrisons and patrolling the borders. Fourth century B.C.

(d) Part of the cavalry archive, fourth century B.C. One example of several dozen recovered from a well in the Agora. A thin strip of lead, found tightly rolled up, with a man's name inscribed on the outside (Conon). Within, is the inscription: 'A chestnut, with a centaur brand, value 700 drachmae.' These tablets were used for the annual assessment of the cavalry and would form the basis of a reimbursement by the state should the horse be lost in battle.

(Stoa of Attalos Museum, Athens IL 1575, 1573, 1572 (**a**); MC 1187, 1189, 1190 (**b**); MC 1245 (**c**); IL 1563 (**d**))
J.H. Kroll, *Hesperia* 46 (1977) 83–140 (**d**). *Idem, ibid.*, 141–6 (**a**). J. Kroll and F. Mitchell, *Hesperia* 49 (1980) 87–91 (**b, c**).

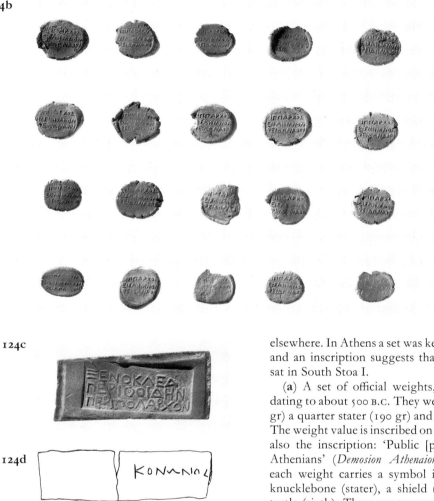

124c

124d

|_____|_____|_____|_____| 5 CMS.

elsewhere. In Athens a set was kept in the Tholos and an inscription suggests that the *metronomoi* sat in South Stoa I.

(a) A set of official weights, of bronze and dating to about 500 B.C. They weigh a stater (795 gr) a quarter stater (190 gr) and a sixth (126 gr). The weight value is inscribed on each and there is also the inscription: 'Public [property] of the Athenians' (*Demosion Athenaion*). In addition, each weight carries a symbol in high relief: a knucklebone (stater), a shield (quarter), and a turtle (sixth). These are presumably for convenience and perhaps for the illiterate: each symbol corresponds to a specific weight. Numerous other weights, mostly in lead, also bearing these or symbols for other fractional weights, have come to light.

(b) A sample of official clay measures used for both dry goods (grain, nuts) and liquids (wine, oil). They carry stamps as well as a painted inscription: 'demosion' (public property). Two similar measures of bronze, bearing the same inscription, were found in a well not far from South Stoa I, probable office of the *metronomoi* (inspectors of weights and measures). An inscription of the second century B.C. gives some idea of how the market must have been regulated in earlier times: 'Sellers of Persian nuts, almonds, hazelnuts, pine nuts, chestnuts, Egyptian beans, dates, and any other dried fruits normally sold

125. Commercial activity in the Agora was closely regulated. By the 370s official testers sat at tables in the Agora to ensure that only acceptable currency circulated in the market-place. In addition, other officials, the *agoranomoi* (market inspectors) and *metronomoi* (inspectors of weights and measures) were appointed to protect the consumer. Official sets of weights and measures of various types have come to light in Athens and

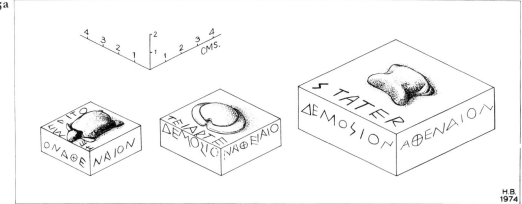

125a

125b

125c

with these, also lupines, olives and pine kernels should use a measure of the capacity of three half-choinikes of grain levelled off, selling them heaped up in this choinix which shall be five fingers deep and have a lip one finger wide'. The specifications listed match almost exactly the third measure from the left. The inscription continues: 'If anyone sell in a smaller container, the appropriate authority shall immediately sell the contents by auction, pay the money to the public bank, and destroy the container' (*IG* 11² 1013).

Standards for other items are known as well. Marble slabs carved with representations of roof-tiles are known from Athens (**c**) Assus and Messene. These set the standard sizes for both broad tiles as well as the cover tiles which protected the joints.

(Stoa of Attalos Museum, Athens B497, 492, 495 (**a**), AP 1103, P3559, P14431, P13429 (**b**), A1283, A1133 (**c**))

(**a**, **b**) M. Lang and M. Crosby, *The Athenian Agora* x, *Weights, Measures, and Tokens* (Princeton, 1964). (**c**) G.P. Stevens, *Hesperia* 19 (1950) 174–88.

5. SOCIAL LIFE IN CLASSICAL GREECE

JOHN BOARDMAN

Our view of the daily life of a Greek family in the Classical period will vary with our sources, none of which were designed to inform us on the matter. A morning looking at the boys in the palaestra, followed by some hours debating affairs of state in the *ekklesia* or of criminality in the law-courts, and an evening of music, philosophy and wine, while madam dressed her hair, plied her loom and strummed on her lyre in the company of her neighbours and handmaidens, was diet enough for a nineteenth-century view, fostered by selective use of the best literature and abetted by Victorian painters. Fifth-century Athens could be viewed as a somewhat more rarefied version of what was hopefully attributed to civilized life in Pompeii. Better, probably, to follow the asides and vignettes of life in Aristophanes, for a view of a knockabout, blustering, dirty and sometimes violent society. The material record is silent about behaviour, but can tell something, because behaviour is constrained and sometimes dictated by environment, and the physical trappings of life are some sort of guide to the manner in which they might have been used. And for Athens there are the vase-paintings, but here we should be as much concerned with what is not shown, as by the probability that there is a degree of idealization in the scenes, and certainly a great deal of ambiguity. That there should also be a great deal of subtlety in the commentary they offer on status, gender or belief is improbable given the nature and value of the medium. But the higher visual arts seem to have ignored such subjects altogether and we must be grateful for the insight offered by the ubiquitous painted pot.

Excavation has yet to yield any useful account of the domestic architecture of Athens. We here turn rather to the northern Greek town of Olynthus, whose destruction (even if partial and followed by localized and limited reoccupation) in the middle of the fourth century has preserved a full ground plan and much individual detail of housing in a Classical Greek city. This is, in modern terms, suburbia, and not even suburbanism centred on a great city. But once we allow for the cultural advantages enjoyed by an Athenian citizen, through the quality of the architecture of his city and the cosmopolitan nature of its commerce, we can at least in Olynthus glimpse something of the conduct of everyday life in any Classical society of moderate prosperity. So the houses of Olynthus constitute our text, while consideration of the life they and similar dwellings allowed can lead us to look at the representational and physical evidence from other parts of Greece, especially Athens. This is surveyed, as it were room-by-room, with some more general aspects of Classical life appended.

126. The Classical city of Olynthus in north Greece (Chalcidice) was laid out in the later fifth century after an access of population called for a large new area of housing outside the old walled hill-site (**a**). It was destroyed by Philip II of Macedon in 348 B.C. and reoccupation thereafter was slight and localized, so that we have essentially a Classical city of less than upper-class but decidedly not poor homes. The rectilinear plan was divided into blocks of about 300 × 120 feet, each with two rows of five houses, roughly 60 feet square. Little space seems unoccupied – areas for an agora and sanctuary – but there may have been other public buildings in the upper town. Conditions look very crowded, the planning mechanical. Although the houses are uniform in size there are individual variations in plan, but keeping the living quarters in the north (to catch the sun across the courtyard) and with the same basic sets of rooms. As time passed some houses were joined and factory or workshop areas were laid out within them. Classical houses have seldom been so thoroughly excavated – and published – and these are important because the well-known later houses at Priene and Delos show the same basic plans but with more variety

126a

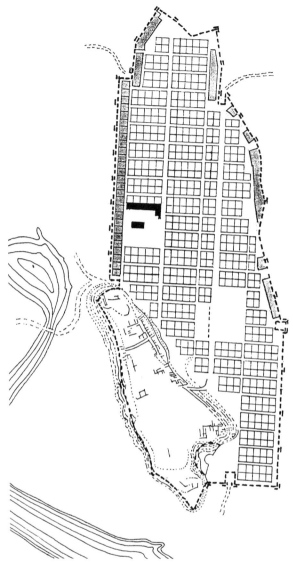

126b

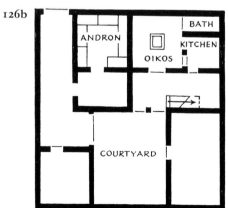

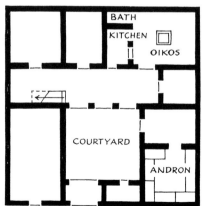

ANDRON
BATH
KITCHEN
OIKOS
COURTYARD
BATH
KITCHEN
OIKOS
COURTYARD
ANDRON

and generally more spaciousness and implied wealth. Olynthus houses must have closely resembled much of the new middle-class housing in Athens or any other Greek city, though there would have been regional preferences and in the long-established towns space must have been at a premium and orderly layouts like this rarely possible to achieve. This seems certainly true of Athens.

Two typical plans are shown (**b**), one of a house on the north side of a block, the other on the south. The floor area, including the small court and allowing for an upper floor over the living quarters, was close to that of a modest middle-class home in modern Europe or the USA. But there was no garden, just a narrow alley (about 1.5 m wide) at the back for drainage over cobbles, sometimes helped out with pipes and with soakaways. Street widths were about 5 metres, which just accommodates passing wheeled traffic; nearly 9 for Main Street – quite generous. House walls were of brick (sun-dried) on rubble foundations, with clay rooftiles. Privacy within the home was (if desired) fairly readily achieved, and the rooms were relatively spacious for the style of life. We should probably think away the excess of furniture with which most of us live as well as spaces occupied by gadgetry and the trappings of leisure. On the other hand, there may have been greater need for capacity to store supplies. Inner walls were at best plastered and some painted in panels. There were enough trinkets and clay figures found (about a half dozen figures per house on average) to suggest that they were somehow placed to be visible (in niches or on shelves) and we cannot easily judge how much decoration there could have been in painted wood (panels etc.) nor the elaboration of the furniture or rugs and textiles. There are a few mosaic floors. There is no reason to think that home life was unduly austere or colourless, but the furnishing even of Alcibiades' house in Athens, as revealed by the sale catalogue of his effects, suggests nothing very elaborate by way of interior decoration, and there are several comments in literature about the relative modesty of even upper-class housing in Classical Athens.

In the following entries we look at the forms and functions of individual rooms, illustrating their use often by recourse to representational evidence from elsewhere in Greece.

Olynthus VIII (The Hellenic House, 1938); XII (1946), *Haus und Stadt* with ch. 2 on Olynthus, whence our (**a**) and (**b**) from figs. 22 and 29/30. Houses in Athens: *Athenian Agora* XIV (1972) 173–83, 182 for Alcibiades' home. R.E. Wycherley, *CAH* v², 199–202.

127. The entrances to Olynthus houses were usually through double wooden doors, leading into the court or *pastas* (verandah), either directly or through a corridor between or beside living rooms. There was only one entrance except for corner houses which might have two. There is nothing in excavational evidence to suggest that Greek houses were normally provided with two entrances, nor, where they are, that this was deliberately to segregate inferiors (women and servants). The desire to keep the noisy or smelly areas (cooking, children) away from the prime living rooms is one that determines the plans of most homes of any period before controlled air-conditioning. On the Athenian vase shown here the master arrives home late and a maid or his wife is apprehensively approaching, holding a lamp, to let him in. The door has a single leaf and the roof of clay tiles is effectively sketched with an odd perspective. Note that the man is essentially naked, surely a common condition for males of various ages in Classical Greece and not confined to athletic occasions. We learn from texts that finer Greek houses might have porches and doormen, and that balconies might over-hang the streets, though these were discouraged wherever planning was taken seriously. Roof-tiles, for temples or houses, were enormous by modern standards, their sizes publicly authorized by standard reliefs against which moulds could be measured (see **125c**).

(New York, Metropolitan Museum 37.11.19)
    Robertson, *HGA* pl. 132e; J. Bazant, *Les citoyens sur les vases athéniens* (Prague, 1985) fig. 12.

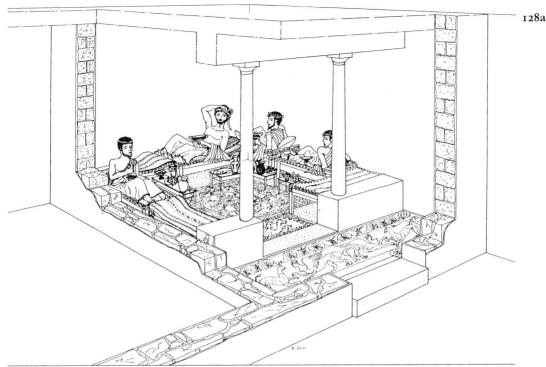

128. The *andron*, men's room, is laid out like a dining room. At Olynthus it was always sited beside an outer wall, probably to ensure lighting through high windows. Access was usually from the courtyard through an anteroom. There was a low platform 0.90 to 1.0 m wide around the walls to provide a level base for couches (*klinai*). The number of *klinai* determined the size of the room; at Olynthus there could be any number from three to twenty, five being the commonest. The ordinary *andron* at Olynthus (as in **126b**) was barely 5 metres square; allowing for the width of couch and individual side table this left about 1.5 m clear at the centre. There was certainly no room for a floor show, or even usually for the wine-mixing bowl (*krater*) which must commonly have been outside in the anteroom or court where there was room to manoeuvre wine and water jars and where any livelier behaviour would have taken place – the *komos*, which is not usually shown in an immediate symposion setting. Scenes on Athenian vases commonly show the cup-boy leaving the couch area to refill. A meal and drinking party was very much a nose-to-nose affair (there could, if necessary, be two men on one *kline*), with, at best, room for a

music-maker. The game of *kottabos*, flicking cup lees at a target (more often, no doubt, at each other), would have been fairly easy at this range. Spacious domestic symposia must have been quite exceptional even in Athens, and were held in larger rooms – these are the focus of most recent discussions of the symposion and its significance; the ordinary meal and party took place in something more like the modern 'smoke-filled room'. *Andron* and anteroom were the most decorated places in Olynthus houses, sometimes with mosaics, and normally a drain in the middle of the main room. The reconstruction drawing of the *andron* of a wealthy early-fourth-century house at Eretria shows just how crowded it might be with only four of the seven (or more) symposiasts in place (**a**). Here the vestibule gave directly on to the court.

The scene on the Athenian vase (**b**) is of a symposion, with two to a couch, and room for a girl to perform a pyrrhic war-dance. Note that side tables are never too high to be pushed under the *klinai* when need be; they are three-legged to stand more sturdily on an irregular floor – only the *klinai* commonly had prepared platforms and at any rate they were larger.

((a) After P. Ducrey, *Eretria. A Guide to the House with the Mosaics* (1991) fig. 12, drawing by Alfred Liver. (**b**) Naples, Museo Nazionale Stg 281; *ARV* 1045, 9, by the Lykaon Painter; about 440 B.C.)

For the practice of reclining to eat and drink see *Pls. to Vol. IV*, pl. 188; *CAH* IV², 429–30. Bibliography and discussions: *Sympotica* (ed. O. Murray, Oxford, 1990); F. Lissarrague, *The Aesthetics of the Greek Banquet* (Princeton, 1987); on *kottabos*, B.A. Sparkes, *Archaeology* 13 (1960) 202–7.

129. A courtyard was almost invariable in a Classical house, to provide light and air. The larger and wealthier had elaborate peristyles, with decorative paving and cistern below. At Olynthus they were simply cobbled and drained into the street or alley. One side was open, through a row of pillars or columns, to a verandah (*pastas*), a useful covered area that caught the sun and could serve for various activities, from convivial to funerary (cf. *Pls. to Vol. IV*, pl. 217). It would have marked the edge of the upper floor and there may have been a balcony above, overlooking the court. The stairway up was usually at one end of the *pastas*, or into the court, as shown in this restored drawing of an Olynthus house. There would be an altar in the court – at Olynthus few were elaborate (as the one shown), many were miniatures of clay or stone, adequate focuses for daily rites.

(Court of house A.vi.5 at Olynthus, restored drawing by A.R. Curry)

Olynthus VIII pl. 73.

130. By the Classical period the core of a house, the *oikos*, where the family hearth stood and which in earlier, simple buildings was often the only major room, remained the principal living room and the focus for domestic industry and cooking. At Olynthus some *oikoi* have fixed hearths, mainly for heating. The cooking was done on portable stoves and braziers. At Olynthus one end of the *oikos* might be partitioned off as the cooking area, beneath a large flue, running up through the house; elsewhere normal chimneys were installed, the chimney-pot often just a broken pot. Plain, handmade pottery proved the most fire-resistant, and Athens has yielded a considerable range of standard cooking pots. Decorated Athenian red-figure pottery was in common use in the houses, as well as plain black pottery, much of it of local manufacture. We show cooking pots and braziers from Classical Athens (**a**). (**b**) shows a view of one of the finer country houses at Olynthus (the Villa of Good Fortune). The *oikos* is in the foreground (b), with the partition for the cooking area and flue at the bottom of the picture (c). Beyond is the *andron* (a)

130a

with its anteroom at the left (g), both decorated with mosaic floors.

Heat in other rooms of Classical houses was normally provided by portable stoves and open braziers; light by window-openings in upper walls. At Olynthus four or five clay lamps were found in each house (for the use of these small, open oil lamps see **127**).

((**a**) Athens, Agora Museum P 21948/21958, 14655/16521; (**b**) *Olynthus* VIII pl. 51, 2)

The *oikos*: G. Mylonas in *Olynthus* XII (1946) 369–98. For kitchen pottery: B.A. Sparkes and L. Talcott, *Athenian Agora* XII (1970); *Pots and Pans of Classical Athens* (Agora Picture Book no. 1; 1958); B.A. Sparkes, *JHS* 62 (1982) 121–37.

131. Many Olynthus houses had clay bathtubs (sit-up style) embedded in the floor in a corner of the *oikos*, beside the flue/cooking area, for warmth and hot water, and against the outer wall, for drainage. Otherwise there were standed lavers of stone or clay, found in various places in the house and especially in the court and kitchen, and well documented in Athenian vase-painting (e.g., *Pls. to Vol.* IV, pl. 183). The simplest way to bathe was to crouch and have a companion pour water over one's hair and body – a posture adopted by women in many bathing scenes in Greek art (**a**), and by Aphrodite herself in a much-copied Hellenistic statue (by 'Doedalsas': R.R.R. Smith, *Hellenistic Sculpture* (London, 1991) fig. 102). Few Olynthus houses had cisterns and the water source must have been public fountains to which water was piped from outside the town. There was a water tunnel into the town 3 to 6 metres below the surface. There were no installed latrines at Olynthus, just the occasional clay seat (**b**). All liquid and solid waste (most solids could be usefully burnt and there were

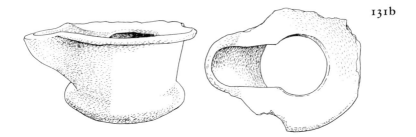

131b

131c

fewer problems then of disposable packaging!) must have gone into the back alley, with minimal drainage. We can recapture the flavour of Classical urban life in some under-privileged towns or town quarters in various parts of the world today.

The bath in (c) is unusually placed, beside a side entrance, in what appears to have been a workroom containing a mortar, millstone, and group of thirty-nine loomweights. It drained via a pipe through the outer wall, and over a tile into the main room.

((a) Athens, National Museum 1472; *ARV* 1477, 1; R. Ginouvès, *Balaneutike* (1962) pl. 25, 79. (b) *Olynthus* VIII pl. 56, 1. (c) *ibid.*, pl. 53, 1, House ESH 4)

132. Storage in a Greek house was managed in skin and wooden containers (chests rather than cupboards), baskets and clay vessels. *Pithos* storage jars could be sunk into the ground for liquids or solids. At Olynthus there were several, some carefully mended with lead clamps, and some

marked on their rims with their prices, which are notably high (between about 31 and 55 drachmae), indicating what important furniture they were and how difficult they were to make. How domestic supplies of grain were kept, or indeed transported in bulk, is not clear. Wine was kept in the familiar large knob-footed amphorae but they were not that common in Olynthus houses and concentrations of them suggest shops. The illustration is of a number of amphorae recovered from destruction levels of the Persian sack of Athens in 480/79 B.C., Corinthian (at the left) and Attic.

(Athens, Agora Museum)
V. Grace, *Pots and Pans* (Princeton, 1961) fig. 35. *Pithos* prices: D.A. Amyx, *Hesperia* 27 (1958) 169–70.

133. Loomweights were found all over all the Olynthus houses, a fair indication of the commonest, indeed inevitable, domestic industry. The women's quarters (*gynaikonitis*) could not be identified as such but the *oikos* accommodated some domestic industry such as weaving, while sleeping and dealing with children were mainly activities for upstairs. The domestic group shown in (**a**) is set in the *oikos*, with a loom at the left, nurse, mother, baby and older son(?). Rooms were differentiated by function here, as probably in most Greek houses – even grander ones – rather than the sex or status of their occupants, although this was inevitably reflected. It is difficult to determine, even roughly, whether there was any substantial slave population in houses of the Olynthus social level, and we would not look for special accommodation for slaves anyway. The 'women's life' that seems to have occupied the interest of Athenian vase-painters increasingly in the later fifth and fourth centuries, and of modern commentators of the current generation, is partially and ambiguously documented. Few scenes are devoted to domestic industry – hardly any looms except in myth contexts, and where a spindle is carried it seems almost as much an attribute of a basically domestic scene rather than a deliberate study of the activity involved. But there is much to glean from such scenes of textile production at home. Otherwise, so many scenes dwell on women dressing, often with intimations of approaching marriage and sometimes in the presence of an Eros, that there is uncertainty about which allude deliberately to some heroic marriage, and which simply assimilate the mortal to the heroic in the usual Greek manner. There are comparable problems with scenes of women playing music. Most relevant scenes appear on shapes which might be judged appropriate for women's use – pyxides (boxes for trinkets), miniature hydriae, and vases associated with marriage (the so-called loutrophoros and lebes gamikos for which see pl. **134**).

Child-care is archaeologically almost completely inaccessible as a subject, though an Athenian
vase shows how a baby could be accommodated
(b), and children at play appear on small jugs
(*choes*) of the end of the fifth century, associated
with the Anthesteria festival (*CAH* v², 254, fig.
33).

((a) Harvard, Sackler Museum 60.342; *CVA* Robin-
son Collection 2, pl. 43. (b) Brussels, Musées Royaux
A 890; *ARV* 771, 1, Sotades workshop, about 460
B.C.)

H. Rühfel, *Kinderleben im klassischen Athen* (Mainz,
1984). D. Williams, in A. Cameron and A. Kuhrt
(eds.), *Images of Women in Antiquity* (London and
Canberra, 1983) 92–106.

134

134. An Athenian wedding. The scene is from
the side of a cylindrical box (pyxis), a receptacle
for trinkets and commonly decorated with scenes
of women's life. The procession to the new home
is here shown leaving the bride's home rather
than arriving, which is the more usual. At the left
the bride's mother stands at the open two-leaf
door. The groom mounts a chariot with his
bride, behind him a torch-bearer (normally the
bride's mother in other scenes), a woman carrying a box (for dress probably) and another
carrying a lebes gamikos. This is a ritual vase
thought to be a container for the bridal bath.
Collecting water for the bath (in Athens from
Enneakrounos) was an important ceremony and
the vessel commemorates it. Real examples are
found in tombs, possibly for the unmarried
whose nuptials are with Hades, and were dedicated at the sanctuary of the Nymphs on the
slopes of the Acropolis. The woman with a torch
by the chariot should be the groom's mother and
a young man leads. The chariot lends a heroic
touch but they may have been used in Athens for
such special processional occasions; other scenes
show a mule cart (*Pls. to Vol. IV*, pl. 186).

(London, British Museum 1930.12–21.1; *ARV* 1277,
23, Marlay Painter; about 430 B.C.)

135. Formal education for at least some levels of
society is suggested by the scenes of school life,
where music, reading and writing seem the
activities most readily portrayed by the vase-
painter. Women were by no means excluded
from such activity. The dancing classes shown
may have been more often for the training of
Athenian geishas, but there are other scenes of a
more conventional character. On (**a**) one young
lady drags another off to school, clutching her

13

writing tablet, and on (**b**) one is reading from a
scroll before an open box – which incidentally
may offer a clue to the assumed contents of some
of the many other boxes shown in vase scenes,
generally thought to be full of jewellery or
clothes – even if, in this case, the lady might be
taken for a Muse.

((**a**) New York, Metropolitan Museum of Art
06.1021.167; *ARV* 908, 13, cup by the Painter of
Bologna 417. (**b**) Paris, Louvre CA 2220; *ARV* 1199,
25, lekythos by the Klügmann Painter)
   F.A.G. Beck, *Album of Greek Education* (Sydney,
1975).

6. CLASSICAL RELIGION

ROBERT PARKER

'Everything is full of gods', said Thales: certainly, Greek religion penetrated and was penetrated by almost every aspect of Greek life. As a result, innumerable phenomena that are also of interest to the religious historian appear elsewhere in these volumes. The history of early Greek architecture is, almost exclusively, a history of temple-building; most of the masterpieces of Greek sculpture were created specifically in order to be dedicated to gods (others were to stand on tombs); and mythology early became the most important theme for the vase-painter, and long remained so. One can scarcely stress enough how important it is that the principal imaginative and pictorial world of the Greeks was that of mythology, which was inextricably intertwined with the gods and so with cult. Everywhere he looked an Athenian saw images of that Heracles, son of Zeus, whom he also on occasion worshipped. It is as if the images that are so perpetually present in modern tabloids and television were literal 'cult-figures'. Of course, we cannot begin to review all that evidence here. But if we leave famous temples and sculptures on one side, this is not through any belief that they were somehow less religious than humbler places or objects. It was the opinion of one observer (Quintilian) that Phidias' monumental chryselephantine statue of Zeus at Olympia 'added something to religion'.

GENERAL BIBLIOGRAPHY

W. Burkert, *Greek Religion: Archaic and Classical* (tr. J. Raffan, Oxford, 1985); E. Simon, *Die Götter der Griechen* (Munich, 1969); C. Bérard *et al.*, *A City of Images* (tr. D. Lyons, Princeton 1989); *LIMC*; T.H. Carpenter, *Art and Myth in Ancient Greece* (London, 1991).

Sanctuaries

The Greek for sanctuary is *temenos*, that is to say an area 'cut off' (*temno*) from ordinary use (and often in fact marked off by boundary markers, *horoi*). At its grandest, such a *temenos* could be a large area containing numerous buildings, as is the case, for instance, with the precinct of Zeus at Olympia (see *CAH* v², 194, fig. 17). But the only indispensable element was an altar for sacrifice; and when we find that the calendar of an ordinary Attic deme or village (Erchia) in the fourth century mentions at least a dozen sacred sites, it is clear that, even in the great temple-building centuries, a number of *temene* continued to consist of little more than a altar, accompanied perhaps by a very modest building, in a field.

The illustrations show some of the kinds of sacred site that lacked monumental temples. We might also mention here, as instances of simple sanctuaries, the many precincts of Zeus on mountain-tops, where for obvious reasons monumental temples were seldom built; and also the characteristic examples of small temples that are illustrated in *CAH* v² 210, fig. 26 (very modest) and 219, fig. 31 (much more refined and expensive, but still small).

(On sanctuaries see R.A. Tomlinson, *Greek Sanctuaries* (New York, 1976); on mountain cults of Zeus, M.K. Langdon, *A Sanctuary of Zeus on Mount Hymettos Hesperia* Suppl. 16, (Princeton, 1976).)

136. Part of the sanctuary of Aphrodite at Daphni, which lay directly on the Sacred Way that led from Athens to Eleusis. According to Pausanias, the precinct contained a temple, but this was evidently very small; the plate shows a feature quite often found in architecturally simple sites, a set of niches cut into the rock at the back of the sanctuary to receive votive offerings.

Travlos *Attika* 184–5: for such votive niches see, e.g., *idem*, *Athens* (New York, 1971) 418–19, 570.

137. 'Goddess' carved inside the cave of the Nymphs at Vari in Attica. Many caves were sacred to the cult of the Nymphs and Pan: the Corycian cave, for instance, which can still be visited above Delphi, or the Nymphaeum at Phyle which is the scene of Menander's *Dyscolus*. The Vari cave is a particularly curious example, because it contains a series of crude carvings in the rock, the work (as we learn from an inscription of the fifth century in his own hand) of one 'Archedemus of Thera who was seized by the Nymphs' and 'fashioned the cave on the instructions of the Nymphs'. To confront the figure shown here, apparently a goddess, was perhaps the culminating experience for a visitor to the cave.

Travlos, *Attika* 462–5; *L'Antre corycien BCH* Suppl. 9, (Paris, 1984); W.R. Connor, *Classical Antiquity* 1988, 155–89.

138. A hero-sanctuary in the Agora at Athens. Hero cults seldom attracted elaborate architecture, and tend as a result to leave few traces archaeologically. This, however, shows a striking discovery made in the Agora excavations of 1972. An outcrop of living rock has been framed in a small, man-made enclosure; one can see clearly in the photograph fragments of the many votive offerings (small pots, lamps, loomweights and the like) that the excavators found heaped over the sacred rock. Such an earth-rooted cult must have honoured a hero or heroine or underworld power.

The Athenian Agora, a Guide, (3rd edn, Athens, 1976) 87–90; J.M. Camp, *The Athenian Agora* (London, 1986) 79.

Rituals

Greek artists were not concerned with documentary realism; their portrayals of religious scenes are not, as it were, photographs of actual practices, but an evocation that is largely dependent on conventional symbols. That does not make their work any the less important for the study of Greek ritual, harder though it doubtless becomes to use. Pictorial evidence often adjusts the

nuances of the impression created by literary sources, and sometimes in fact reveals ritual practices otherwise unknown. Above all, it presents religious conceptions, a vision for instance of Dionysus and his world, in a different medium. We will look first at scenes that relate to the basic rituals of Greek cult, procession (**139–40**) and sacrifice (**141–2**); then at some more specialized and unusual rituals and sacred myths.

139. Athenian black-figure band-cup of the middle of the sixth century, which splendidly illustrates the formal civic procession, *pompe*, to a place of sacrifice. Ready to receive the procession there stand, behind the burning altar, a priestess and the goddess Athena herself, who is imagined as present in person at her rite. Among the figures in the procession, note the discriminations of status, the way in which individuals participate in virtue of their civic or military role: hoplites march as hoplites, cavalry as cavalry . . . In this treatment of the procession as a form of civic display, we already find pre-figured such characteristic rites of the Classical period as the great Panathenaic procession at Athens. For a procession of a very different type see *Pls. to Vol. IV*, pl. 225, where six youths struggle beneath the

burden of a giant phallus. There is doubtless comic exaggeration here, but 'escorting the phallus' was a regular element in festivals of Dionysus (at the City Dionysia, for instance, before the tragedies started); Aristophanes' *Acharnians* contains (247ff.) a charming evocation of a rustic phallic procession.

(Private Coll.)

E. Simon, *Festivals of Attica* (Madison, 1983) 63, pls. 16.2, 17.2.

140. The centrepiece of the Parthenon frieze, which – unusually, since temple sculptures did not normally portray the rituals of the cult – depicted (or at least evoked) the Panathenaic procession. The scene shown is the central section of the east frieze, and its special importance is marked by the presence of the twelve gods on either side, seated at their ease and, we must suppose, enjoying the procession. Almost everything about the scene is controversial: we do not know, for instance, why the bringing of stools by two girls to a figure who is perhaps the priestess of Athena is given such prominence; and even the sex of the small figure on the right is in dispute. But there is little doubt that the object held by this small figure and the mature man beside it (often taken to be the *archon basileus*, the magistrate in charge of the procession) is the peplos, the elaborate robe which was woven for Athena every four years by specially designated young girls. It was embroidered with traditional scenes of the battle of the Gods and the Giants, among which Athena's victory over Enceladus doubtless had a special prominence; and the presentation of this holy of holies to Athena marked the climax of the great procession. The scene portrayed here is apparently a preliminary, a formal folding or inspection, rather than the actual presentation.

(London, British Museum. East Frieze Slab V)

F. Brommer, *Der Parthenonfries* (Mainz, 1977) 263–70; E. Simon, *Ath.Mitt.* 97 (1982), 127–44; W. Gauer in E. Berger (ed.), *Parthenon Kongress Basel* I (Mainz, 1984) 220–9; J. Boardman, in *Kanon. Festschrift E. Berger* (Basel, 1988) 9–13; O. Palagia, Ὁ Γλυπτὸς Διάκοσμος τοῦ Παρθενῶνα (Athens, 1986), 66–7.

140

141

141, 142. Athenian red-figure bell-craters that show typical sacrificial scenes. In **141**, a procession escorting a sacrificial sheep has reached the altar. (The sheep was always the commonest victim, though here the more expensive and prestigious cow sacrifice is also evoked by the suspended skull.) The participants wear garlands, as was normal on festal occasions; and a flute-player accompanies the procession as was, again, common. The central scene probably alludes to the two preliminary rituals that are invariably mentioned in detailed literary accounts of sacrifice: the distribution to all participants of lustral water, for purification, and of barley-grains which were 'thrown forward' just before the kill. Here the main sacrificer seems to be dipping his hands in a lustral water bowl held by an assistant; there will therefore be grain in the container in the assistant's other hand. (But some suppose that the 'lustral water bowl' contains the grain.) Interestingly, in scenes of animal sacrifice the actual moment of killing is almost never

shown (in strong contrast to portrayals of mythological *human* sacrifice). The pictorial evidence therefore works against the theory which sees aggression, ritually channelled against an animal, as the very essence of sacrifice. Instead, some of the acts that followed the killing are often shown, as if these mattered more than the actual moment of ritual violence. 'Bloodying the altar' was a symbolic means of, as it were, presenting the death to the deity: blood had duly been poured over the altar in **142**, as we see from the stains on its side. The officiant is apparently depositing the portion of the victim that was burnt for the god (note his serious gaze directed to the statue of Apollo); in one hand he holds a roll of fat or meat, while the boy attendant is reaching out to him the chine and tail on a platter. He is probably about to draw omens from the way that these portions, particularly the tail, burnt in the altar-fire; the 'thumb up' gesture of his left hand is often seen at such moments of sacrificial divination. The giant shish-kebab carried by the naked youth behind him consists of the spitted entrails (*splanchna*) of the victim, which are about to be roasted on the altar fire and distributed to the inner circle of participants to be eaten on the spot. (For a remarkable vase which shows in detail the various stages of sacrifice and sacrificial cuisine see *Pls. to Vol. III*, pl. 324.) Third quarter of the fifth century B.C.

(**141**. Boston, Museum of Fine Arts 95.25; *ARV* 1149, 9, manner of Kleophon Painter. **142**. Frankfurt, Mus. Für Vor-und Frühgeschichte B 413; *ARV* 1115, 31 bis, Hephaistos Painter)

W. Burkert, *Homo Necans* (tr. P. Bing, Berkeley, 1983); M. Detienne and J.-P. Vernant, *La cuisine du sacrifice en pays grec* (Paris, 1979); J.-L. Durand, *Sacrifice et labour en Grèce ancienne* (Paris and Rome, 1986) figs. 52, 62; M.H. Jameson in *Greek Tragedy and its Legacy* (*Essays presented to D.J. Conacher*; Calgary, 1986) 59–66; F. van Straten in R. Hägg *et al.* (eds.), *Early Greek Cult Practice* (Stockholm, 1988) 51–68.

143. This is one of a small group of Athenian black-figure skyphoi that show a scene unknown from literary sources, Dionysus in a 'ship-chariot'. The ship-chariot is at the centre of a sacrificial procession; it carries the god himself, wrapped in a himation, and two flute-playing satyrs. Most scholars assume that what is portrayed, rather freely, is a 'bringing in' of Dionysus performed (possibly for a short period only, around 500 B.C.) at one of the god's Athenian festivals, probably the Anthesteria. The point of such a ritual would be to dramatize the idea (which runs right through Euripides' *Bacchae*, for

example) that Dionysus is the 'stranger' god, the god whose temporary presence in a city is always the product of a more or less dramatic 'arrival' from afar.

(Bologna, Museo Civico 130)

CVA 2, pl. 43; *LIMC* III *Dionysos* no. 829; H.W. Parke, *Festivals of the Athenians* (London, 1977) 109.

144. An Anodos or 'coming up', the emergence of a goddess from the earth, on an Athenian red-figure crater. Often in such portrayals the goddess is surrounded by capering satyrs, who may wield mattock-like objects; a ritual of 'calling up' the goddess, possibly by means of sounds made by the 'mattocks', is perhaps reflected. Here, however, the scene is certainly on a primary level one of myth: Persephone, having spent her annual four months in the Underworld, is returning to earth to rejoin her mother Demeter (the sceptre-bearing figure on the right). Hecate escorts her with torches, while Hermes the guardian of transitions looks on. In the case of Persephone, the motif has a double significance: the goddess' 'coming up' certainly has a connexion, though a looser one than is often suggested, with the annual return of vegetation from below the earth; but her regular movement from one world to the other also makes the opposition between life and death less absolute. It was therefore to Persephone that mortals appealed (above all through the Mysteries at Eleusis) in hopes of a better lot in the afterlife. About 440 B.C.

143

144

145

(New York, Metropolitan Museum of Art 28. 57. 23)
  ARV 1012, 1, Persephone Painter; C. Bérard, *Anodoi* (Rome, 1974) 129–30.

145. This Athenian white-ground lekythos shows, enigmatically, a very different form of passage between the two worlds. Two souls, *psychai* (represented, as often, in the form of a tiny winged figure), emerge from a half-sunken jar, watched by Hermes 'the escorter of souls' (*psychopompos*); a third seems to be going back in. Why the jar? Obviously such a partly sunken vessel could be imagined as a channel between above and below, but it is hard to be more precise; possibly libations were poured to the dead through such jars. About 460 B.C.

(Jena Univ. 338)
  ARV 160, 41, manner of the Tymbos Painter; *LIMC* v Hermes no. 630; L. Deubner, *Attische Feste* (Berlin, 1932), 95.

146. The Athenian red-figure pelike from Kerch (Panticapaeum, in the Crimea) is as important as it is controversial. The crucial action is that of the left foreground. Again we see a goddess emerging from the earth, through a kind of cave, but in this case she is handing a baby to Hermes. The baby is wrapped in a fawnskin and wears (as does his mother) a crown of ivy, traditional Dionysiac symbols; he should be Dionysus himself. Who is his mother? Not Semele, who notoriously was destroyed by a thunderbolt at the moment of birth. Perhaps therefore the emergent goddess is again Persephone, and the vase depicts the 'Orphic' myth which made Dionysus her child and not Semele's. As the other side of the vase shows a scene relating to the mystery cult at Eleusis, the important inference seems to follow that Eleusinian and Orphic mythology had become in some measure intertwined. About 350 B.C.

(St Petersburg, St 1792)

ARV 1476, 1, Eleusinian Painter; E. Simon, *AK* 9 (1966) 72–92; F. Graf, *Eleusis und die orphische Dichtung Athens* (Berlin, 1974) 66–78; C. Bérard, *Anodoi* (1974) 147–51.

147. The 'Lovatelli urn' is a Roman copy of another Eleusinian scene, the initiation of Heracles (the first foreigner, according to tradition, to be admitted to the Mysteries). On the left is Demeter enthroned, with Persephone behind her; mysteriously, a young man (not necessarily Heracles) extends his hand towards a snake in the goddess' lap. In the centre, a priestess holds the sacred winnowing-fan over the veiled, seated initiate (betrayed as Heracles by the lion skin on which he sits); the ram's head beneath his right foot hints at the 'fleece of Zeus' which was supposedly used in purifications at Eleusis. To the right Heracles holds a pig (a traditional preliminary offering at Eleusis) over a low altar, while an older man pours something from a jug. We cannot be sure that mortal candidates for initiation underwent exactly the same preliminaries as are shown here; but in other contexts too 'seating' is mentioned as a technique of purification and initiation. (There is a parody of such rituals in Aristophanes, *Clouds* 250–60.)

(Rome, Museo Nazionale 11301)

W. Burkert, *Homo Necans* (tr. P. Bing, Berkeley 1983) 266–9; *LIMC* IV *Herakles* no. 1410.

148. The Athenian red-figure oinochoe illustrates an important religious practice that is attested by some seventy vases but is virtually unknown from literary sources: the use of masks of the god himself in the cult of Dionysus (who was, of course, the patron of masked drama). The mask rests in a *liknon* or winnowing-basket, an object often employed in ritual, on a table; to the left a woman holds out a kantharos, Dionysus' characteristic vessel, while on the right another woman, ivy-crowned, brings offerings of grapes and fruit. Much more commonly, as on the vase shown in *CAH* v² 253, fig. 32, the mask hangs on a pillar, in front of which women distribute wine from large jars; on the reverse, other women dance with varying degrees of wildness. (Another type just shows dancing around the pillar; *Pls. to Vol. IV*, pl. 223.) Despite a century of debate, these scenes cannot be reliably associated with any particular Athenian festival (Lenaea and Anthesteria have long been candidates); but they hint at the form, a domesticated one, that 'maenadism' may have taken among the women of Athens. The mask served to evoke, once again (cf. on **143**), the presence at the festival of the 'stranger' god, the god of advents; it also, with its direct frontal gaze, challenged the worshipper to see and be seen by the disconcerting god (who similarly gazes straight at the viewer out of the François vase, alone of the many figures represented there). About 430 B.C.

(Athens, National Museum, ex Vlastos Collection)
ARV 1249, 13, Eretria Painter; F. Frontisi-Ducroux, *Le Dieu-masque* (Paris and Rome, 1991) 159–61.

149. This is a detail from a remarkable Athenian red-figure crater which shows 'Dionysiac' dancing in its most extreme form: a castanet-player provides accompaniment (elsewhere on the vase we see flutes and tambourines), and the dancers, heads thrown wildly back, are even shown handling snakes, like the mythical maenads of Euripides' *Bacchae*. But this 'Dionysiac' dancing did not in fact honour Dionysus, or not at least in a familiar way: for men too are involved, and the dance is linked to a procession (not shown here) which approaches a god and goddess enthroned together. This divine couple cannot be identified with any certainty, and the vase reminds us yet again how much we do not know about Greek religion. About 430 B.C.

(Ferrara, Museo Nazionale T 128)
ARV 1052, 25, Group of Polygnotos; C. Bérard *et al.*, *A City of Images* (tr. D. Lyons, Princeton 1989) 23–30.

150. Here is a final scene of cult, on an Athenian red-figure lekythos. A woman mounted on a ladder bends down to receive, from a Cupid-like figure, a half-amphora from which little plants are growing; other such amphora flower-pots are shown on the ground. These pots are almost certainly 'Adonis gardens': that is to say, little collections of fast-sprouting seeds which Athenian women grew in preparation for the annual mourning for Adonis which many of them performed on the roofs of their houses (whence the ladder). The fast-growing, fast-withering seeds symbolized, it seems, lovely Adonis' brief career; and the Cupid who hands over the garden evokes the erotic atmosphere of this festival which honoured Aphrodite's own lover. Early fourth century B.C.

149

(Karlsruhe, Badisches Landesmuseum, B 39 (278))

CVA 1, pl. 27; *LIMC* I *Adonis* no. 47; W. Atallah, *Adonis dans la littérature et l'art grec* (Paris, 1966); M. Detienne, *The Gardens of Adonis* (tr. J. Lloyd, Hassocks, 1977).

Votive Reliefs

We turn now to evidence of a quite different type, dedications of actual worshippers. Objects of almost any kind could serve as 'gifts' to the gods, but we are concerned here with a special kind of commemorative dedication: a plaque or tablet or sculpted relief showing the god or his worshippers or, most commonly, the two together, as the worshippers bring an offering to the altar. Such a representation as it were freezes the moment of encounter between god and worshipper, and so seeks to perpetuate the divine goodwill that the mortals hope to achieve through their offerings. (But perhaps one might also compare the 'me and the Parthenon' photos of modern tourists.) Votives of this kind are extremely common. Most surviving examples, of clay or marble, date from after 500; but the characteristic scene of worshippers bringing their victims to an altar already appears on a fine painted wooden specimen from Pitsa, dated to around 540 (*Pls. to Vol. III*, p. 323).

U. Hausmann, *Griechische Weihreliefs* (Berlin, 1960); G. Neumann, *Probleme des griechischen Weihreliefs* (Tübingen, 1979); F.T. van Straten, 'Gifts for the gods', in H.S. Versnel (ed.), *Faith, Hope and Worship* (Leiden, 1981) 65–151.

151. One of a series of superb specimens found in the sanctuary of Artemis at Brauron in Attica. Like many dedications to Artemis, it was made by a woman, Aristonike the wife of Antiphates, and women are prominent in the long procession of worshippers (an 'extended family' group, plus servants?) that it portrays. Artemis is identified by her attributes, the bow in her left hand and the little deer peeping out behind her; she is shown pouring a libation at her own altar. As is usual in such scenes, the worshippers are humbly depicted as much smaller than the deity. The victim is a bull, a costly offering for private individuals to bring (it was about six times as expensive as a sheep, the commonest victim); but, if Aristonike's family could afford such a fine marble dedication, they were evidently not poor. Second half of the fourth century B.C.

(Brauron Museum 1151 (5))
LIMC II *Artemis* no. 974.

15

152. This is a much humbler votive, of a very characteristic type, one dedicated to the Nymphs and Pan. Three Nymphs are dancing by an altar, accompanied by Pan on his pipes, in a cave-like enclosure (we noted earlier that caves were the normal cult-sites for these rustic deities). Above the cave Pan's goats appear; the giant head on the left (as we know from many related portrayals) is that of the river-god Achelous, constantly associated with the water-loving Nymphs. Such a little marble votive, designed to be hung up by the hole in its back, could evidently be bought ready-made; no worshippers are shown, and it bears no dedication. Fourth century B.C.

(Athens, National Museum 1445, from Eleusis)
   C.M. Edwards, *Greek Votive Reliefs to Pan and the Nymphs* (diss. New York, 1985).

153. This fragment of a painted pottery votive plaque is from the Athenian Acropolis, showing Athena herself in her aegis. It was, therefore, like **152**, a 'ready to dedicate' votive, a simple image of the relevant deity. About 500 B.C.

(Athens, National Museum)
   B. Graef, E. Langlotz, *Die Antiken Vasen von der Akropolis zu Athen* (Berlin, 1933) II pl. 81, no. 1038.

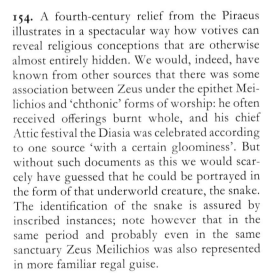

155. A specimen from the Athenian Agora of a characteristic type of 'hero-relief', variants of which have been found in great abundance from about 500 B.C. down to the Roman period (cf. *Pls. to Vol.* VII. 1, pl. 239). A male figure reclines on a couch, with drinking-vessels in his hands, a table of foodstuffs beside him. A woman sits submissively beside him, and two female worshippers approach from the left. Often in such reliefs a horse's head is included in the relief, antinaturalistically, in a window-like frame. Similar scenes often appear on tombstones (from the fourth century), but it is now accepted that the iconographical type belongs originally to heroes; and this bears a dedication, 'Chrysis to the hero'. The interpretation is disputed: does the hero's feast evoke (1) his lot in the afterlife, or (2) the actual food offerings made to him by his worshippers, or (3) the luxurious lifestyle of that socially superior order to which the hero is conceived as belonging? Analogy with other votive reliefs supports (2); but the history of the reclining banquet motif speaks for (3), as does the horse's head (horses being a supreme symbol of wealth for the Greeks). The two explanations are, in fact, perhaps not incompatible: the worshippers bring offerings appropriate for a member of a superior order.

(Athens, Agora Museum Inv. 1. 4707)
  AJA 41 (1937), 184–7; J.-M. Dentzer, *Le Motif du banquet couché dans le proche orient et le monde grec* (Rome, 1982) 584 R. 143.

154. A fourth-century relief from the Piraeus illustrates in a spectacular way how votives can reveal religious conceptions that are otherwise almost entirely hidden. We would, indeed, have known from other sources that there was some association between Zeus under the epithet Meilichios and 'chthonic' forms of worship: he often received offerings burnt whole, and his chief Attic festival the Diasia was celebrated according to one source 'with a certain gloominess'. But without such documents as this we would scarcely have guessed that he could be portrayed in the form of that underworld creature, the snake. The identification of the snake is assured by inscribed instances; note however that in the same period and probably even in the same sanctuary Zeus Meilichios was also represented in more familiar regal guise.

(Berlin, Staatliche Museen K 91 (inv. SK 723))
  Van Straten, *op. cit.* (**150**) 82; M.H. Jameson, *BCH* 89 (1965) 159–66.

156. One of a superb series of tablets from the famous sanctuary of Persephone at Locri in South Italy, which appear to open a window onto a distinctive local mythology and set of practices, concerning in particular marriage and the underworld. This is an instance of a characteristic scene-type, in which one of a variety of gods (here it is Dionysus) pays homage to the enthroned Persephone, who is often accompanied by her husband Hades. The occasion is probably their wedding; and the scene may derive cult significance from Persephone's role as a paradigm for mortal brides. About 460 B.C.

(Reggio, Museo Nazionale)

    LIMC III *Dionysos* no. 538; H. Prückner, *Die lokrischen Tonreliefs* (Mainz, 1968) 78; C. Sourvinou-Inwood, *JHS* 98 (1978) 101–21 = '*Reading' Greek Culture* (Oxford, 1991) 147–88.

157. This is one of a large number of votives honouring the Dioscuri found at Tarentum in South Italy, where their cult seems to have been even more important than in Sparta, Tarentum's mother-city and the Dioscuri's mythological home. Numerous iconographic types are found; this one evokes the panhellenic practice of honouring the Dioscuri by a rite of 'god-entertaining' (theoxeny): the twin gods, who were closely associated with horses, are arriving at the gallop over a table laid for their entertainment. At the edges appear two of the Dioscuri's characteristic but enigmatic symbols: two amphorae, and two bossed phialae.

(Taranto, Museo Nazionale 4118)

L.P.B. Stefanelli, *Archeologia Classica* 29 (1977) 356 and pl. 89.3.

158. This famous dedication was made by one Archinus at the healing shrine of the hero Amphiaraus at Oropus, on the borders of Attica and Boeotia. In such a cult, the vital encounter that the votive commemorates is not normally the sacrificial procession but the god's act of healing. Here the representation is very complex. The cult at Oropus was one of incubation, and on the right we duly see the patient asleep on a couch. In the left foreground, the hero Amphiaraus, like a human doctor, is actually treating the patient's right shoulder: this scene represents the supposed content of Archinus' dream. But in the scene on the right a sacred snake, a healing animal, is also shown licking or biting the same, right shoulder of the sleeping patient: this is the same cure as it would supposedly have appeared to a waking observer. Behind can be seen, on a pillar, a votive stele – like the one dedicated by Archinus himself. And perhaps the figure on the far right is yet a third representation of Archinus, in this case gratefully dedicating his stele. About 370 B.C.

(Athens, National Museum 3369)

van Straten, *op cit.* (**150**) 124.

158

7. THE THEATRE

J.R. GREEN

Material remains provide our fullest and most direct evidence for the non-textual aspects of theatre of the fifth and fourth centuries, that is for the way performances were staged and costumed, as well as for questions of reception such as the popularity of the various forms or genres of performance and audience reaction to them, and, through inscriptions, for records of performances and the victories won by playwrights and actors. Our surviving dramatic texts or scripts contain no original stage directions or instructions from the playwrights. On the other hand the interpretation of the archaeological evidence is not a simple matter either. Vase-painters, for example, were not photographers and the pictures they created were governed by complex artistic and social conventions which need to be understood if their evidence is to be used. At the same time, recognition of these conventions can tell us a lot about the way Athenians, and Greeks in general, regarded theatre.

GENERAL BIBLIOGRAPHY

A.W. Pickard-Cambridge, *Dithyramb, Tragedy and Comedy* (2nd edn rev. T.B.L. Webster, Oxford, 1962); *id.*, *The Dramatic Festivals of Athens* (2nd edn rev. J. Gould and D.M. Lewis, Oxford, 1968, 1988); T.B.L. Webster, *Greek Theatre Production* (2nd edn, London 1970); A.D. Trendall and T.B.L. Webster, *Illustrations of Greek Drama* (London, 1971); E. Simon, *The Ancient Theatre* (London, 1982); J.R. Green, 'On Seeing and Depicting the Theatre in Classical Athens', *GRBS* 32 (1991) 1–36.

159. Nothing is less certain than the physical form of the theatre in the fifth century, and especially that of the Theatre of Dionysus at Athens (**a**) which was re-modelled and re-developed, sometimes drastically, over the 800 or 900 years of its use. It now seems probable that the older idea of a theatre developed around a circular dancing floor has to be abandoned. We should think, rather, along the lines of the surviving later fifth- and early fourth-century theatres at Thorikos (**b**) and Trachones in rural Attica, or even that at Syracuse. They have roughly rectilinear seating arrangements and a space for the chorus, the orchestra, which is a little over twice as wide as it is deep (although the one at Syracuse is squarer). Some doubt the existence of a stage in the early years, but there must have been one by 458 B.C., the date of Aeschylus' *Oresteia*. It must have been about 25 m long. Evidence datable near the end of the fifth century suggests that it was about a metre high with a stairway in the centre leading up from the orchestra. The stage itself was of wood (which by no means implies an impermanent structure) and it is quite possible that the façade of the stage building was of timber also. The details of the appearance of the stage building are uncertain, but there must have been a central door which served as the palace-entrance in many tragedies, as the main house door in comedies, or as a sanctuary or cave in tragedy (e.g. *Philoctetes*), in satyr-play or in comedy (e.g. *Birds*). Not far from the door there was (as we know from Aristophanes and early fourth-century vase-paintings) a window, and given the Greek sense of symmetry, perhaps one each side as in **c**. It is debated whether there were balancing doors at the ends of the stage-building in the fifth century and whether they were emphasized architecturally. Arguments in favour of wings (*paraskenia*) include the parallels in the late fifth century of the newly constructed Stoa of Zeus in the Athenian Agora (see **82b**) and the modification of the Royal Stoa; wings give architectural definition to a long straight building, and when built at each end of a stage would frame the area of action and help to set it apart from the ordinary world. We know from a vase-painting (**160**) that the theatre at Tarentum in South Italy had wings with side-doors by the middle of the fourth century. As to the treatment of the façade of the building, it is certain that the Theatre of Dionysus had an arrangement of semi-columns

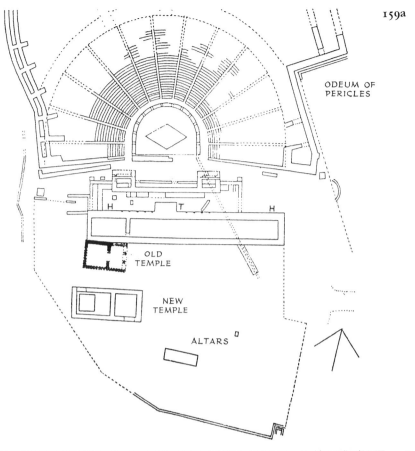

159a

ODEUM OF
PERICLES

H   T   H

OLD
TEMPLE

NEW
TEMPLE

ALTARS

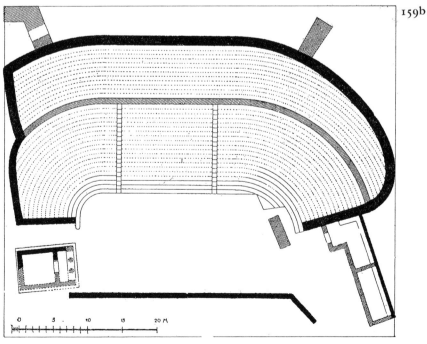

159b

0   5   10   15   20 M

in the later fourth century and it is tempting to suppose them earlier, as **160** also implies.

Other features certain from the literary evidence include the *ekkyklema*, a wheeled platform perhaps between two and three metres wide and one and a half metres deep which could be rolled forward onto the stage through the central doors. It was supported by the stone platform T which projects forward from Wall H in **a**. The *ekkyklema* was used in tragedy to present set-pieces showing the key figures and objects of an event that had happened indoors (i.e. within the palace) as if outdoors (i.e. forward of the building, on the stage). On the only occasions where we are clear about its use in comedy, it was used to parody tragedy. Similarly with the other major device, the crane. One can only guess at its structure and mechanics, but its use was to transport actors in the role of heroes or divinities from behind the façade of the stage building over onto the stage. In many cases this was seen as more effective than the alternative of having them appear on the roof of the stage building: it brought them into the realm of man whereas the roof was regarded as the territory of the gods. It was probably located towards the right-hand end of the stage as the audience looked at it. The notion of scenery in fifth-century theatre, though commonly assumed, rests on very doubtful evidence, and it is likely that settings were largely created in the mind of the audience by the words of the play.

In the course of the fourth century the role of the chorus was steadily reduced while the attention given to actors increased. The most popular became superstars who were able to command huge fees and attract large audiences. The increased popularity of theatre is seen for example in country Thorikos (**b**) where the extension of the seating area was carried out fairly soon after the middle of the century (despite a probably reduced population). In other centres monumental theatres were constructed, such as the well-known example at Epidaurus, perhaps about 330 B.C., and the Theatre of Dionysus at Athens, traditionally associated with Lycurgus (in power 338–326 B.C.). It has been suggested that their arrangement about a circular orchestra was prompted by contemporary theory on acoustics. The other typical feature of these theatres is the high stage for the actors: it removed them from contact with the orchestra but made them more visible to the large audience.

W. Dörpfeld and E. Reisch, *Das griechische Theater: Beiträge zur Geschichte des Dionysos-Theaters in Athen und anderer griechische Theater* (Athens, 1896); E. Fiechter, *Das Dionysos-Theater in Athen*, I–IV (*Antike griechische Theaterbauten*, 5–7, Stuttgart 1935–50); A.W. Pickard-Cambridge, *The Theatre of Dionysus in Athens* (Oxford, 1946). Also E. Gebhard, *Hesperia* 43 (1974) 428–40; W.W. Würster, *Architectura* 9 (1979), 58–76; L. Polacco, *Il teatro di Dioniso Eleutereo ad Atene* (Rome, 1990); on the *ekkyklema* and crane, H.-J. Newiger, *Dioniso* 59 (1989) 173–85 = *Würz.Jb.Alt.Wiss.* 16 (1990) 33–42.

160. Fragmentary Tarentine calyx-crater, about 350 B.C., decorated in added colour (Gnathia technique). The left part of the scene is the best preserved but was balanced equally on the right. The precise import of the picture is uncertain (arrival of Jason in Iolcus?) but it shows a theatre performance with two figures in the centre between wings containing doors through which women emerge. Note the elaborate treatment of the architectural detail; it is difficult to know how literal the painter was in his depiction but the principle of wings at the side doors should hold good.

(Würzburg, Martin-von-Wagner Museum H 4696 + 4701, from Taranto)

H. Bulle, *Berliner Winckelmannsprogramm* 94 (1934) pls. 1–2; *IGD* III.3, 43; Simon, *Theatre* 23 fig. 3, pl. 10; *MTS*² GV 1.

161. Athenian red-figure pelike, about 470 B.C. On each side a maenad dances to the music of a piper. The piper is shown in elaborate costume and is used as a conventional symbol that the scene is a theatrical performance. The maenad has a sword in the right hand and a half fawn or kid in the left, and is shown as 'real'. Yet since the piper signifies that the figure is a chorusman, the figure should, in the actuality of the stage performance, have had footwear and, as a young man, cannot have had a naked feminine breast. The question then arises whether the half fawn or kid is a literal depiction of a piece of stage property, or is an insertion by the vase-painter as something that maenads normally have, thus characterizing the maenad, or if it is something that the vase-painter was persuaded to imagine was there by the words of the script. It is certain that in the theatre this torn animal did not have blood pouring out of it as we see here. The frontal face, uncommon in art at this period, was perhaps inspired by thinking of the mask. And then, although one cannot see it in the reproduction, the painter wrote about the figure the word *kalos*: the boy (rather than the girl) is fair.

The vase is unique in its uncertain handling of the ambiguity between the actuality of the performance as put on in the theatre, and the further

161b

reality of what the performers were persuading the audience to believe in.

(Berlin, Staatliche Museen inv. 3223)

ARV 586, 47 (Earlier Mannerist), *Para* 393; *Add²* 263; J.D. Beazley, *Hesperia* 24 (1955) 312–3; *MTS²* AV 15; Pickard-Cambridge, *Festivals* 182, fig. 35; Simon, *Theatre* pl. 1.

162. Athenian red-figure column-crater, about 490 B.C. In the early fifth century theatre was just being invented and there is good reason to suppose that it was highly experimental as playwrights and (by their negative or positive reaction) audience worked out the most effective content, structure and style of performance within the setting and expectations of the time. Early tragedy had only one actor to exchange word and song with the chorus. The stage action must therefore have been limited.

This vase exemplifies one solution that seems to have been popular with audiences. The chorus is represented by the six young men who sing (unintelligible words, invisible in the photograph, are shown coming from their mouths), dance and lift their arms in their attempts to raise

162

a hero from his tomb. It is a theme known later, from Aeschylus' *Persae*, and that play gives a good idea of how the motif was used and the style of song employed. At a time of crisis (in the *Persae* brought about by military disaster) the population, as represented by the chorus, feels lost and leaderless. They therefore seek advice from one of the great heroes of the past and with great effort and lamentation bring him up from the Underworld. We have vases reflecting use of the motif in at least three other plays, one earlier and two later than this.

(Basel, Antikenmuseum BS 414. Height 36.5 cm)
   CVA 3, pl. 6, 1–2, pl. 7, 3–5 (with further refs.); F. Jouan, *Revue de l'Histoire des Religions* 98 (1981) 403–21; J.R. Green, *GRBS* 32 (1991) 1–36.

163. Athenian white-ground calyx-crater by the Phiale Painter, about 445 B.C. The clearest and most convincing example of depictions derived from the theatre is a series which seems to relate to Sophocles' *Andromeda*. This example shows Andromeda tied to stakes, exposed for the mon-

ster and explaining her situation to her saviour Perseus.

Other vases of the same date show different moments from this exposure scene but certain features remain the same, for example her costume with its eastern hat, short tunic and trousers, the attendants shown as blacks, and in some cases the objects carried by the attendants, objects which suit both a funeral and a wedding, an ambiguity which one might guess was deliberately evoked by the playwright.

These vases stand apart from the rest of the iconographic tradition. The fact that this tight series is the work of different painters also helps to persuade us that this version derives from the stage rather than a pictorial tradition developed within a workshop. Later depictions mostly have her chained to a rock, perhaps a feature of the Euripidean version but also the rule in other artistic interpretations.

By the head of Perseus are the words 'Euaion kalos Aischylou' (Euaion son of Aeschylus is fair). He must have played the role of Perseus here, just as he seems to have played in Sopho-

163

cles' *Thamyras* (**164**). Family tradition was strong in classical theatre production and was largely in the hands of the upper classes, as the use of the patronymic here shows for Euaion.

(Agrigento, Museo Nazionale AG 7, from Agrigento. Height 44.4 cm)

ARV 1017, 53 (Phiale Painter); *Para* 440; *Add²* 315; *MTS²* 116, AV 53; *IGD* III.2, 1; J.H. Oakley, *The Phiale Painter* (Mainz, 1990) no. 53, pl. 37; J.R. Green, *GRBS* 32 (1991) 1–36.

164. Athenian red-figure hydria by the Phiale Painter, about 440–430 B.C. This is a good example of translation of stage performance into the reality created in the mind of the audience. The scene almost certainly draws on Sophocles' *Thamyras*. The play does not survive but the subject was a Thracian poet who boasted that he could defeat even the Muses; he was headstrong enough to do so, whereupon they not only blinded him but, more importantly, took away his ability to sing and play. The vase shows a critical moment: the contest must be just over, for his white-haired mother Argiope approaches from the right to crown and congratulate him. Behind, two Muses express agitation.

Over the poet's head is the inscription THA-MYRAS, over Argiope EUAION KALOS, over the Muses CHORONIKA. Sophocles himself is thought to have played Thamyras, but the actor playing Argiope appears to have been Euaion (cf. **163**). The painter's introduction of actuality here is also seen in the line that runs from the chin to her hair, suggesting a mask. The

inscription over the Muses should refer to the play's victory in the contest.

By the same painter as **163** and **165**. They are useful evidence of the way one individual reacted to the theatre.

(Vatican Museums 16549, from Vulci. Height 42.8 cm)

ARV 1020, 92; *Para* 441; *Add²* 316; *MTS²* 117, AV 58; *IGD* III 2.9; Oakley, *op. cit.*, 20–2, 81 no. 92, pls. 72a and 73a–b.

165. Athenian red-figure pelike by the Phiale Painter, about 440 B.C. The only occasions when one has literal depiction of tragic theatre in the Classical period are those which show the figures outside the theatre proper. Two chorusmen dressing as maenads. The one on the right already wears his chiton and is pulling on his boots. His mask lies on the ground in front of him. It is an excellent profile view of a mask showing how it was designed to cover the head to well below the crown; it often seems to have been held down by a hidden tie-string secured under the performer's chin. The boots (*kothornoi*) were regular wear.

The young man on the left has finished dressing and goes to put his own clothing away, but he starts to dance the part. This is a normal phenomenon: once one puts on the mask, one takes on the persona and behaves appropriately (compare the chorusman from satyr-play on **169**). It is indicative of the realism and power attributed to masks.

By the middle of the fourth century, when

164

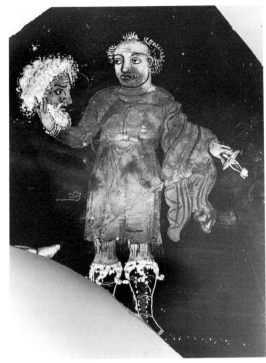

classic tragedies were being re-staged in competition and performance was more important than the message, we find occasional explicit depictions of tragedy in performance: see the *Oedipus Tyrannus* on a Sicilian vase about 340 B.C. (*Plates to Vol. VII.I* pl. 190).

(Boston, Museum of Fine Arts 98.883, from Cervetri. Height 24.1 cm)

ARV 1017, 46; *Para* 440; *Add²* 315; *MTS²* 47, AV 20; Pickard-Cambridge, *Festivals* fig. 34; Oakley, *op. cit.*, 73, no. 46, pl. 26a.

166. Fragment of a Tarentine bell-crater, about 350–340 B.C., decorated in added colour (Gnathia technique). This is one of the finer examples of Greek vase-painting, both in the skill of the drawing and in its depiction of the contrast between the shabby person of the tragic actor and the heroic quality of the figure he has just portrayed. The clothing for the part is a rich purple-red with a fringe at the hem. Note that the mask does not have the crest of hair – *onkos* – popularly associated with tragic masks, a feature not introduced before the late fourth century

when it was presumably developed to suit larger theatres. The actor is now a professional: by contrast with the actors on **169, 170**, he cuts his beard close so that it will not interfere with his mask. The figure played has been thought to be Tereus, from Sophocles' play of that name.

(Würzburg, Martin-von-Wagner Museum H 4600 (L.832), from Taranto. Height 18.5 cm)

H. Bulle, *Festschrift für James Loeb* (Munich, 1930), 5–37; *MTS²* 80, GV 3; Pickard-Cambridge, *Festivals* fig. 54; P. Ghiron-Bistagne, *Recherches sur les acteurs dans la Grèce antique* (Paris, 1976) frontispiece (colour); Simon, *Theatre* pl. 4, 3.

167. Fragment of an Athenian marble relief, about 350–340 B.C. Young man wearing female clothing and carrying a female mask from tragedy. The figure is usually taken as an actor, but he is young and is perhaps to be interpreted as a chorusman: compare **165** and contrast **166**.

(Copenhagen, Ny Carlsberg Glyptotek inv. 465. Height 0.78 m)

MTS² 34, AS 4; Pickard-Cambridge, *Festivals* fig. 52.

167

interpreted reality is the depiction of Aeschylus' *Sphinx* of 467 B.C. (*Pls. to Vol. IV*, pl. 200).

The play from which the scene derives is not known. Hardly any texts of satyr-plays survive, but to judge by the pictures, they were much more uninhibited in the early days than later in the fifth century. (Compare *CAH* v 271, fig. 36, for a satyr player.)

(Boston, Museum of Fine Arts 03.788, probably from Greece)

ARV 571, 75 (Leningrad Painter); *Para* 390; *Add²* 261; L.D. Caskey and J.D. Beazley, *Attic Vase Paintings in the Museum of Fine Arts, Boston* III, 51–2 no. 151, pl. 86; Brommer, *Satyrspiele²* no. 1, fig. 6; *MTS²* 46, AV 14; Pickard-Cambridge, *Festivals* fig. 40.

169. Athenian red-figure volute-crater by the Pronomos Painter, end of the fifth century. Named after the piper depicted at the bottom of the scene in the centre. Compare the prominence given to him (note too that he is placed directly under Dionysus) with that given to the playwright Demetrios who rests idly on a stool somewhat to the left, the papyrus roll with the script in his left hand. The occasion depicted is the celebration of victory after the performance of a satyr-play which had presumably been staged as the concluding element after a set of three tragedies. The chorusmen, who are of the age of ephebes (cf. **165**), wear the shorts with phallus and tail like those of **168**. They stand and chat, mask in hand, with the exception of the one immediately behind the piper who is wearing his mask and therefore takes on the persona of the character and acts the part (cf. **165**).

In the upper register and closer to the god are the actors. They are bearded mature men wearing elaborate theatre costume. To the right is the Papposilenos or Father-Satyr in his suit with white wool tufts and mask with bald head and full white beard, and next to him the actor who played Heracles carrying a dark-bearded mask with the jaw of the lion-head visible above. The setting is the sanctuary of Dionysus (cf. **170**) as is indicated by the victory tripods at each side and by the presence of the god himself. It is where the performers continued the celebration of the god initiated by the performance in the theatre, joining him in drinking his magic gift of wine. It is also where they dedicated their masks in tribute and perhaps as a sign that they left here with the god the other world of the characters they represented.

168. Athenian red-figure hydria by the Leningrad Painter, about 480–470 B.C. This is the fullest literal depiction we have of a satyr-play. On the right is the piper in his elaborate costume and behind him a man who may be the producer or the playwright. In front of him five satyrs of the chorus dance vigorously and begin to erect the various parts of a symposium couch and, at the far left, perhaps a table. The painter has made the artificiality of the masks evident as well as the typical drawers with a tail attached at the back and a phallus at the front.

Depictions of satyr-play hover between the literal style of depiction typical of comedy and the interpretive depictions of tragedy. This is consonant with the position of satyr-play as a genre. An excellent example of the further or

(Naples, Museo Nazionale inv. 81673 (H 3240), from Ruvo)

ARV 1336, 1; *Para* 480; *Add²* 365–6; *IGD* II, 1; *MTS²* AV 25; Pickard-Cambridge, *Festivals* fig. 49 (opp. p. 188).

170. Athenian red-figure bell-crater, from Spina, end of the fifth century. The scene here too is set in the sanctuary of Dionysus after a performance and it again echoes the rocky site of that sanctuary on the slope of the Acropolis (note especially the figure on the upper right). Two actors are represented in company with the god and his entourage of satyr and maenads. The elaborate costume is in contrast to the impression one has from earlier in the century. The man, who is bearded, holds a sceptre and must have played the part of a king. The other figure should also be a male (there were no female actors) but, like the figure who sits on the end of the couch on **169**, has been transformed by the painter into something of the role played. Both the masks 'she' holds are female, the one in her left hand a principal character with long hair, the one in her right with ivy in the hair (as she has) either a young woman taken with the cult of Dionysus or a maenad from the chorus.

(Ferrara, Museo Nazionale T 161 C, from Spina)

F. Berti and C. Gasparri (eds.), *Dionysos. Mito e mistero* (Bologna, 1989) 132–3, no. 63 (ill.).

171. Athenian black-figure jug, about 490 B.C. Piper with two chorusmen as Birds set against a background of ivy. Their human faces have red beards and large pointed noses; on their heads are red crests or combs. They wear body tights decorated with feathers, the one nearer the piper with the softer feathers of the underbody on his front. This figure also shows how the wings work: they fall over the arm and are gripped by a strap near their ends and a further strap holds them in place at the elbow. On the other dancer it is just possible to see where the painter outlined the figure's arms through the wings, suggesting that the wings were somewhat transparent and certainly lightweight so that they floated. The figures have protrusions at each knee (in most cases red): these must be the Birds' feet so that here they are conceived of as flying. When they came to rest, the chorusmen knelt and the feet were on the ground.

The scene is decorated in a standard convention for scenes of comedy with a piper and members of the chorus (cf *Pls. to Vol. IV*, pls. 198–9, and here **172**). By contrast with tragedy, pictures of comedy are always literal, showing actors acting, and painters are generally careful to show the particulars of costume. The playwright evidently put great effort into presentation (the appearance of the chorus characterized the play in Old Comedy) and the vases show that the audience watched their efforts carefully.

(London, British Museum B 509)

E. Haspels, *Attic Black-Figured Lekythoi* (1936) 214, 187; *ABV* 473; *Para* 214; *Add²* 119; *IGD* 1 12; J.R. Green, *GV Getty* 2 (1985) 101, no. 8, figs. 11a–c.

172. Athenian red-figure calyx-crater, about 414 B.C. The chorus of Aristophanes' *Birds*. Iconographically it belongs within the same convention as **171**, one that had been in place since the middle of the sixth century and would continue in quasi-official monuments until the middle of the fourth. The painter had an awkward hand but seems to have been careful in his depiction.

Birds had been a much-used type of chorus over the generations (cf. **171**) and it is probably for that reason that Aristophanes designed a highly stylized and very clever costume that is both a parody of that of satyr-play (cf **165**, **169**) and, with the dot-filled circles, usable as the basis of varied jokes such as the reminiscence of eastern clothing, peacocks, or the moulted or plucked-chicken effect. One should perhaps imagine that different members of the chorus had the costume in different colours, although the pattern for all would have been the same. The chorusmen of comedy (as distinct from the

172

actors) were not normally phallic. The use of the central door of the stage building as a cave in the *Birds* was a normal feature of satyr-play and was perhaps another aspect of Aristophanes' parody of the genre.

Pipers for drama are normally mature men (i.e. bearded), and Pronomos on **169** is unusually young. It must have been a highly skilled and at times gruelling job.

(Malibu, The J. Paul Getty Museum 82.AE.83. Height as preserved (without the modern foot) 18.7 cm)
J.R. Green, *GV Getty* 2 (1985) 95–118.

173. Tarentine red-figure bell-crater by the Choregos Painter, about 380 B.C. Scene from an Athenian comedy of the late fifth or very early fourth century. The principal figures are two play sponsors (*choregoi*, each of them labelled), one of them old, the other younger. Between them, and apparently officiating over the proceedings as he stands on his overturned basket, is a slave (Pyrrhias). For a slave he wears rather elaborate dress and one suspects that he has engineered himself a role beyond his station. To the left is a figure labelled Aegisthus who stands by an open door, his hand to his head, possibly in surprise, wonder or a lack of understanding as the older *choregos* addresses him. One thinks of the contrast between the characters Aeschylus and Euripides in the *Frogs*. The subject must concern the production of tragedy of a traditional kind (plays concerning Agamemnon seem to have been somewhat out of fashion by now) and is a good example of paratheatricality in comedy at this period.

The costume of the two *choregoi* and the slave is typical and closely comparable to that of the terracottas (**175**). The figure of Aegisthus is shown as 'real', i.e. as the part played, something which is normal in representations drawn from tragedy.

Note the wooden stage with its strong supports, and the steps. There is no strict logic here. The steps are shown in the middle, as they were in the theatre, but the door is shown at the end

173

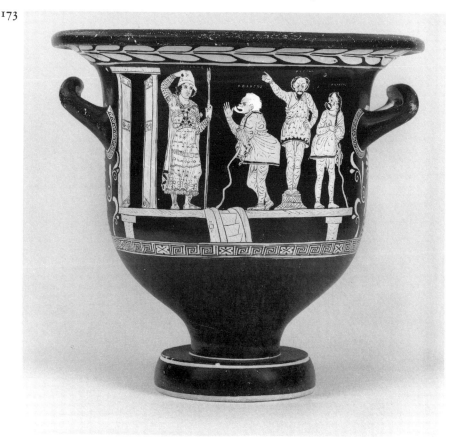

because the composition of the scene as shown demands it.

Aristophanes wrote a play called *Proagon*, or 'the parade before the performance'.

(New York, priv. coll.)
RVAp Suppl. 2, 7, no. 1/124, pl. 1, 3. More generally J.R. Green, *Numismatica e Antichità classiche* 20, 1991, 49–56, and O. Taplin, *Comic Angels and Other Approaches to Greek Drama through Vase Paintings* (Oxford, 1993). For a full catalogue and discussion of vases with comic scenes, see A.D. Trendall, *Phlyax Vases* (3rd edn rev. and enlarged by J.R. Green with the assistance of A.D. Trendall, forthcoming).

174. Tarentine red-figure bell-crater by the Schiller painter, about 370 B.C. Aristophanes' *Thesmophoriazusae*. At lines 689 ff. Mnesilochus snatches a woman's baby and seeks refuge at the altar, sword in hand and using the child as hostage. On being unwrapped, the baby turns out to be a wineskin, complete with Persian slippers. At line 753 Mnesilochus proceeds with the sacrifice of the 'infant' and (at 755, the moment shown here) the woman runs up with a bowl to catch the wine as it squirts out. That done, he finally gives her the empty skin back (which is also a means of getting it off stage). All this by-play takes a mere seven lines of text and is a good instance of the elaboration that takes place in performance.

The pose of Mnesilochus at the altar is a direct parody of scenes of the Euripidean *Orestes* with Telephus at the altar. The anti-hero is dressed as a male in woman's clothing (the skirt shorter than that of the real woman) and he wears a beardless mask that is grubby about the chin, a remnant of the shaving scene. The humour does not rest only in Mnesilochus. The woman, who earlier had presumably hidden her face modestly with her veil as she held her 'child', now lets it loose in her eagerness to get to the wine she had lost and so reveals what a drink-sodden hag she is.

The vase was made in Tarentum and the play presumably performed when it was already some thirty years old, but the vase need not reflect the play's first performance there. It is a clear demonstration that the local audience could enjoy a fairly high level of Athenian content in its plays and that it must have been sophisticated enough in its knowledge of Euripidean tragedy to appreciate the parodies, even if one supposes that some elements of the play could have been modified to suit local conditions.

(Würzburg, Martin-von-Wagner Museum H 5697. Height 18.5 cm)
RVAp I, 65, no. 4/4a (Schiller Painter); A. Kossatz-Deißmann in H.A. Cahn and E. Simon (eds.), *Tainia. Festschrift Roland Hampe* (Mainz, 1980) 281–90, pl. 60; E.G. Csapo, *Phoenix* 40 (1986), 379–92; O. Taplin, *Proc.Camb.Phil.Soc.* 213 (1987) 92–104. Comparative discussion of Telephus scenes, E.G. Csapo, *Quaderni Urbinati di Cultura Classica* 34 (1990) 41–52.

175. Terracotta figurines of actors were introduced in Athens in the late fifth century. Best known is a carefully made series known as the New York Group, named after a set of fourteen figurines said to have been found in a grave in Athens. Others can be added on grounds of style. They are solid mould-made figurines, modelled back and front, and most were reproduced in considerable numbers. They are about 10–12 cm high and are characterized by very sharp and lively detail in the modelling. They originally had bright colours; red-brown for the faces and hands of the men and slaves, pink for the women's, black, white or red hair depending on the character, yellow on dresses, blue on cloaks. They wear all-over body-suits with padding on the rump and belly and a phallus attached at the front. This is stage-naked and over it are worn whatever clothes, male or female, that are appropriate to the part.

These are not individual characters from single performances, but standardized types common to all comedies of the late fifth and the first half of the fourth century. They have been found all over the Greek world, both as imported Athenian and as local reproductions. These and

174

pottery with scenes from comedy made in such centres as Corinth, Olympia, Tarentum, Metapontum, Syracuse and Paestum show that Athenian comedy was becoming Greek comedy and that it was quickly becoming enormously popular.

Figurines were probably acquired as souvenirs of performances, whether as single pieces reminding one of particular characters, or in whatever combinations suited a particular play. They were made for fans and at the same time encouraged people to be fans. In the grave (where the chance of excavation has dictated that most of them were found), they must have symbolized happy times and have evoked the world of the god for whom the plays were produced, Dionysus.

*MMC*³ 45ff., AT 9–23; *BICS* 27 (1980) 123–31.

176. Fragmentary marble relief from the Ceramicus cemetery in Athens, about 340–320 B.C. Portrait of comic writer. As a mark of his trade he held in his left hand a roll of papyrus, now largely broken away; in his right he holds a mask of a slave from comedy. On the wall in the background hangs a mask of an old man.

The relief dates shortly before the appearance of New Comedy and is important evidence for the style of mask Menander must have used at the beginning of his career. It is also a good example

of the function of the mask in society now. The types are readily recognizable as representing defined characters from the stage. They can therefore serve as a cast-list and so commemorate a comedy, as they do on the Aixone relief, probably to be dated 340/339 (*Pls. to Vol. VII.1*, pl. 192). Here the sculptor has chosen to typify comedy by the masks of a slave and an old man, one of our earliest instances of this usage. The poet contemplates the mask not simply because it was his habit but because he uses the characters to work out the plot of his play. This is a motif which is picked up in the later Menander reliefs (e.g. *Pls. to Vol. VII.1*, pl. 206).

Depiction of masks as opposed to whole figures becomes increasingly popular, as is evident too on pottery where comic scenes disappear at precisely this period and are replaced by masks shown in a Dionysiac setting.

(Stockport, Lyme Hall. Preserved height 1.19 m)

E. Strong, *JHS* 23 (1903) pl. 13; G. Dontas, *Eikones pneumatikon anthropon* (Athens, 1960) pl. 3b; Pickard-Cambridge, *Festivals* fig. 88; *MMC³* 117, AS 1; N. Himmelmann in *Kotinos* (Festschrift E. Simon) (Mainz, 1992) 267–9.

177. Tarentine red-figure bell-crater by the Choregos Painter, about 380 B.C. Head and shoulders of Dionysus in three-quarter view. Over his left shoulder is a staff or pole; around it grows the trunk of a vine which then spreads out behind and above his head and is laden with grapes. At the left, by a *thymiaterion* in which incense is burning, an actor dressed as a slave from comedy stands on tip-toe reaching up to and seemingly exclaiming about a bunch of grapes. On the right an actor dressed as Papposilenos stands on a small platform holding a very large skyphos. On the other side of the vase, a youth with thyrsus, presumably again Dionysus, moves right in procession with a satyr and maenad.

169, 170, 177–8 can be read as a sequence showing the changing relationship between Dionysus and his actors and therefore the changing function of theatre in society. On **169** and **170** the actors enter the realm of Dionysus but they do not interact with him. Here the iconography – and therefore the thought process that lies behind it – is taken a step further. It develops the notion of the linking of wine and theatre and symposion by having not satyrs picking grapes and remarking on the god's wondrous gift of wine (a traditional theme for satyrs), but actors. Note that on **169** too, Dionysus' thyrsus sprouts a vine.

(Cleveland, Museum of Art 89.73)

Bulletin of the Cleveland Museum of Art 78:3 (1991) 73; *RVAp* Suppl. 2, 493, no. 1/125.

178. Paestan red-figure bell-crater by Python, about 330 B.C. An actor dressed as a Papposilenos walks along with Dionysus. Dionysus carries a kantharos and a thyrsus tied about with a red sash. The actor plays the pipes and carries a situla full of wine. Above them there hangs from an ivy-spray and set about with a red sash the mask of a slave from comedy. The actor figure has now become a full companion of the god, like a satyr or maenad, just as the actors themselves are referred to as 'artists of Dionysus'.

The relevance of the scene to the purchaser is that the actor provides a link with the happy world of Dionysus, typified by enjoyment of wine in the context of the kind of celebration we see first on the Pronomos vase, and the freedom from care typified by comedy and satyr-play. The vase itself was made for the symposium, and symposia were also accompanied by masks hung about the walls like that above the scene here. The symposium room is thereby equated with the sanctuary of Dionysus, a motif which is echoed or reinforced by pieces such as this. Python painted many vases of this kind.

(Sydney University, Nicholson Museum 47.04)

A.D. Trendall, *The Red-Figured Vases of Paestum* (London, 1987) 158, no. 269, pl. 99c–d; A.D. Trendall, *Phlyax Vases*[2] (London, 1967) no. 171.

178

8. CLASSICAL WARFARE

N. V. SEKUNDA

Throughout the Archaic period the dominant form of warfare was hoplite warfare. To a certain extent 'hoplite warfare' is a modern construct. Apart from the battles of Marathon and Plataea, which were fought against Persian non-hoplite armies, the first descriptions of hoplite battles come in Thucydides, well after hoplite warfare had started to change. Even so, it seems that at the start of the fifth century battles were a fairly simple affair of two long lines of hoplites advancing against each other over any flat piece of ground that was available. Why did the Greeks bother with such formal battle procedures when most of the terrain of Greece is extremely mountainous and rugged: ideal guerrilla country? Why didn't the Greeks retire behind their city-walls and harry the invading army using guerrilla tactics?

The main limitation in the techniques of warfare which determined the retention of hoplite warfare was the backward nature of siege-warfare. At the beginning of the Classical period cities could only be taken by escalade, which was enormously costly in casualties, and very rarely successful, or by investment. Investment was also rarely successful, for it would take months for the city to run out of its stored food, and it was much more probable that the besieging army would run out of food first. Thus, when a dispute had arisen between two states, the ability of the militarily stronger to impose its will on the weaker was limited. The defender could always withdraw behind his city-walls, where he was virtually invulnerable to all forms of attack other than starvation. This led to the development of the 'Strategy of Devastation'.

The most tangible determinant of the nature of warfare was the need of the ancient Greek state to defend its cultivable land. Inter-state disputes frequently arose over the ownership of bordering tracts of cultivable land. Therefore the aim of an invading army was often to destroy the produce of such territory before the inhabitants of the defending state could harvest it. In many cases ancient Greek states designated these areas as holy land, in dispute at an earlier period, but which had subsequently been consecrated to a deity to avoid conflict between the two states. If one state was driven, either by want or by greed, to occupy and sow the land, this would inevitably bring about a retaliatory invasion designed to forestall the harvesting of the crop. Invasions always occurred at harvest time. If a crop could not be harvested and brought back it would at least be destroyed. Corn would be trampled underfoot or fired and fruit trees would be chopped down. In some cases we even hear of invading armies bringing wagons with them to carry back the rooftiles and timbers of dismantled houses. The loss of agricultural produce for even one year could mean widespread hunger or even starvation for the invaded city state. Even if this could be avoided without eating the seed corn stored for next year's planting, an invasion brought enormous long-term economic damage. Repeated invasions increased the risk of being compelled to eat the seed-corn and so of future starvation, and state finances had not developed sufficiently for the invaded state to arrange for the continuous importation of needed food. The imposition of emergency taxation to deal with the crisis might well lead to internal conflict within the state between rich and poor. The aim of the 'Strategy of Devastation' was to force the enemy out from behind his city-walls, onto the battlefield, where he could be defeated and forced to sue for terms.

The defender, for his part, was compelled to secure his crops. An invasion, therefore, had to be resisted at all costs. In this respect the great fault of guerrilla methods of warfare, then as now, is that they can only be used offensively: they can never defend ground and property. When Thucydides (II.19–21) describes the invasion of Attica during the opening stages of the Peloponnesian War, he tells us that the

Spartan King Archidamus, by making his camp at Acharnae, the biggest and most prosperous town of Attica outside Athens, hoped to force the Athenians to battle. He knew that the Acharnians supplied 3,000 hoplites to the Athenian army, and he hoped that they would not be able to stand by idly as he destroyed their farms and crops, but would force the whole Athenian army outside the walls of the city to oppose him. The aim of warfare was, then, in the enemy's case to devastate the defender's crops, or by the threat of taking this action force him to come to terms. In the defender's case, unless he decided to stand by as his land was ravaged, it was to meet with the invader before he had time to destroy the crops. In view of this an invader usually tried to mount an invasion as rapidly as possible to avoid opposition, and to catch the farmers in the fields before they had the time to bring their livestock and property to safety inside the city-walls. For this reason an early warning system to tell the invaded state that the enemy was on his way was essential.

Most ancient Greek states consisted of a central plain ringed about with mountains. The mountain passes leading from one state to another, along which the invading army would come, would usually be guarded by forts and patrol-posts manned by the young men of the state performing their compulsory military service. These would, it was hoped, give a warning of the invader's approach, and give sufficient time to mobilize the army and take the field. If this could be achieved the invader was usually prevented from devastating the crops, as the threat of action on the defender's part forced him to keep his forces together. If an invading army was unable to spread out and devastate the land it was unable to achieve its objective. In some cases a 'staring match' developed, if neither side wished to risk a pitched battle. Opposing armies would face each other for days until one side ran out of supplies or courage and retired from the field; but in other cases a full-scale pitched battle took place. If a pitched battle did take place, however, it was always fought in the plain, the possession of which was the strategical aim of invader and defender alike.

Hence warfare in Greece was always fought between lines of armoured spearmen drawn up in the plain, fighting over the agricultural land. Once efficient artillery was developed under the patronage of Philip II of Macedon the days of hoplite warfare were numbered. It was no longer necessary to threaten a defender's agricultural land in order to tempt him out onto the plain to give battle, for he was no longer safe if he remained behind his city-walls. The 'Strategy of Devastation' was replaced by the 'Strategy of Overthrow'. In fact the 'Strategy of Devastation' was not a successful form of warfare. The defending state could rarely be persuaded to take the field, as the damage the invader could inflict was insufficient to force the defender out from his walls. However, given the lack of development in siege-techniques, this strategy was the only one which an invading army could follow. This guaranteed the existence of the Greek political system of the city state, and of the cultural life which it underpinned, until the middle of the fourth century. In the following pages we shall discuss, through the medium of representational evidence, the attempts of the Greek world to develop techniques in warfare to overcome the limitations of the 'Strategy of Devastation', and to come to terms with the 'Strategy of Overthrow' which replaced it. The limiting factor in this process was the inability of the Greek city state to develop fiscal systems which would provide the necessary finance to implement military reform on a continuous basis.

The model outlined above is, of course, a generalization specific to no time or place. The first hoplite battle of which we have a reasonably complete description is Delium in 424 B.C., long after the Archaic period to which the model of 'hoplite warfare' truly belongs. Recent revisionist work has done much to illuminate inconsistencies and contradictions within the model as it broke down during the Classical period, and to show how social and ideological impulses forced the Greek citizen to defend his land. The validity of the model as an explanation of the practical determinants of hoplite warfare still, however, stands.

GENERAL BIBLIOGRAPHY

W.R. Connor, 'Early Greek land warfare as a symbolic expression', *Past and Present* 119 (1988) 3–27; V.D. Hanson, *Warfare and Agriculture in Classical Greece* (Pisa, 1983); V.D. Hanson, *The Western Way of War: Infantry Battle in Classical Greece* (New York, 1989); ed. V.D. Hanson, *Hoplites: The Classical Greek Battle Experience* (London, 1991); P. Krentz, 'The Nature of Hoplite Battle', *Classical Antiquity* 4 (1985) 50–61; Josiah Ober, *Fortress Attica* (Leiden, 1985).

and almost certainly of Laconian manufacture, probably represents a Spartan officer. The unusual transverse crest is probably a badge of rank, as the Greeks generally wore insignia of rank on the helmet. The helmet is of the Corinthian type, almost universal at this period, offering good protection but restricted vision and hearing. Spartan society became increasingly conservative owing to its militarization, and this is reflected in the Archaic braided long hair and in the retention of the enveloping himation, which was being replaced by another type of cloak, the chlamys, elsewhere in Greece.

(Wadsworth Athenaeum, Hartford, Conn. 1917.815)

D.G. Mitten and J.F. Doeringer, *Master Bronzes from the Classical World* (Cambridge, Mass., 1968) 62, no. 49.

180. Throughout the Archaic period even the armour of the Greek hoplite had remained more or less unchanged. The Corinthian helmet was used almost exclusively, as was the muscle-cuirass, hammered from sheet bronze, and so called because it was worked to represent the musculature of the torso. From the middle of the sixth century onwards we also come across representations of the composite cuirass in Greek art (**180a** cf. A.M. Snodgrass, *Arms and Armour of the Greeks* (London, 1967) 90–1). This was a borrowing from the East, which may be representative of a spread of increased knowledge of how to work iron. The composite cuirass was made of small scales, most probably of iron, either left exposed, or covered with a layer of stiffened leather, usually shown as white, which

179. The dominant military power at the beginning of the Classical period was Sparta. The Spartan army was an entirely hoplite army, and the Spartans were masters of hoplite tactics, which had been developed for wars exclusively between Greeks. Throughout the Archaic period the basic form of hoplite warfare had remained unchanged, and Sparta, though far from being the richest state in Greece, had remained dominant through an increasingly severe militarization of its society (J.F. Lazenby, *The Spartan Army* (Warminster, 1985)). This bronze statuette, dating to the early fifth century

180a

was presumably applied to the armour to prevent rusting. A new form of composite-helmet, made from combined iron scales and plates (**180b**), also appeared at this time.

((**a**) Fiesole, Collezione Constantini; *CVA* Fiesole, Collezione Constantini I, pl. 15, 2.
(**b**) Paris, Cab. Méd. 537+598; *ARV* 429, 19; *LIMC* I pl. 143)

181. Until the sixth century the strategic foundations of hoplite warfare had remained in place, but the rise of first the Lydian Kingdom, and then of the Persian Empire, overturned these certainties. The Greek states now came into contact with a potentially hostile power possessing much greater financial resources than any enemy they had faced before. The option of retiring behind impregnable city-walls was no longer as secure as it had been, for the Persians had the financial power to carry through a siege to the end. A Lydian siege-mound, constructed by Alyattes around 600 B.C., has been uncovered by archaeological excavations at Smyrna (*CAH* III².3, 197; J. Boardman, *The Greeks Overseas* (London, 1980) 96–7). This later siege-mound, constructed by the Persians with massive effort in order to take Paphus in Cyprus in 498 B.C., is preserved where it fills the defensive ditch surrounding the city. It vividly conveys the increased scale of effort in siege-warfare of which the Persians were capable, which rendered the fortifications of the Greek cities vulnerable, and forced the Greeks to take the field against the Persian army.

(Franz Georg Maier, *Alt-Paphos auf Cypern* (Trierer Winkelmannsprogramm 6, 1984) pl. 11, 3)

182. The rise of the Persian Empire also forced the Greeks to modify their battlefield tactics to cope with massed archery. In order to avoid casualties when encountering archer-based armies, hoplites would now hope to charge their enemies at a run, minimizing their exposure to archery (A.M. Snodgrass, *Archaic Greece* (London, 1980) 151–3). At both Marathon and Plataea the Greeks charged the Persians at a run. This Attic black-figure amphora, dating to the last decade of the sixth century, shows two ranks of hoplites charging at the run. At this period the individual hoplite was allowed to chose his own shield-blazon. The white-leg shield-blazon may be a family device used by members of the Alcmaeonid family. An athletic competition, the *hoplitodromos* or armed race (see *Pls. to Vol.* IV, pl.

180b

181

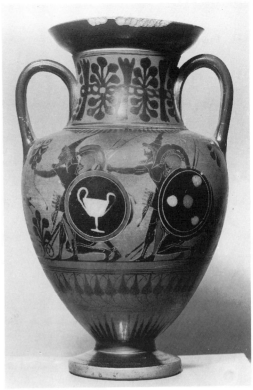

210), was developed to train the citizenry in this new military requirement. The race was originally run over a distance of 400 metres, just long enough to carry the hoplite line through the 'beaten zone' of enemy archery and up to the enemy line. The *hoplitodromos* was first run at Olympia in 520, and at Delphi in 498.

(Munich, Staatliche Antikensammlungen 1510)
ABV 375, 203; *CVA* Munich 9, pl. 2,2.

183. The tyrant Pisistratus did not enjoy the political support of the Athenian hoplites, and was swift to incorporate archers, practically unknown in Greek armies previously, into his largely mercenary army. Scythian mercenary archers are shown on numerous Athenian vases shooting from beneath the cover of a line of hoplite shields. Polycrates of Samos, another tyrant, is also known to have maintained a corps of a thousand archers (Hdt. III.39, 45). Following the Persian conquest of Thrace in 514 B.C., lines of communication and recruitment with Scythia were cut, and Greek archers, frequently wearing mixed elements of Greek and oriental dress, start to appear on Athenian vases (cf. François Lissarrague, *L'Autre Guerrier, Archers, Peltastes, Cavaliers dans l'Imagerie attique*, Paris, 1990). It seems that Pisistratus' son Hipparchus had started to equip and train the Athenian poor (*thetes*) as archers: thus the Athenian corps of archers was born. In 510 the Pisistratid tyranny fell, but the corps of archers was maintained by the democratic regime which replaced it. We do not hear of the Athenian archers participating in the battle of Marathon, but they were probably kept away from the battle for political reasons (they were

potential supporters of the exiled Athenian tyrant Hippias).

(Berlin, Staatliche Museen F 1865)
M.F. Vos, *Scythian Archers in Archaic Attic Vase-Painting* (Groningen, 1963) 86, pl. 6b.

184. In 483/2 Themistocles persuaded the Athenians to spend the revenues derived from the discovery of a rich vein of silver in the mining district of Laurium on the expansion of their fleet of triremes. Recent work on reconstructing a trireme has added much to our knowledge of this vessel (cf. *Pls. to Vol. III*, pls. 180–1; add J.F. Coates, S.K. Platis, J.T. Shaw, *The Trireme Trials 1988* (Oxford, 1990)). One of the principal archaeological sources used in reconstructing the Athenian trireme is a drawing, made in Rome between 1610 and 1635 for the Cavaliero dal Pozzo and now in the British Museum, recording an ancient relief sculpture, now lost. The drawing shows the starboard bow of the Athenian state trireme, the Paralos, under oar, with the bow officer (*prorates/proreus*) looking and signalling aft. The defeat of the Persians left the Athen-

184

ians in control of the sea, enabling them to establish an empire, and to expand the revenues available for military expenditure.

(London, British Museum, Dal Pozzo-Albani fol. 171; no. 201)

    C.C. Vermeule, *The Dal Pozzo-Albani Drawings of Classical Antiquities in the British Museum* (= American Philosophical Society, Transactions n.s. 50 (1960) part 5) fig. 79; J.S. Morrison and J.F. Coates, *The Athenian Trireme* (Cambridge, 1986) 13, fig. 11, 141–2.

185. The revenues generated by this empire not only allowed Athens to maintain her fleet and expand her light infantry: the cavalry, previously the weakest branch of the army, was expanded to 300 around 457 (G.R. Bugh, *The Horsemen of Athens* (Princeton, 1988) 39–78, 221), and then to 1,000, probably around the year 442 (Albert Martin, *Les cavaliers athéniens* (Paris, 1887) 132–4), when a unit of 200 horse-archers was also raised. This funerary marble lekythos, shows an Athenian cavalryman wearing a *petasos* hat, a thin sleeveless tunic and a bronze muscle-cuirass (without shoulder-guards, which would have inhibited the ability of the rider to cut downwards with his weapons, or to throw his javelins). The expansion of the cavalry was facilitated by the introduction of the *katastasis*, or 'establishment grant', which guaranteed the replacement cost of any mount lost on service, and the introduction of an allowance for fodder. An inspection (*dokimasia* – see *Pls. to Vol. IV*, pl. 194) was introduced to assess the value of each horse.

185

The Athenians, under the leadership of Pericles, now possessed a cavalry arm equal to that of Sparta's principal ally, Boeotia, and inferior only to that of Thessaly. This meant that the Athenians could now challenge the Spartans for the leadership of the Greek world. Pericles intended to retire behind the fortifications of Athens, using his cavalry to harry the invading army, and prevent it from dispersing to ravage the countryside (I.G. Spence, *JHS* 110 (1990) 91–109 with refs.). Meanwhile the superior fleet was used to launch a series of seaborne raids on the enemy.

(Athens, National Museum 835)

B. Schmaltz, *Untersuchungen zu den attischen Marmorlekythen* (Berlin, 1970) A 7, pl. 4.

186. During the fifth century, as the revenues of empire grew, the Athenians made increasing use of their corps of archers (A. Plassart, 'Les Archers d'Athènes', *Revue des Etudes grecques* 26 (1913) 151–213), to supply each trireme with its complement of four archers, and to provide garrisons and units for campaigns on land. By the beginning of the Peloponnesian War the corps of archers stood at 1,600, but even this figure was found to be inadequate, and the corps had to be supplemented with mercenaries, frequently called barbarian archers in the texts and inscriptions. Representations of archers are very rare during the Classical period, especially in Athenian art. This Attic vase, an oinochoe attributed to the Disney Painter (*c.* 430–420 B.C.), may possibly represent an Athenian archer, and though Richter, owing to his 'untidy hair and unmartial look', thought him to be Odysseus returned to Ithaca, he may rather be one of the enigmatic barbarian archers!

(New York, Metropolitan Museum of Art 28.97.24)

G.M.A. Richter, *Red-Figured Athenian Vases in the Metropolitan Museum of Art* (New Haven, 1936) 187, pl. 150 (152); *ARV* 1265, 15.

187. Another type of foreign mercenary employed by the tyrant Pisistratus was the Thracian peltast (J.G.P. Best, *Thracian Peltasts and their Influence on Greek Warfare* (Groningen, 1969)). The peltast was a javelin-man, but equipped with a small shield to afford him some protection from enemy missiles. The peltast could now stalk a hoplite line with more confidence than if he were unprotected. The peltast's finest hour came at the Battle of Lechaeum in 390 B.C., when, under the leadership of the Athenian general Iphicrates, an army of peltasts managed to destroy an entire regiment of Spartan hoplites. The *pelte* was a lighter shield than the hoplite shield, usually made of wood and leather, and without the hoplite shield's distinctive offset rim, which kept the bronze outer layer of the shield under stress. The shield was frequently decorated with apotropaic 'eyes' to look out for incoming missiles, as here. The top of the shield was cut-out, giving the *pelte* a crescentic shape, to afford the user a clear field of vision. This Attic skyphos, painted by the Brygos Painter about 480 B.C., and excavated from a grave at Rhitsona in Boeotia, shows a peltast wearing Thracian boots, a Thracian cap and a wrap-round apron,

186

187

or *perizoma*. The *perizoma* was originally worn by hoplites under the groin-flaps of the cuirass for extra protection, but when armour started to be discarded for extra mobility the *perizoma* was frequently used as a substitute. This peltast then, is wearing mixed dress: the fox-skin cap with earflaps (*alopekis*) and the boots are Thracian, but the *perizoma*, though made of Thracian material, is a Greek concept. Therefore this peltast may be a Greek, possibly an Athenian, in Thracian dress, rather than a Thracian mercenary.

(Thebes Museum)
    ARV 381, 177; *BSA* 14 (1907/8) pl. 14.

188. During a time of crisis, even if the city did not possess a regular corps of peltasts, the poorer citizens might be pressed into service, fighting as irregular light-armed troops, or *psiloi*, with whatever weapons might lie to hand. In 457 B.C., when the regular Athenian army had been committed to a campaign in Boeotia, the Corinthian army descended on Megara. The Athenians mobilized their young hoplites and old men, and all other forces available. At Cimolia the Corinthian hoplites were driven back into a ditched agricultural enclosure and stoned to death by the Athenian *psiloi*. This Attic skyphos, not far in date from the battle of Cimolia, shows a peltast on one side, and a *psilos* on the other. Note the handle arrangement of the *pelte*, and the sword and skin-shield worn for protection by the *psilos*.

(Vienna, Kunsthistorisches Museum, Inv. IV 1922)
    CVA Vienna 1, pl. 40.

189. Only a rich state such as Athens could afford to train and maintain large corps of specialist troops drawn from her citizenry. Other states had to rely on mercenaries. In 424 B.C. the Spartans organized, for the first time, a corps of cavalry, and made use of archers. While the horsemen were citizens, the archers were almost certainly mercenaries, most probably coming from Crete. The Cretans were one of the few ancient Greek peoples to practise archery regularly, and were in great demand as mercenary archers. Depictions of Cretan archers are rare. This example, now lost, a tombstone from Kantanos in the White Mountains of western Crete, dates to the start of the third century B.C. The turban wrapped round the head is the ancestor of the *sarikaki* worn in modern times as part of Cretan folk dress.

(*Inscriptiones Creticae* 2 vi 7, p. 88)

188

189

190. The hoplite line had to make some response to the increased potential of missile troops, but the solution was far from obvious. If body-armour were reduced to increase the hoplite's mobility, he would be rendered more vulnerable to missiles, but if armour were increased, his mobility would be further reduced. Two features which appear in the literary and archaeological record are best interpreted as attempts to give hoplite troops an advantage against missile troops. First we hear of troops selected from the hoplite line, and usually from the younger age-classes, designated *ekdromoi* or 'runners-out'. Their job was to dash out of the line, all together on a given order, in order to catch and kill a few of the nearer light-armed enemy troops, thereby intimidating the rest from further missile-attacks on the hoplite line. Secondly, as the fifth century goes on, we frequently see representations of hoplites who have abandoned metal armour in favour of lighter and non-metallic substitutes. The *perizoma*, or apron, has already been mentioned. On some vases we see hoplites wearing a jerkin of thickly woven coarse material, usually decorated in the Thracian manner, as a substitute for the cuirass. This jerkin is probably to be identified with the enigmatic *spolas*, which is mentioned in texts. This Attic vase was painted by the Nikon Painter around 460 B.C. Note that the greaves have also been abandoned by this date.

(Providence, Museum of the Rhode Island School of Design 23.323)

ARV 653, 1; *CVA* Providence, pl. 15, 2b.

191. The middle of the fifth century also saw attempts to develop lighter substitutes for the helmet. For comfort, hoplites would frequently wear a coarse felt cap, of the type normally used by shepherds or hunters, under the helmet (cf. *Pls. to Vol. IV*, pl. 149). The hoplite on (**a**), shown on a vase painted a little before the outbreak of the Peloponnesian War, is about to set out for

190

191b

war. He has already put on his cuirass, and he is
shown taking his shield out of its protective
cover. To the right his attendant is about to hand
him his helmet and spear. The attendant wears a
felt cap and an animal-pelt as a cloak. On another
fragment (**b**) a hoplite is standing on guard with
shield and spear only; his helmet has been discarded and only the felt cap is retained. We may
compare modern practice, where the steel helmet
is used in combat, but the lighter plastic helmet-
liner is substituted for guard-duty and the like
away from the front line. Homer (*Il.* x.258) uses
the word *kataityx* to describe a helmet made from
bull's-hide. This word has been falsely applied to
some varieties of cap-comforter. There seems,
however, to be no specific word attached to these
'cap-comforters', which were simply called *piloi*,
or felt caps.

((**a**) Bern, private. (**b**) Berlin, Antikensammlungen F
2535)
   AK 7 (1964) 48–50, pl. 14. 1b, 2; *ARV* 825, 11;
CVA Tübingen 5, 35, fig. 15.

192. The felt-cap varied in shape from region to
region: for example we hear of Laconian, Arcadian and Macedonian *piloi*. The Laconian variety
was of a pointed sugar-loaf shape, normally
shown in ancient art being worn by the Laconian
heroes Castor and Polydeuces (Pollux). This
Attic grave stele, from Megara and possibly
dating to the 420s, shows an example of a
Laconian *pilos*, clearly of felt, being held in the
hoplite's right hand. In his left hand he holds a
spear, in a position suitable for the march, with
the front handle (*antilabe*) of his shield held with
the index-finger. Thucydides (IV.34.3) describes
how in 424 B.C. the Spartan hoplites garrisoning
the island of Sphacteria suffered greatly as their

192

piloi offered little protection against the arrows of
the Athenians. Clearly the sacrifice of protection
in search of mobility had gone too far.

(Worcester Art Museum (Mass.) 1936.21)
   JHS 49 (1929) 3, fig. 4; *AJA* 60 (1956) 325; C.
Vermeule, *Socrates to Sulla* (Boston, 1980) 179, no. 32.

193. From some date in the second half of the fifth century onwards, a new helmet-shape becomes increasingly popular. The *pilos*-helmet was a skeuomorph, reproducing the shape of the Laconian *pilos* in bronze. The protection offered by the cheek-pieces, nasal and nape-piece of more traditional helmet types had been abandoned in favour of lightness, but bronze still offered more protection than felt. This example comes from Upper Egypt, where it had perhaps been lost or discarded by a Greek mercenary in Persian or Egyptian service.

(Berlin, Staatliche Museen, Inv. L 41)
    P. Dintsis, *Hellenistische Helme* (Rome, 1986) 362, no. 120, pl. 22, 3; H. Pflug, *Antike Helme. Sammlung Lipperheide und andere Bestander des Antikenmuseums Berlin* (1988) 437, no. 48.

194. On this Apulian calyx-crater, painted by the Painter of the Berlin Dancing Girl around 420, the long-haired naked warrior wearing the *pilos*-helmet may be a Spartan. The wearing of long hair and beards by adult males was a Spartan practice, to make their warriors 'look taller, more dignified and more terrifying' (Xen. *Lac. Pol.* x.3). The vase may depict a historical incident, perhaps an intervention by the Spartan army in South Italy. The hoplite is shown under attack from a mounted javelin-man, usually interpreted as an Amazon, but more probably a native Italian cavalryman. The increased mobility afforded to the hoplite on the battlefield also enabled the Spartan phalanx, for the first time, to manoeuvre in battle and develop new tactics (J.K. Anderson, *Military Theory and Practice in the Age of Xenophon* (Berkeley/Los Angeles, 1970)).

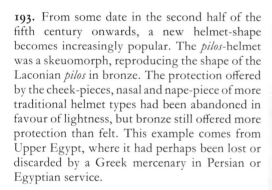

(Wellesley College (Mass.))
    A.D. Trendall and Alexander Cambitoglou, *The Red-Figured Vases of Apulia* I (Oxford, 1978) pl. 2, 5.

195. Spartan influence was at its strongest among the armies of the Peloponnesian League. This tombstone, of Lisas the Tegean, was discovered in the course of terracing work undertaken at the royal estates at Tatoi in Attica around 1874.

Lisas probably served in the garrison of the nearby fort established by the Peloponnesian League army at Decelea in 413, and died in an engagement fought during the 'Decelean War' of 413–404. He is shown at the moment of his death: his spear has either fallen from his hand, or was perhaps once painted in. He wears the *pilos*-helmet and *exomis* tunic, left free at the right shoulder for ease of movement, both once distinctive of the Spartan army, but now rapidly spreading to other armies allied to the Spartans. When victory was achieved in the Peloponnesian War the influence of the Spartan army on Greek warfare reached its zenith. Just as Prussian victories during the last century guaranteed the spread of the spiked helmet throughout the armies of the world, the Spartan victory ensured the spread of the *pilos*-helmet and *exomis* tunic outside the Peloponnese. We are still a very long way away from military uniform, however, for Attic funerary monuments of the period show hoplites still wearing other styles of helmet. Rather the adoption of the *pilos*-helmet would have been through widespread personal choice.

(At Tatoi?)

  IG II² 10436; *BCH* 4 (1880) 408–15, pl. 7.

196. Warfare in Sicily and South Italy had developed somewhat differently, largely owing to contact with native Italian military systems. Emphasis was especially given to the development of cavalry. The city of Tarentum in particu-

lar was renowned for its horsemen, armed with a number of javelins and small 'fist-shields', trained to jump off their horses, throw their javelins, and then re-mount and gallop away. The establishment of military training pro-

196

196

196c

grammes for the first 'Tarentines' may well date to this period. From the middle of the fifth century onwards, the coins of Tarentum start to show light horsemen engaged both in throwing javelins (**a**), and also in vaulting from horseback in an athletic competition (**b**), armed with a shield and baton or javelin (G. Brauer, *Taras, its History and Coinage* (New Rochelle, N.Y., 1986) 27–8, 54). The athletic competition was first known as the mare's race, *dromos kalpes*, during the last stage of which the riders leapt down and ran alongside their horses. The race was introduced as an event at Olympia in 496 and continued until 441 B.C. The athletes were later called *anabatai* and rode stallions, as on this crater (**c**) by the Anabates Painter, a Lucanian artist active in the first quarter of the fourth century. In the painting the various stages of the competition are telescoped: the *anabates* dismounts, passes the finishing post and is crowned by Nike, the goddess of victory, all at once. Units of 'Tarentines' started to appear in other armies of Italy and Sicily first, but only spread to the Greek mainland during the Hellenistic period. In 369 B.C. Syracuse sent a small unit of fifty mounted javelin-men to help the Spartans: Xenophon (*Hell.* VII.1.21) describes with wonder the way these horsemen harried the Theban hoplite line, wheeling round in front of the enemy and throwing their javelins, then dismounting and resting.

((**a, b**) London, British Museum. (**c**) London, British Museum 1978.6–15.1)

(**a, b**) cf. O.E. Ravel, *Descriptive Catalogue of the Collection of Tarentine Coins formed by M.P. Vlasto* (London, 1947) nos. 538–59, 530–5. (**c**) A.D. Trendall, *The Red-Figured Vases of Lucania, Campania and Sicily* Suppl. 3 (London, 1983) 40.

197. The principal threat to the Western Greeks, particularly to those of Sicily, was Carthage, not Persia. The response to this threat led to different forms of development in political life and military organization. The Sicilian Greeks, however, proved unable to combine against their enemy. Hippocrates the tyrant of Gela managed to exploit these circumstances to found the powerful centralized Deinomenid state. His policies involved a programme of relocating the citizenry of the small city states into expanded concentrations of population. In 492 B.C. Camarina, originally founded as a Syracusan colony, passed from Syracusan to Deinomenid control. Its population was expelled to be replaced by a new citizen body, formed from the large force of mercenaries at Hippocrates' disposal. Contingents drawn from the new citizenry of Camarina participated in Hippocrates' subsequent military campaigns. This didrachm, struck by Camarina after 492, may commemorate one of these military victories. The obverse of the coin shows a shield decorated with the blazon of a Corinthian helmet, clearly a reference to the mercenary origins of the citizen contingent. The reverse of the coin shows a dwarf palm (*chamaerops humilis*), a plant common in Sicily, flanked by a pair of greaves, all in a circular incuse. The symbolism of the palm, other than perhaps as a general reference to victory, is obscure. In 491/0 Hippocrates was succeeded by Gelon, his master-of-horse, who finally achieved the conquest of Syracuse in 485. During his lifetime Gelon enrolled more than 10,000 mercenaries as citizens of Syracuse (Diod. XI.72.3). The fiscal resources of this new kind of state allowed the expansion of military and naval resources, and

197

the introduction of military reforms diversifying the army at his disposal. Prior to the Persian invasion of Greece the Spartans appealed for Gelon's help, and Herodotus (VII.158) informs us that Gelon's army stood at 200 triremes, 20,000 hoplites, plus 2,000 cavalry and 2,000 light infantry trained to fight alongside them (*pezoi hippodromoi*). This is the first mention of such troops, who seem to be the ancestors of the *hamippoi* who appear afterwards in the armies of mainland Greece. In 489 Gelon was able to mobilize an army of 50,000 foot and 5,000 cavalry (Diod. XI.21.1) to thwart a Carthaginian invasion at the Battle of Himera. The Sicilian mercenary became a figure of proverb (H.W. Parke, *Greek Mercenary Soldiers* (Oxford, 1933) 10–13).

(Kraay–Hirmer, fig. 146)
P. Franke and M. Hirmer, *Die Griechische Münze* (Munich, 1964) 88–9, pl. 52; U. Westermark and K. Jenkins, *The Coinage of Kamarina* (London, 1980) 18–21.

198

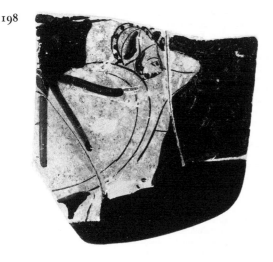

198. By the later fifth century the application of some degree of uniformity in dress and equipment was becoming general in most armies of Greece under the influence of the Spartan army. First came a uniform shield-blazon, usually either the badge of the patron deity of the city state or league, or the initial letter of its name. This fragment from an Attic skyphos, dated about 430 by Beazley, shows a hoplite whose shield (held upside-down) is decorated with the letter *chi*. This could be the blazon used by the army of the Chalcidian League, which was formed when the cities of the Chalcidice revolted from Athens in 432/1 B.C. The complete vase may have originally shown an engagement between Chalcidian and Athenian hoplites. The Chalcidian League was one of the first examples of such federal political organizations, which became increasingly popular as an alternative to the Greek city state during the fourth century. Given the absence of centralized states of the Western Greek type in mainland Greece, the federal league offered the smaller Greek states an opportunity to combine their financial and military resources.

(Oxford, Ashmolean Museum 1966.709)
ARV 1281; *Sir John and Lady Beazley's Gifts to the Ashmolean Museum 1916–1966* (Oxford, 1967) no. 271.

199. The dominance of the Spartan army in Greek warfare was eventually overturned by the Thebans. The Thebans had for a long time employed a depth of fifty ranks in their hoplite line. This checked the tendency for the phalanx to peel off at the back, and ensured that the phalanx advanced unfalteringly against the enemy. Now the Theban general Epaminondas developed new tactics, striking at a single point in the enemy line with overwhelming force. In addition the morale of the army was raised by an

199

intense period of physical training. These and other factors resulted in the Theban victory over the Spartans at Leuctra in 371 B.C., which shattered Spartan military supremacy for ever. Unfortunately our knowledge of the Theban army is limited by the paucity of representational evidence recovered by excavation. This Cabiric vase, dating to the early fourth century and showing a comic scene, is one of the very few contemporary representations of a Theban warrior. He can be identified as such by the club of Heracles, the patron god of the Thebans, used as a shield-blazon by the Theban army (Xen. *Hell.* VII.5.20). The helmet-type is obscured by a break. During the early part of the fourth century the Thebans used the *pilos*-helmet, but it is unknown whether this was replaced by the Boeotian helmet when Thebes rose as a military power.

(Boston, Museum of Fine Arts 563)
P. Wolters and G. Bruns, *Das Kabirenheiligtum bei Theben* I (Berlin, 1940) M34, 112–13, pl. 37, 4.

200. A principal role in the Theban victory was played by their cavalry. Outside Thessaly the Boeotians possessed the strongest force of cavalry in all Greece. The Boeotians had originally been slow to implement new developments. There may have been some diversity in cavalry equipment however, for while one Boeotian kantharos (**a**) shows a heavily equipped cavalryman, armed with a cuirass, a fighting-spear, and a sword, a second (**b**) shows another cavalryman with much lighter equipment. Both date to the early years of the fourth century. Sometimes the *petasos* hat was replaced with a version in bronze, retaining the same shape, as in this case. The helmet can be distinguished from the hat as it lies flat on the head, rather than being pushed forward at a rakish angle. An actual example of such a *petasos*-helmet (**c**) has been excavated in Athens. Though the helmet is bronze, the small holes round the rim indicate that the helmet was originally covered in felt. In the opinion of the author, the *petasos*-helmet, with its horizontal rim with single fold at each side, should be distinguished from the Boeotian helmet, with its sloping rim with at least two folds on each side.

200a

200b

((**a, b**) Athens, National Museum 1097, 1099; *Ath.-Mitt.* 65 (1940) pls. 19. 2, 22.2. (**c**) Athens, National Museum)
O. Alexandri, *Arch.Eph.* 1973, 93–105, pls. 51–4.

201. The Boeotian helmet was based on a local Boeotian version of the *petasos* (**a**); shown here on an Attic vase painted by the Niobid Painter in the 450s. The Boeotian hat was fitted with two straps, normally placed above the head and attached to a button. If the hat needed to be held in place securely, one strap could be passed under the chin, and the second could be passed under the nape of the neck. The two straps produced the distorted rim associated with the Boeotian helmet. The Boeotian helmet was simply a Boeotian hat in bronze (Andreas Rumpf, 'Kranos boiotiourges' = Abhandlungen der Preussischen Akademie der Wissenschaften 1943, Phil.-hist. Klasse nr. 8). A white-ground lekythos (**b**), painted by the Phiale Painter in the 430s and found in a tomb at Oropus on the Attic-Boeotian border, shows Hermes wearing a Boeotian hat with the chin-strap pulled down. One example of a Boeotian helmet (**c**) was found in June 1854 in the bed of the Tigris river near Tille in present-day Turkey. Mr R.B. Oakley of Oswaldkirk, Yorkshire, was travelling to Mosul by raft. One of the boatmen pushed his boathook into the stream to keep the raft from running ashore, and when he lifted it out of the water this helmet was caught on the hook. Helmets of this type were formed by hammering sheet bronze over a workshop model. This example (**d**), dating from the Hellenistic period, is of limestone and was recovered from a workshop in Memphis in Egypt. The success of the Boeotian cavalry led to a spread in the use of the Boeotian helmet by Greek cavalry.

reform. In 374 B.C. Jason was elected *tagos* or king of Thessaly, which gave him access to the considerable financial resources of the Thessalian League and established his military reforms on a more secure basis. Jason now commanded, as well as his own army of 6,000 mercenaries, 6,000 Thessalian cavalry and 10,000 hoplites plus an unspecified number of peltasts from surrounding subject peoples (Xen. *Hell.* VI.1.5, 8–9). He hoped to unite the rest of Greece under him in a crusade against the Persians, but was assassinated in 371 before he could put his grandiose plans into effect. The role of Jason in Greek warfare has been underestimated, and in many ways his career foreshadowed that of Philip of Macedon. Jason is credited with the invention of the new cavalry formation known as the Thessalian rhomb (Aelian, *Tact.* VII.4–5, 46; Arrian, *Tact.* XVI.3), which allowed Greek cavalry to break away from their linear tactics, and to manoeuvre on the battlefield, for the first time. He is also credited with the invention of a new piece of armour, the half-cuirass (*hemithorakion*: Pollux, *Onomast.* 1.134). Further information can be gleaned from contemporary coinage. A heavy cavalryman, equipped with Boeotian helmet, is shown on this coin (a) struck by one of Jason's successors, Alexander of Pherae, and an interest-

((**a**) Leiden, Rijksmuseum van Oudheden PC 78; *ARV* 605, 58 and 1702; *CVA* Leiden 3, pl. 132.5. (**b**) Munich, Antikensammlungen 2797; *ARV* 1022, 135. (**c**) Oxford, Ashmolean Museum; P. Dintsis, *Hellenistische Helme* (Rome, 1986) 200, no. 3, pl. 3, 4–5; cf. *Pls. to Vol.* VII. *1*, pl. 107. (**d**) Amsterdam, Allard Pierson Museum Inv. 7864; C.S. Ponger, *Katalog der Griechischen und Römischen Skulptur, der Steineren Gegenstände und der Stuckplastik im Allard Pierson Museum zu Amsterdam* (Amsterdam, 1942) no. 179)

202. A principal role in the development of Greek cavalry was played by the Thessalians. They had always possessed the most powerful cavalry arm in all Greece, but had previously played an insignificant role in the history of Greece due to inter-state rivalries. During the 370s Jason tyrant of Pherae concentrated his efforts on uniting Thessaly under his rule. The first part of his career was marked by desperate struggles to raise enough finances to pay his mercenary army (Polyaen. VI.1). As always, developments in military technique were held back by lack of finances to implement military

ing example of a Boeotian helmet with cheek-pieces is shown on a coin of Scotussa (**b**). Cavalry and light-infantry (*hamippoi*) fighting together are shown on a Pharsalian coin (**c**), and a Thessalian peltast is shown on a coin of Pelinna (**d**).

((**a–d**) London, British Museum)
(**a**) *BMC* Thessaly to Aetolia (1883) 47, no. 14, pl. 10.11. (**b**) E. Rogers, *The Copper Coinage of Thessaly* (London, 1932) no. 548. (**c**) *BMC* 45, no. 21, pl. 9.17; Rogers, no. 502. (**d**) *BMC* 38 no. 2, pl. 8.2.

203. Developments had been taking place in Persian warfare which were eventually to have a dramatic effect on the Greeks. The principal type of infantryman employed by the Persians was the *sparabara* (*gerrhophoros*), literally a wicker-shield-bearer. He carried a large shield made from rawhide, strengthened with osiers woven through the leather when wet. When the leather dried out and tightened the result was a light shield of considerable strength. The leather and osiers would frequently be dyed in contrasting colours, imparting a V- or W-shaped pattern to the shield, a detail observed on this skyphos in

Berlin, painted about 450 B.C. The front of a Persian infantry regiment would frequently be made up of a line of these shields pitched together.

(Berlin, Antikensammlungen 3156)
   CVA Berlin 3, pl. 141.5.

204. Once the shield-wall was cast down the Persian *gerrhophoros* was placed at a great disadvantage in combat with more heavily armed troops, such as the Greek hoplite, who had a more manoeuvrable shield which could be used to greater effect at close quarters. Therefore, in the years following the Persian Wars, we start to find representations of Persian infantry using another type of shield, crescentic and similar to the Thracian *pelte* in shape, but equivalent to the hoplite shield in size. The Greek sources call these troops *peltophoroi*, which may be a semantic translation for the original Old Persian *takabara* (cf. *Archäologischen Mitteilungen aus Iran* 21 (1988) 74–6). This oinochoe, dated 410–400, shows a fight between a Greek hoplite and a Persian *peltophoros*.

(Paris, Louvre G 571)
   Ath.Mitt. 90 (1975) pl. 26, 4; A. Lezzi-Hafter, *Der Schuwalow-Maler* (Mainz, 1976) pl. 161.

205. This Attic calyx crater, one of the few Greek vases depicting peltasts of any type, shows a combat scene between one group of warriors, both cavalry and peltasts of the new type, wearing distinctive striped tunics, and an opposing group of hoplites. It dates to the last decades of the fourth century, and may represent a combat

204

between Greeks and Thracians belonging to the army of the Odrysian King Seuthes. If this speculation is correct, we may assume that the use of the new type of peltast initially spread to areas on the periphery of the Achaemenid Empire.

(Sarajevo, Bosnia-Herzegovina State Museum 28)
CVA Sarajevo (Jugoslavia 4) pls. 171–2.

206. As far as Greek armies were concerned, the great advantage of the new type of peltast was that his equipment, especially the shield, cost much less than the equipment of the hoplite. In the aftermath of the Peloponnesian War it seems that an increasing number of Greek citizens were compelled by economic necessity to enter Persian service as mercenaries. Many of these individuals were, however, unable to provide themselves with hoplite armour. Prior to the Persian invasion of Egypt in 373, the Athenian general Iphicrates had been placed in command of the Greek mercenary contingent which numbered 20,000 men. Diodorus (xv.44.2) tells us that he substituted for the traditional hoplite shield a *pelte*, increased the length of the spears by half, and almost doubled the length of the swords. Nepos (xi.2.4) tells us that Iphicrates commanded a force of 12,000 'Iphicrateans', so it may

205

be that only 8,000 of the Greek mercenaries had
been able to equip themselves as hoplites, and
Iphicrates had been constrained to equip and
train the remainder as *peltophoroi* to enable them
to fight in the front line. Many texts mention
peltasts fighting in Greek armies in the 360s and
350s, and these are best understood as 'Iphicrateans'. Representations of such troops are, however, rare. This carved base from the Academy in
Athens, showing an Athenian cavalryman riding
down an 'Iphicratean' peltast, may possibly
record an action in the Peloponnese during the
360s.

(Athens, National Museum 3708)
 Die Antike 17 (1941) 37, fig. 3.

207. This gravestone of Panaitios of the deme
Hamaxanteia, possibly a relative of the Panaitios
known to have served as hipparch in 425/4,
shows us the equipment of an Athenian cavalryman during the early years of the fourth century.
The secondary role of Athenian cavalry in battle
is amply demonstrated by his mixed weaponry.
The principal cavalry-spear, or *kamax*, simply a
variant of the hoplite-spear, was designed to be
able to reach enemy infantry during the pursuit,
rather than as a weapon suitable for the cavalry
mêlée. The *kamax* is supplemented with javelins,
again weapons used for harassment rather than
for a charge. Xenophon (*On Horsemanship*
VIII.10), writing about 367, describes a practice
cavalry pursuit undertaken at Athens. The

defender holds his blunted *kamax* pointing back-
wards, while the pursuer attempts to hit him with
blunted javelins. The ability of the Athenians to
institute further military reform was severely
constrained after the Peloponnesian War when
the revenues of empire were lost. Athenian
generals were expected to finance military
expeditions from the proceeds of booty, and
some were even forced to hire out their soldiers
as agricultural labourers in times of military
inactivity.

(*IG* II² 5601; Athens, National Museum 884)
 G. Kokula, *Marmorlutrophoren* (Berlin, 1984) 165–6,
G3.

208. In 409 B.C. the Carthaginians started to
launch a series of massive assaults against the
Greek cities of Sicily. The Carthaginians had the
financial resources to attempt to reduce the
fortified towns of the island by direct assault. Six
siege-towers, weapons previously unknown to
the Greeks, were brought up against the walls of
Selinus. The *helepolis* was a huge wooden tower,
dwarfing the walls of the city under attack,
mounted on wheels and containing an integral
ram. The attackers could now dominate and clear
the circuit wall of defenders with their superior

missile power, and prevent the defenders dropping objects onto the head of the ram, or between the ram and the wall. Only a single example of a battering-ram has been preserved, a dedication from Olympia dating to the first half of the fifth century. The rams' heads which decorate either side of the ram allude to the name (*krios*) and function of the weapon.

(Olympia, Archaeological Museum B 2360)

E. Kunze, *V. Bericht über die Ausgrabungen in Olympia* (Berlin, 1956) 75–8; Y. Garlan, *Recherches de Poliorcétique grecque* (Paris, 1974) 156–69.

209. Selinus soon fell, and the cities of Himera, Acragas and Gela followed in turn. In 399 B.C. Syracuse fell under siege, and Dionysius I, who had by now made himself tyrant of Sicily, gathered together a large group of military engineers to devise new weapons to defeat the besieging forces. Out of their frantic activity arose the *gastraphetes*, or 'belly-bow', a form of crossbow and the first catapult (Y. Garlan, *Recherches de Poliorcétique grecque* (Paris, 1974) 164–6). The *gastraphetes* greatly increased the power with which an arrow could be shot, and, although its invention was one factor which enabled Dionysius to foil the Carthaginian siege of Syracuse, the weapon ultimately swung the balance further in favour of the attacker. (Our illustration shows a model *gastraphetes* being loaded.) Dionysius gradually extended his power, eventually ruling most of the Western Greeks. Using the Deinomenid kingdom as his model, he attempted the creation of a centralized state, making heavy use of mercenaries. He also increased the efficiency of his citizen troops by selecting out of the masses units of *epilektoi*, or picked troops. *Epilektoi*, already known on the Greek mainland, were selected hoplites, permanently embodied and permanently paid.

E. Schramm, *Die antiken Geschutze der Saalburg* (Bad Homburg, 1918; ed. D. Baatz 1980) 16, fig. 3; cf. E.W. Marsden, *Greek and Roman Artillery. Historical Development* (Oxford, 1969) 6 fig. 1.

210. Greek fortifications had already started to respond to the developments in siege techniques. The curtain-walls of a city no longer simply enclosed the inhabited buildings which comprised the city; they now stretched for miles seeking out any advantage in height in the local topography, giving the defender maximum advantage. Thus huge areas of uninhabited land, as well as the actual city itself, could be enclosed by the 'GeländermauerTrace', as these walls are known ('contour-trace' or 'cross-country trace'). This tendency, already present in the fifth century (F.E. Winter, *Greek Fortifications* (London, 1970) 304) developed apace in the early fourth century as siege techniques progressed. The fortifications of Messene extend for 9 kilometres, winding along the tops of the slopes and spurs of Mount Ithome. The date of the city-walls of Messene is disputed. Whilst they seem to have been laid out originally shortly after 370, many features, such as the chisel decoration shown here on the gate above tower 24 (see **213b**), suggest modifications later in the century (A.W. Lawrence, *Greek Aims in Fortification* (Oxford, 1979) 382–5).

P. Themelis, *Praktika* 1986, 75, fig. 1; cf. P. Ducrey, *Warfare in Ancient Greece* (London, 1986) fig. 103.

211. The next ruler to attempt the creation of a centralized military state was Philip II of Macedon, initially under the compulsion of dire necessity. When Philip gained the throne in 359 B.C. Macedonia had been devastated by a Dardanian invasion and her army all but destroyed. Philip set about creating a new army to face the next invasion. The finances to procure hoplite equipment were absent, so Philip re-equipped the Macedonian phalanx as 'Iphicratean peltasts', and set about a gruelling retraining programme (Diod. XVI.3.1–2; Polyaen. IV.2.10). Next year the Dardanians were defeated and Philip set about expanding his power base. He soon gained control of the rich Pangaeum mines, which yielded an annual revenue of a thousand talents. With these increased resources the army was further strengthened, but further enemies were made. As Jason of Pherae had found, the only way Philip could hold on to his tenuous power was to increase the extent and resources of the state: thus was born a cycle of military expansion, and Macedon became a paradigmatic example of a military state, a process described in J.R. Ellis, *Philip II and Macedonian Imperialism* (London, 1976). Philip also developed the power of his cavalry arm, borrowing the tactical formation of the wedge, even more flexible than the Thessalian rhomb, from the Scythians to the north (Arrian, *Tact.* xvi.6). This relief from Pelinna in Thessaly probably shows a Macedonian cavalryman, as he wears a cloak of the Macedonian, not Thessalian, type. Note the helmet of Phrygian type (J. Vokotopoulou, 'Phrygische Helme', *AA* 1982, 479–520), overwhelmingly popular at this time, and also leather straps (*pteruges*) at both shoulder and groin of the cuirass.

(Paris, Louvre, MA 836)

H. Biesantz, *Die Thessalischen Grabreliefs* (Mainz, 1965) K 34, 21, pl. 14.

212. Philip also invested much effort in the further development of siege weapons, in order to extend his power over the fortified Greek cities lying to the south. Torsion artillery, powered by springs of sinew, seems to have been developed by artificers working under the direction of Philip's chief mechanic, the Thessalian Polyidus, between 353 and 341 B.C. (E.W. Marsden, *Greek and Roman Artillery. Historical Development* (Oxford, 1969) 60). This new artillery could no longer be held by hand, but had to be mounted on frames. The size of the bolt which could be propelled was greatly increased. Numerous heads from catapult-bolts, marked with the legend 'Philip's', have been recovered during excavations at Olynthus, a city which Philip successfully besieged in 348 B.C. (cf. *Pls. to Vol. VII.1*, pl. 112). City-walls were now modified to take full advantage of this increased missile-power. One feature which appears at this time is the 'jogged trace', which was also developed, according to Philo, by Polyidus, and which is first encountered in extant fortifications at Priene which date to about 350 B.C. (A.W. Lawrence, *Greek Aims in Fortification* (Oxford, 1979) 349–51). The 'jogged' or 'indented' trace was designed to provide defending artillery with as many shooting positions as possible from which to attack the flank of an enemy assault group. Each jog was, in effect, a substitute tower. This plan shows the line of the jogged trace in the walls of Samikon in Triphylia, lying between Messenia and Elis.

(After J.-P. Adam, *L'Architecture militaire grecque* (Paris, 1982) 66, fig. 30)

213. In 346 Philip conquered Phocis, and the fortifications of that country were razed or at least slighted. Following his victory over the Greeks at Chaeronea in 338, however, Philip found it expedient to build up the power of Phocis as a counter-balance to that of Thebes, his

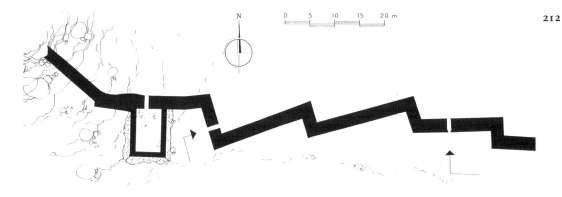

principal enemy. The Phocians were allowed to rebuild their cities, and the new fortifications in Phocis provide well-dated evidence for the extent to which artillery was influencing military architecture. The artillery tower (**a**) from the fortifications of the Phocian city of Lilaea is provided with square windows in the second

storey enabling artillery to be placed within the tower in order to shoot down on attackers (cf. *Pls. to Vol. VII.1*, pl. 115), as well as with arrow-slots in the wall below.

Decorative surface treatment of the masonry is very much a feature of fortifications dating to this period and later. The West Tower of the plateau wall at Thisbe in Boeotia (**b**) was built at the same time as the Phocian fortifications, and shows 'broached' surface decoration.

R.L. Scranton, *Greek Walls* (Cambridge, Mass., 1941) 21–2, 76–7; L.B. Tillard, *BSA* 17 (1910–11) 54–75.

214. From the 360s onwards Athenian state revenues started to grow again, principally because of an increase in activity in the silver-mines of Laurium. Military reform again became financially viable, and started to enter the political debate. Around 367 Xenophon produced two pamphlets, *On the Duties of the Hipparch* and *On Horsemanship*, recommending reform in cavalry tactics and equipment. In chapter 12 of the second pamphlet he advocates, among other things, an increase in the body-armour to be carried by the Athenian cavalry, the attachment of *pteruges* (leather flaps) at the shoulder of the cuirass as well as at the groin, and the adoption of the Boeotian helmet. From this date onwards we begin to find representations of Athenian cavalrymen with heavier body armour, sometimes

with *pteruges* attached to the shoulder-pieces (cf. **211**), and Boeotian helmets.

(Athens, National Museum 2586)

B. Schmaltz, *Untersuchungen zu den attischen Marmorlekythen* (Berlin, 1970) 144, no. A 270; *Arch.Eph.* 1973, pl. 54 b.

215. In his *On the Duties of the Hipparch* (v.13, IX.7) Xenophon also recommended that a corps of *hamippoi* should be raised from among the exiles and other foreigners resident in Athens who had special reason to hate the enemy. It seems that the Athenian state was fast to act on Xenophon's recommendations, for Diodorus (XV.85.4) implies that *hamippoi* were present at the Battle of Mantinea in 362 B.C., though inferior in tactical skill to those fighting with the Theban cavalry. *Hamippoi* were trained to run alongside the cavalry, holding onto the tails of the horses and the hems of the riders' cloaks, as this Athenian relief shows. In the mêlée they would attack horse and rider alike with daggers and other weapons.

(Paris, Musée du Louvre 744)

N. Sekunda, *The Ancient Greeks. Armies of Classical Greece, 5th and 4th Centuries B.C.* (London, 1986) 57.

216. The equipment of the Athenian infantry also changed in the 360s. From this time onwards hoplites are shown on Athenian sculptures, such as this Athenian marble funerary loutrophoros, wearing a muscle-cuirass with *pteruges* at the groin, usually, though not always, accompanied by a helmet of the Phrygian type. It may be that heavy body armour had been re-introduced into

Greek warfare by the Thebans along with their new tactics of attack in depth. The Athenian military reform may perhaps be alluded to by Plutarch (*Mor.* 193F) who tells us that the Athenians entered the Mantinean campaign with new weapons. Another reform carried out at about this time was the creation of a corps of Athenian *epilektoi*. They are not mentioned in any account of the Battle of Mantinea in 362, and first appear in the literature at the Battle of Tamynae in 349.

It may be that they were created around 354/3 from volunteers willing to serve under the Athenian general Chares, who was sent to help the rebel satrap Artabazus. Despite these strenuous attempts to raise their military potential, the tide of history was running against Athens and the other Greek city states. Advances in siege techniques developed by the centralized Macedonian military state had removed one of the underlying precepts of hoplite warfare, that city-walls were effectively invulnerable. The strategy of devastation had now been replaced by the strategy of overthrow, and the Classical age of Greek culture, based around the city state, was now drawing to a close.

(Athens, National Museum 3473)

IG II² 12658; G. Kokula, *Marmorlutrophoren* (Berlin, 1984) 178, L 81.

217. The infantry the Macedonians were fielding against the Athenians were, it seems, no longer peltasts of the 'Iphicratean' type. Contemporary representations of Macedonian infantry, such as this one taken from the so-called Alexander Sarcophagus, show them in full hoplite panoply. The issue of peltast equipment to the Macedonian phalanx in 359/8 B.C. had been a

stop-gap measure. As soon as Philip had the resources available, it seems, the phalanx was given hoplite equipment.

(Istanbul, Archaeological Museum)

K. Schefold, *Der Alexander-Sarkophag* (Berlin, 1968) pl. 49.

218. Hoplite infantry had ceased to be the queen of the battlefield. The decisive blow was now delivered by the cavalry, in command of which Alexander showed himself a master (cf. J.F.C. Fuller, *The Generalship of Alexander the Great* (London, 1958); E.W. Marsden, *The Campaign of Gaugamela* (Liverpool, 1964)). This relief from Bursa, though probably illustrating an incident from the civil wars which followed the death of Alexander, shows cavalry and infantry equipment as would have been worn in the final years of Alexander's reign. The cavalry was not too heavily armoured, with cuirass and Boeotian helmet, so as to preserve its manoeuvrability. As far as infantry equipment is concerned, it seems that the pressure of long relentless campaigning in Asia had constrained Alexander to reduce the armour carried by at least some of the phalanx battalions (N. Sekunda, *The Army of Alexander*

217

218

219

the *Great* (London, 1984) 31–2). The cuirass has been abandoned, and the hoplite shield has been replaced by a bronze *pelte*.

(Bursa, Archaeological Museum)
E. Pfuhl and H. Möbius, *Die Ostgriechischen Grabsreliefs* (Mainz, 1977) no. 1271.

219. Bronze *peltai* were henceforward used by some regiments of the phalanx. This Hellenistic example, measuring 65–7 cm across, was recovered in excavations at Pergamum. Henceforward, in general terms, the Hellenistic phalanx was divided into two elements, hoplites (or their Macedonian counterparts the *chalkaspides* or bronze-shields) and peltasts of the 'Iphicratean' type.

(Archaeological Museum, Pergamum)
A. von Szalay and E. Boehringer, *Altertümer von Pergamon* x. Die Hellenistischen Arsenale (Berlin, 1937) 33, pl. 27g.

220. Throughout the Classical period it had been the responsibility of the individual citizen to provide his own equipment. True uniformity in dress and equipment could not arise under these circumstances. The only exception to this may have been the militarized state of Sparta. In the new age of the centralized state, issue of uniform dress and equipment perforce became general. A bronze spear-butt seemingly provides us with an example of the process. In the course of cleaning in 1977 the painted letters MAK appeared on the butt underneath the corrosion. The letters, an abbreviated form of Macedonia, are an indication that the weapon was issued by the state.

(University of Newcastle upon Tyne, Greek Museum, Inv. no. 111)

Greek Arms and Armour, The Greek Museum, The University of Newcastle upon Tyne (Newcastle, 1978) 13.

220

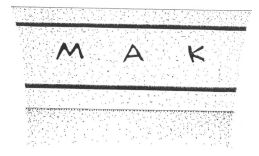

9. CLASSICAL COINAGE

M. JESSOP PRICE

By 480 B.C. the idea of a precious metal coinage had spread to most parts of the Greek-speaking world. The next 150 years saw the establishment of economic systems which required the use of coins for small daily transactions (Plut. *Pericles* 16.4) as well as for accumulating wealth in relatively small units. One small but interesting consequence of the changing pattern is the custom of placing an obol with the dead to pay Charon for the passage across the Styx. It is no coincidence that this appears to have started in the late fifth century B.C. Similarly, the introduction of coinage in bronze and a notable increase in the number of gold coinages alongside massive outputs of silver coins illustrate the development of a fully flexible monetary system.

The creation of a coin issue begins with the requirement that a particular denomination be struck for particular payments. The introduction of 2-obol and 3-obol payments to citizens at Athens, for example, in the second half of the fifth century B.C., is typical of the developments that were taking place all over the Greek world. The need for obols, diobols, and, later, triobols for such payments is obvious. Tetradrachms, pieces equal to 24 obols, do not provide the flexibility required for the system that Athenian democracy demanded to recompense citizens for attendance at the *ekklesia* and for jury service. Plato's comment on such developments is interesting: 'Pericles made the Athenians lazy, miserable, chatter-boxes, and misers by being the first to introduce payment for service' (*Gorgias* 515e). Such easy money is undesirable (*Republic* 421d).

The introduction of bronze coinage was a dramatic development. Hitherto, the silver, gold, and electrum used for coinage were in themselves valuable metals. Although the state usually placed a premium on the precious metal turned into coinage in order to retain the metal within the city's area of jurisdiction, precious metal did have a significant intrinsic value. A small token of bronze on the other hand was

worthless, and circulation of such pieces required legislation and acceptance, sometimes enforced, by the citizen body. At Gortyna, in Crete, an inscription has survived recording a law which forced the new bronze coinage on reluctant citizens (*Inscr. Creticae* IV. 162; cf. A.E. Jackson, *NC* 1971, 37–8). Otherwise, little has survived in other forms of evidence to illuminate the decisions to create coinage, but a great deal may be gleaned from the coins themselves.

The requirement that a particular denomination should be struck is an economic decision brought about by the needs of the state. It reflects the current historical situation and immediately places the resulting coin issue in a historical context. Once the need is established, a decision has to be made on what designs should be placed on the coins. This is clearly a political decision which was normally made by the ruling authority, a dynast or a leading politician, a group of officials or a city assembly. This, too, may reflect current historical events, and so provide a contemporary document which may be studied in its context to further our knowledge of the ancient world. Increasingly it became the norm to place a design on the reverse punch die, an arrangement adopted by Athens, Corinth and others in the late Archaic period. The use of Athenian tetradrachms as 'good money' throughout the Near East in the Persian Empire led to the adoption of the same designs not only by satraps, but even by the Great King himself.

The theme of the design has to be interpreted by the engravers who cut the dies from which the coins were made. The same design cut in very different styles at the same time or over a period of time provides a sequence of closely datable objects illustrating in detail the changing artistic styles of the ancient Greek world. During the later fifth and fourth centuries the inclusion of the engraver's name in the design provides a personal contact with the artist. Best known are those from Sicily and South Italy, but Crete also offers such names, not otherwise recorded for their artistic achievement, and engravers' names are known even from Pamphylia and Cilicia.

The final stage in coin production is the striking of the prepared metal flan between the two dies. The square section of the punch die, which created the reverse, still produced *c.* 480 B.C. an incuse square on the coin, which often did not cover the whole of the flan. By 400 B.C. only a few mints retained the incuse square in a consciously archaizing manner which, by biting into the metal, probably acted as a deterrent to forgery. Rhodes, which only started to coin in the name of all the Rhodians at the very end of the fifth century, instituted the coinage with a deep reverse incuse square, and this continued until the third quarter of the fourth century. Abdera in Thrace, however, abandoned the incuse square in the middle of the fourth century (J.M.F. May, *The Coinage of Abdera* (London, 1966) period VIII, chronology revised by M.J. Price in *Coin Hoards* VII (New York, 1985) 42–4). It was replaced on the small denominations by a linear square, suggesting that the square itself was viewed as part of the reverse design.

In circulation coinage clearly passed easily within the area of origin. An interesting decree of 375/4 B.C. appointing a coin inspector to be present in the Athenian Agora and in the Piraeus (T.V. Buttrey, *Quaderni Ticinesi* 10 (1981) 71–94) throws light on the problems of imported or counterfeit coins being tendered in the city. Although only good Athenian coins should be used, the treasury held quantities of Cyzicene electrum and other foreign coins. Similarly, at Delphi, when there was need to melt silver for a coin issue (P. Kinns, *NC* 1983, 1–22), the treasury provided coins from three other cities, Larissa, Sicyon and Locri Opuntii. There were, however, several areas in which silver was a scarce commodity and coins were overvalued to the extent that pieces rarely passed out of the geographical area of issue. This is notable, for example, in Sicily and Italy, in Thessaly and Crete, and in southern Asia Minor. The large hoards from the Near East containing a mixture of many mainland Greek coinages, which is a feature of the late Archaic period, disappear in the middle of the fifth century. Only the coins of Athens continued to circulate in significant quantities, adopted under the Persian Empire as a form of common currency. This pattern survived until the time of Alexander the Great, when political turmoil is well illustrated by the changes in the minting and circulation of coinage.

GENERAL BIBLIOGRAPHY

C.M. Kraay, *Archaic and Classical Greek Coins* (London, 1976); I.A. Carradice and M.J. Price, *Coinage in the Greek World* (London, 1988); G.K. Jenkins, *Ancient Greek Coins* (2nd edn, London, 1990). For continuous updating of bibliography, see the 'Survey of Numismatic Research' published to coincide with International Numismatic Conferences, the latest being for 1985–1990, T. Hackens *et al.* eds. (Brussels, 1991).

Unless otherwise stated, all illustrated coins are of silver and are from the collection of the British Museum.

221. A star of barley grains provided the first reverse design at Metapontum. The obverse die depicting an ear of barley had also been used for the last incuse coinage, on which the reverse was an incuse ear of barley. Traces of earlier designs on this piece, underneath the barley ear and star, show that it has been overstruck on an existing coin, possibly of Corinth. This practice emphasizes the need to retain valuable silver within the territory of the city. Stater, *c.* 460 B.C.

S.P. Noe (A. Johnston ed.), *The Coinage of Metapontum* Parts 1 and 2 (New York, 1984) 70, no. 310; *SNG* Lloyd 323.

222. The owls of Athens, silver from the rich mines at Laurium, spread throughout the Greek world. Their reputation for purity resulted in widespread use, even in the Persian Empire. Their designs remained the same throughout the fifth and fourth centuries, with only minor changes in detail. Tetradrachm *c.* 450 B.C.

BMC 41; C.G. Starr, *Athenian Coinage 480–449 B.C.* (Oxford, 1970) 59, no. 178.

223. The fourth-century owls differ in style from the earlier pieces, and the incuse square on the reverse becomes less prominent. On the obverse, Athena's eye is clearly shown in profile, with the inner end wide open. Punch marks test the metal of the coin while in circulation. Tetradrachm *c.* 350–325 B.C.

BMC 138. Cf. J. Bingen, 'Le trésor monétaire Thorikos,' *Thorikos VI, 1969* (Brussels, 1973) group IV.

221

222

223

224   225

226

224. A 4-drachma piece was worth four days pay for the architect of the Parthenon, and so the eighth of an obol (a forty-eighth of a drachma) was needed for small payments in the Agora, despite its impractical size (0.097 g). Like the obol and other small coins, it was probably carried in the mouth, under the tongue (cf. Aristophanes, *Wasps* 608–9, 790–1 and *Birds* 503). Hemitetartemorion with head of Athena and facing owl, *c.* 410 B.C.

BMC 207.

225. Gold coinage was struck at Athens only in times of emergency. This is the first such issue, well documented in the annual Parthenon inventories inscribed in stone. The Spartan capture of Decelea in 413 B.C. cut Athens off from Laurium and her silver mines. In 407/6 B.C., in a desperate effort to raise funds for the defence of the city, an

issue of gold coins was made in six denominations from stater (= 6 silver tetradrachms) to hemiobol (= 1 silver drachma). Seven gold statues of Victory, 14 talents in all, disappear from the accounts at this time, and were clearly used to provide some of the gold for this issue. On completion of striking the dies for this issue were placed in an alabaster box in the Parthenon treasury (*IG* II².2 665). Gold stater.

PCG Add. 17.

226. When the gold was exhausted, the Athenians resorted in 405 B.C. to an issue of bronze tetradrachms, drachmae, and hemidrachms, plated with a thin film of silver, much to the chagrin of Aristophanes, *Frogs* 717–25. These were withdrawn *c.* 394 B.C. (*Eccles.* 815–22). A previous attempt to introduce bronze at Athens *c.* 445 B.C. was rejected by indignant citizens (Athenaeus XV.669D).

Plated drachma from the Piraeus, 1902 hoard (*IGCH* 46); J.H.Kroll, *GRBS* 17, no. 4 (1976) 329–41.

227. Timotheus the Athenian general, when besieging Olynthus in the Chalcidice 363–359 B.C., found himself short of silver coin and struck an issue of bronze coins to pay his troops ([Aristotle] *Oeconomica* II.2.23.1). These coins differ from all other Athenian Hellenistic coins in depicting the owl standing on a corn grain, and in having marks of value – (**a**) two dots, (**b**) one dot. The designs of Athena head and owl are distinctively Athenian. Six examples were found in the excavation of Olynthus (*Olynthus* III, 41.82; VI, 46.59–61; IX, 245.1). Only rarely are they found in Athens. These pieces are without question the issue of Timotheus, token 1- and 2-obol pieces specifically issued for the corn subsidy of his army. Regular bronze coinage at Athens itself only started after 350 B.C.

E.S.G. Robinson and M.J. Price, *NC* 1967, 1–6; J.H. Kroll in O. Mørkholm and N.M. Waggoner ed., *Greek Numismatics and Archaeology: Essays in honor of Margaret Thompson* (Wetteren, 1979) 146–8.

228. This example of the early issue of Aenus, Thrace, with the head of Hermes and a he-goat, has been struck upon a tetradrachm of Abdera with a seated griffin design and an added symbol cock and the letters *ΔEO*, which represent the name of the official responsible for the issue. The original coin can be dated *c.* 460 B.C. on strong

227a,b

a   b

228–31

228

229

230

231

358). It is clear that the city was striking large quantities of coins in the period 450–425 B.C. The hoard was buried in 423 B.C. at the time of the recapture of the city by the Athenians. Tetradrachm.

S.P. Noe, *The Mende (Kaliandra) hoard* ANS Numismatic Notes and Monographs 27 (New York, 1926) no. 66.

230. Silver 'tetrobol' of Aphytis, Macedonia, clearly influenced by the coinage of Mende (**229**). The prominent incuse makes a date of 450–425 B.C. most probable. There was found at Aphytis a fragment of a weights and currency decree preventing Athenian allies from striking local silver coinage and arranging for general use amongst the allied states of the Attic weight standard. This has traditionally been placed in the 440s, but there was clearly no effect on coinage at Abdera, Aenus (**228**), Mende (**229**), Acanthus, Samos (**231**) and other cities of the Athenian League during the third quarter of the fifth century. All these, however, do have a break in coinage in the 420s, and this must be the period in which the decree was promulgated. It no longer seems to be an imperialistic measure, but rather a practical arrangement during wartime. Compare the Peloponnesian League, below nos. **232–3**.

I.A. Carradice ed., *Coinage and Administration in the Athenian and Persian Empires* BAR Int. series 343 (1987) 45–51 (M.J.Price), 53–63 (D.M. Lewis), 65–71 (H.B. Mattingly).

231. In the fifth century, Samos produced a series of tetradrachms of the normal types of lion scalp and forepart of an ox, but distinguished by a sequence of letters from *B* to *Ξ*. This is clearly a sequence of numbers, 2–15, and may be interpreted as dates on annual issues during the period when oligarchs were in power 454/3–440/39 B.C. Tetradrachm of Samian weight, year 9 (446/5 B.C.).

J.P. Barron, *The Silver Coins of Samos* (London, 1966) 191, no. 85.

232. The coinage of Corinth played a major role in Magna Graecia where it was often overstruck to produce local coinage (cf. **221**). It was struck on a local standard different from the 'Aeginetic' standard used by other Peloponnesian states. The abundant coinage of the Corinthian 'foals' with Pegasus and head of Athena came to an

hoard evidence. It is now certain that the coinage of Aenus must have started no earlier than 460 B.C. and continued without break until the third quarter of the fifth century. Tetradrachm, 460–455 B.C.

J.M.F. May, *Ainos: its History and Coinage* (London, 1950) 27.9; *id., The Coinage of Abdera* (London, 1966) 106.92. On the evidence for later dating at both mints, M. Price in I. Carradice ed., *Coinage and Administration in the Athenian and Persian Empires* BAR Int. series 343 (1987) 45–6.

229. Dionysus reclining on an ass, and a vine with the grapes to make the famous wine from Mende, Macedonia. Most surviving coins of this type come from the Kaliandra hoard (*IGCH*

232

233

234

235

236

237

abrupt stop *c.* 430 B.C., at the very time that the Peloponnesian War was beginning and funds would seem to be needed for military expenditure. This coinage did not resume until the end of the century. Stater, 435–430 B.C.

O. Ravel, *Les 'Poulains' de Corinthe* I (Basel, 1936) 91–2, no. 306; Kraay, *ACGC* 83–5.

233. The meagre fifth-century coinage of Sicyon blossoms from *c.* 425 B.C. into one of the major coinages of the Peloponnese, with the exciting designs of a chimaera and dove in wreath. This coinage on the Aeginetic standard flourished during the Peloponnesian War, while that of Corinth (**232**) on its individual standard waned. Such a phenomenon makes an interesting parallel to the Athenian currency and standards decree (**228–31**) which appears to have been enacted at about the time of this issue. Stater, *c.* 425 B.C. with a dot graffito dedicating the piece to 'Artemis in Lakedaimon'.

C.M. Kraay, *ACHG* 99 following the chronology of Mrs J.A.W. Cargill Thompson (Warren), *NC* 1968, x. G.F. Hill, *JHS* 1898, 302–5.

234. The Persian adoption of Athenian tetradrachms as a form of currency which could be used throughout their empire resulted in strong influence of the designs on coinage struck in the Near East. A fine portrait of a Persian, traditionally associated with Tissaphernes, is accompanied by an 'Athenian' reverse inscribed with the title of the Great King. Tetradrachm from the Karaman hoard (*IGCH* 1243), which may now be dated to the middle of the fifth century, too late for Tissaphernes. Early portraiture on coins

is a phenomenon of the Persian Empire, particularly prevalent in Lycia.

NC 1948, 48–56; H.A. Cahn, 'Le monnayage des satrapes: Iconographie et signification', in R. Descat ed., *L'or Perse et l'histoire grecque, Revue des Etudes Anciennes* 91 (1989) 97–106; I. Carradice and M. Price, *Coinage in the Greek World* (London, 1988) 84–5.

235. The only coins to be produced with an inscription giving the name of a Greek King are this issue of tetradrachms of Athenian types struck at Memphis and using Egyptian demotic script. A recent hoard from Syria has added sixteen examples to the two known previously, some of them with added names in Aramaic. The demotic reads 'Artaxerxes Pharaoh', and the issue is to be linked with the successful expedition of Artaxerxes III Ochus in 343 B.C. to retake the satrapy of Egypt after a period of revolt.

O. Mørkholm and A.F. Shore, *NC* 1974, 1–8.

236. Local coinage flourished in the western Persian Empire, although no coinage was struck in Babylonia itself. In addition to city issues, there were satrapal or provincial issues which reflect Persian imagery. The bowman and horseman-satrap staters were widely used in the fourth century. A number were found in a hoard from Calymna (*IGCH* 1216), with silver sigloi of Sardis and Carian coinages. This new variety, inscribed in Aramaic, gives the name of Gerashtart in monogram, and letters indicating that he was dynast of Aradus, Phoenicia. This is the Gerostratus (339/8–332 B.C.) who surrendered the city to Alexander.

237. The Persian gold darics played a major role, even in Greece itself. From the time of Xerxes the design remained constant – the symbolic figure of the king, and a rough incuse rectangle, here bearing in countermark, a head of Pan. This variety is unique both in the countermark, and in having a beardless king wearing a decorated robe (*kandys*). This has led to an attractive attribution to Cyrus the Younger (405–401 B.C.), which can be neither proved nor disproved on present evidence. The issue is linked by reverse die to pieces of normal obverse style and so was probably made in Sardes.

BMC Persia 61; I.A. Carradice, 'Coinage of the Persian Empire', in *Coinage and Administration in the Athenian and Persian Empires* (Oxford, 1987) 73–95.

238. The Persians clearly accepted that subject Greek cities should be able to strike their own coinage. The gold coinage of Lampsacus travelled far beyond north-west Asia Minor. The pieces do not bear an ethnic, but the constant reverse design is the forepart of a Pegasus, the badge of the city. The obverse depicting Victory erecting a trophy may well represent a particular event, but not enough is yet known of this coinage to make for certainty. Stater of daric weight, *c.* 350 B.C.

A. Baldwin, *American Journal of Numismatics* 53 (1924) 27, no. 26; Kraay, *ACGC* 251.

239. Bearded male head wreathed with laurel. The electrum staters of Cyzicus, equal in value to one daric, changed their designs frequently, possibly every year. The great number of different images, and the vast volume of the coinage,

238–9

238

239

together with the absence of an ethnic, make it certain that this should be viewed as a Persian provincial coinage, and not as a city coinage. They are, however, to be identified as Cyzicene by the tunny fish, always present in the design. The electrum coinages of Mytilene and Phocaea show the same characteristics, and a fragment of a decree (J.F. Healy, *JHS* 1957, 267–8) tells us that they even co-operated over the purity of the alloy and minting procedures.

H. von Fritze, *Nomisma* 7 (1912) 14, no. 199.

240. The earliest struck bronze coinage is that of Thurii, the panhellenic colony founded in 443 B.C. on a site close to Sybaris. The head of Athena and the bull are the regular designs for the coinage, the bull providing continuity with the earlier silver coinage of Sybaris. The first coinage in silver shows Athena's helmet wreathed with laurel. This changes to a decorative figure of Scylla (**252**), which regularly appears on the helmet thereafter. This issue of bronze belongs to the period immediately following the foundation. Dionysius of Athens (**226**), who gained the nickname Chalkous ('the bronze'), had already had his proposal for a bronze coinage fiercely rejected by the Athenians. At Thurii he seems to have been more successful.

M.J. Price, 'Early Greek Bronze Coinage', in C.M. Kraay and G.K. Jenkins (eds.), *Essays in Greek Coinage presented to Stanley Robinson* (Oxford, 1968) 90–104.

241. The first bronze coinage of Acragas, Sicily was cast and takes the form of weights rather than struck coins. This reflects the traditional use of bronze by weight in the area. The marks of value on these indicate a denominational system reflected in the pieces themselves and also show

240–3

244

that they were not intended to represent actual weights in bronze. They were, as coins, significantly overvalued. 4-uncia (trias), *c.* 430 B.C.

M.J. Price, *op. cit.*, 95; R. Calciati, *Corpus Nummorum Siculorum: The Bronze Coinage* I (Edizioni G.M., 1983) 143–7.

242. The struck bronze coinage of Acragas began *c.* 425 B.C. using the same eagle on hare and crab designs as the silver tetradrachms which can be closely dated. The marks of value range from one to six unciae. 3-uncia (tetras), *c.* 415 B.C.

R. Calciati, *op. cit.*, 149–93.

243. Gold in Magna Graecia was only struck in times of crisis. This issue of 2-obols from Acragas, found in several varieties, is marked, like the bronze, with a mark of value, each piece the equivalent of a silver tetradrachm. The Silanos who signed this piece is not otherwise known, but the coinage is to be dated immediately before the Carthaginian capture and sack of the city in 406 B.C. Similar emergency issues come from Gela and Camarina at the same time.

SNG Lloyd 815; G.K. Jenkins, *The Coinage of Gela* (Berlin, 1970) 98–9.

244. The magnificent 10-drachma piece of Acragas follows the well-established coinage of Syracuse in displaying a galloping quadriga, which is here linked to Acragas by the symbols crab and

eagle. This is also to be dated in the last decade of the fifth century and reflects the need of the city to amass military materials in the face of the advancing Carthaginians. It may be placed just before the gold issues (**243**) *c.* 408–406 B.C.

SNG Munich 5, no. 89.

245-7

246

245

247

245. The Carthaginian invasion had itself to be financed and large issues of coinage were produced, of Greek form but inscribed in Punic. This issue marked 'the camp' beside the palm tree is undoubtedly a military issue. The inscription below the horse forepart shows that it was struck in Carthage for this campaign. Such coinage was also struck in Sicily itself.

G.K. Jenkins, *Swiss Numismatic Review* 53 (1974) 35, no. 1.

246-7. The decadrachms of Syracuse are amongst the most famous coins from the Greek world, yet it is not often realized that they were made at a time of crisis *c.* 405 B.C., when the Carthaginians were threatening the very existence of the city (above nos. **243-5**). The designs are those regularly used for the large Syracusan coinage of the fifth century – the head of Arethusa and a quadriga. In addition, however, to the victorious chariot there is a panoply of armour, shield, greaves, corselet and helmet, sometimes labelled 'prizes'. This underlines the military nature of the issue. The artists' signatures allow an interesting comparison of contemporary styles. KIM on the hairband of **246** identifies Kimon; EUAINE(tos) places his name below a dolphin – each interpreting the designs in his own distinctive style.

Cf. Kraay–Hirmer, figs. 104–6, 116–21.

248. Kimon produced a tetradrachm with the head of Arethusa depicted facing, a dramatic change in tradition which led the way for a number of similar heads in mainland Greece and Asia Minor in the fourth century. The engraver Eukleidas created a similar head, but with Arethusa helmeted for the war against Carthage. His name appears in small letters across the front of the helmet. Unlikely as it may seem, this design was copied in Lycia under the dynast Zagaba *c.* 380 B.C., testifying to the movement of people between Sicily and Asia Minor in the early fourth century (*NC* 1959, 33–35, no. 15). The quadriga of this piece shows the same movement as the Acragas decadrachm (**244**).

Kraay, *ACGC* 222–3; L.O.T. Tudeer, *Die Tetradrachmenprägung von Syrakus in der Periode der signierenden Künstler* (Berlin, 1913) 42–3, no. 59.

249. When silver ran short, the tyrant of Syracuse Dionysius I (405–367 B.C.) turned to striking several issues of gold. This example is also signed by Euainetos. Dionysius gained a reputation for extorting money from the Syracusans ([Aristotle] *Oeconomica* II.2.20), placing a tax, for example, on the wearing of jewellery. The military symbolism of the Heracles and Nemean lion would be clear to the citizens who saw the threat from the lion of Carthage. Gold 100-litre (= 20 silver drachmae), *c.* 400 B.C.

SNG Lloyd 1122.

248

249

250

251

251

252

250. Euainetos also worked at other cities. This tetradrachm of Catana, Sicily, bears his name on a plaque held by Victory in one hand while she offers a wreath to the charioteer with the other. Both the laureate head of Apollo and the horses of the quadriga as it rounds the turning post provide distinctive hallmarks of the engraver's style. The sacred bell on a taenia and the crayfish accompanying the head of Apollo have local significance and have been consciously included to distinguish the issue. The designs otherwise clearly reflect those of Syracuse and must date soon after the capture of the city by Dionysius I in 403 B.C.

BMC 32.

251. A colleague of Euainetos at Camarina was Exekestidas who signs as the engraver on the line below the fast moving chariot. The city was a colony of Syracuse and adapts the well-known coinage for her own use. Tetradrachm, 410–405 B.C.

G.K. Jenkins, *The Coinage of Camarina* (London, 1980) 190–1, no. 149.

252. *ΜΟΛΟΣΣΟΣ ΕΠ* . . . on the line below the bull must be the signature of the engraver Molossos. Such names are sometimes difficult to distinguish from magistrates names, but the verb *ΕΠ[ΟΕΙ* (made) makes the identification certain. The style of this piece of Thurii is indifferent and the coin is silver plated on a bronze core. The helmet of Athena is decorated with a fine figure of Scylla. Stater, *c.* 400 B.C.

E.S.G. Robinson, *NC* 1927, 301–2, no. 8; S.P. Noe, *The Thurian Di-staters*, ANS Numismatic Notes and Monographs 71 (New York, 1935) 13–15.

253. The cities of Asia Minor under the Persian Empire struck notable coinages in the fourth century B.C. At Clazomenae the facing head of Apollo is an adaptation of the work of Kimon at Syracuse, a fashion that became popular in many areas of the Greek world *c.* 350 B.C. The engraver's signature *ΟΕΟΔΟΤΟΣ ΕΠΟΕΙ* confirms the Sicilian connexion (246–51). The swan was sacred to Apollo, and the verb κλάζω, to be used of the cry of the swan, provides a pun on the name of the city. Tetradrachm, *c.* 375 B.C.

L. Forrer, *Note sur les signatures de graveurs sur les monnaies grecques* (Brussels, 1906) 167–70; Kraay, *ACGC* 258.

253

254

255

256

257

254. The large coinage of Aspendus, Pamphylia, in the Persian period depicting wrestlers also includes on a very few dies an artist's signature, *ΕΛΥΨΑ ΜΕΝΕΤΥΣ*. Only here and at Soli, Cilicia (᾿Απατόριος ἔγλυψεν) does this verb appear in the context of engraving coin dies. Tetradrachm, *c.* 350 B.C.

O. Masson, *Kadmos* 31 (1992) 6–9.

255. The coinage of Crete started fairly early under Aeginetan influence but the earliest coinage at Cnossus is of the late fifth century. The symbolism of the Minotaur speaks for itself. The labyrinth on the reverse takes many forms and acts as a badge for the city.

British Museum (1947), overstruck on a turtle stater of Aegina.

256. Engravers' signatures are also to be found in Crete. Pythodoros made dies for Aptera, his name in the genitive in front of the head of Aphrodite, and for Polyrrhenium. His work has

even been recognized on an unsigned bronze issue of Aptera. The warrior on the reverse of Pythodoros' stater has been identified as the Trojan Aeneas performing the ritual for the foundation of Aptera and labelled founder of cities.

PCG III.B.51; M.J. Delepierre, *Revue Numismatique* 1972, 7–20.

257. At Cydonia, *ΝΕΥΑΝΤΟΣ ΕΠΟΕΙ* in minute letters behind the head on the obverse identifies the work of an engraver not otherwise known. The head is of a fertility deity, possibly Dictynna; the reverse shows a hero stringing his bow, and the issue may be connected with the attack of the Phocian Phalaecus in 346–5 B.C. (Diodorus XVI.62.4).

L. Forrer, *Notes sur les signatures de graveurs sur les monnaies grecques* (Brussels, 1906) 247–9.

258. Telephas, whose name is found in the genitive, retrograde, on a drachma of Pharsalus, Thessaly *c.* 375 B.C., has been identified with the sculptor Telephanes of Phocaea who worked in Thessaly, and whose work was much admired (Pliny, *NH* XXXIV.19.68). The form of the name on the coins makes this impossible. It is, how-

258

259

260

261

troops attempting to regain the sanctuary. The Arcadians siezed metal from the sacred treasury to pay for their troops, and, doubtless, this provided the gold for the coins of Pisa. Obol depicting the head of Olympian Zeus and his thunderbolt.

C.T. Seltman, *The Temple Coins of Olympia* (Cambridge, 1921) 56–8, no. 174.

261. Elis regained control over Olympia in 363 B.C. Their first issue thereafter combines the head of Zeus and the head of Olympia herself with their own ethnic. Stater, 363–360 B.C.

Seltman, *op. cit.*, 58, 175.

262–4. Monetary union is often found to accompany political union (**228–34**). This coinage links cities widely separate geographically, but all sharing the obverse design of the young Heracles strangling the snakes, accompanied by the word *ΣΥΝ(μαχικον)* 'alliance'. The reverse designs follow the normal 'badges' of each city, a rose for Rhodes (**262**), the scalp of a lion for Samos (**263**), and lion's head for Cyzicus (**264**), all familiar from their autonomous coinage. In addition to these three cities, Byzantium, Lampsacus, Ephesus, Iasus and Cnidus were all members of this alliance which has left no other trace in history. The weight of these staters is unusual. They are light Aeginetic staters which equate with tridrachms on the Chian/Rhodian standard. The most convincing reconstruction of events is that this is the coinage of the league formed by the Spartan Lysander *c.* 405–404 B.C.

Coin Hoards v (1980) 17; J.P. Barron, *The Silver Coins of Samos* (London, 1966) 113; S. Karweise, *NC* 1980, 1–27.

265. The Chalcidian League was formed at Olynthus in 432/1 B.C. as a counter-balance to the power of Athens in Macedonia. It issued an important coinage in silver until the sack of Olynthus and the dismembering of the league in 348 B.C. This tetradrachm is signed by the magistrate Ariston and may be dated *c.* 373–370 B.C. The Apollo and lyre are the constant types in silver, gold and bronze.

Olynthus IX (1938) 81, no. 134a; P.A. Clement, 'The Chalcidic coinage: Epilogue', in B. Laourdas and Ch. Makaronas (eds.), *Ancient Macedonia* (Thessalonika, 1970) 252–5.

ever, probable that this is the engraver's signature.

E. Babelon, *Traité des monnaies grecques et romaines* II.4 (Paris, 1932) 269, no. 481.

259. The name Epami . . . is one of a large number of names to be found on the staters of Thebes struck during the Boeotian supremacy in Greece 371–338 B.C. This variety may be connected with confidence with the Boeotarch Epaminondas, who died at Mantinea in 364 B.C. after successfully thwarting the power of Sparta. The distinctive shield is regularly found on the confederate issues of the Boeotians, and the amphora refers to the worship of Dionysus at Thebes itself.

BMC Thebes 135; *PCG* III.B.32.

260. Two coins, a gold obol and a ¼-drachma (1½-obol) are all that survive of the community of the Pisatans. The Arcadian League gave them independent status in 365 B.C. They wrested the presidency of the Olympic Games of 364 B.C. from Elis, and gave pride of place to Pisa. However, the games were interrupted by Elean

262

266

263

267

264

268

264

265

clearly marked with its place of origin and subdivided into issues by letters and symbols.

(**266.** Corinth, stater, *c.* 345 B.C. O.E. Ravel, *Les 'Poulains' de Corinthe* II (London, 1948) 250, no. 999; **267.** Leucas, stater, 350–340 B.C. R. Calciati, *Pegasi* II (Mortara, 1990) 431, no. 150. **268.** Syracuse, stater, 340–330 B.C. R. Calciati, *Pegasi* II, 608, no. 3)

C.M. Kraay, 'Timoleon and Corinthian coinage in Sicily', in H.A. Cahn and G. Le Rider (eds.), *Proceedings of the 8th International Congress of Numismatics* (Paris and Basel, 1976) 99–104; R.J.A. Talbert, *NC* 1971, 53–66.

269. The Syracusans proclaimed the new-found freedom of Sicily and the expulsion of Dionysius II from the city with coinage depicting the head of Zeus Eleutherios, the bringer of freedom. The Pegasus clearly derives from the Corinthian connexion. On this gold issue of 344–340 B.C. there are three pellets below the Pegasus, a mark of value indicating that the piece is worth three silver staters (at a ratio of silver to gold of 12:1). Gold hemidrachm.

BMC 265.

270. Zeus Eleutherios is also celebrated on the bronze coinage of Syracuse, on this piece *c.* 340 B.C. with his thunderbolt and a corn grain on the reverse.

R. Ross Holloway, *Annali dell' Istituto Italiano di Numismatica* 16–17 (1969–70) 130, no. 3.

266–8. The expedition of Timoleon in 345/4 B.C. to free the Greek cities of Sicily from Carthaginian aggression created a flood of Corinthian staters into the area. This coinage was struck for the expedition at Corinth and at her colonies in north-west Greece. These staters had a dramatic effect on the coinage of the region. Several cities in Magna Graecia made their own issues of this coinage. This is a form of monetary federation with a weight standard, as at Syracuse, quite different from that normally used. Each issue is

269

270

271

272

273

274

271. This gold stater of Alexander son of Neoptolemus of Epirus (342–330 B.C.) was probably struck in Italy 334–330 B.C. during his campaign to aid the people of Tarentum against their Italian enemies. The designs reflect the Zeus Eleutherios types of Syracuse, but the weight standard is that of his brother-in-law Philip II of Macedonia (**276**).

Kraay, *ACGC* 192–3.

272. The mines that had provided silver for Alexander I of Macedonia were lost to the kingdom of Aegeae in the 460s. For the whole of the reign of Perdiccas II (450–413 B.C.) only small 4-obol pieces were struck. Archelaus (413–399 B.C.) reorganized the state, moving his court from Aegae (Vergina) to Pella. He reformed the coinage to create a silver 'stater' rather lighter than the tetradrachm of his predecessors. The reverse goat reflects the name of Aegae, the mint of the issue. The horseman continues the motif of earlier coinage from the mint and it is most probable that the mint remained at Aegeae although the administration of the kingdom may have moved to Pella.

U. Westermark, 'The coinage of Archelaus' in M.J. Price *et al.* (eds.), *Essays in honour of R.A.G. Carson and G.K. Jenkins* (London, 1993).

273–4. Pausanias (**273**) and Amyntas III (**274**) were under constant pressure from the expansion of the Chalcidian League (**265**). For a time even Pella was lost to the kingdom. Both these coins are plated on a copper core, suggesting that silver was difficult to obtain.

273. Stater, Pausanias, 390–389 B.C., continuing designs introduced by Archelaus with diademed head of Caranus, founder of the dynasty, and horse.

274. Stater, Amyntas III, 393–370 B.C., introducing the head of his ancestor Heracles onto the Argead coinage for the first time.

275. Perdiccas III (365–359 B.C.) was allied with Timotheus of Athens (**227**) against the Chalcidian League. He struck very little coinage, but there is no surviving example of his debased staters (pentadrachms) quoted by Polyaenus III.10.14. Stater.

BMC 1; *PCG* III.B.18.

276–8. Through the expansion of his kingdom Philip II (359–336 B.C.) was able to secure sources of gold and silver which made his coinage dramatically larger than that of his pre-

275 276 277 278

decessors. He struck at two mints and made a thorough reform of the coinage, raising the weight of the stater to the standard used by the Chalcidian League (**265**). The silver begins with a depiction of the king on horseback (**276**). This changes after a few years to represent a jockey holding a palm of victory (**277**), which remains the constant type for the pentadrachm until the end of the reign. Plutarch, *Alexander* 4 shows that Philip himself chose the designs for the coinage to commemorate his victory in the Olympic games, the horse race in 356 B.C., and the chariot race later in 352 or 348 B.C. The

former victory was clearly the cause for the change of the coin types in silver. The latter was commemorated on his gold staters (**278**) which only began after the fall of the Chalcidian League, but continued the weight standard of the league's gold issues.

(**276**. Silver pentadrachm 359–356 B.C. Le Rider, *op. cit.*, Pella I.A.28a. **277**. Silver pentadrachm 355–350 B.C. Le Rider, *op. cit.*, Pella II.A.2.263a. **278**. Gold stater 348–336 B.C. Le Rider, *op. cit.*, Pella I.4a)

G. Le Rider, *Le monnayage d'argent et d'or de Philippe II frappé en Macédoine de 359 à 294* (Paris, 1977); M.J. Price, *NC* 1979, 230–41.